14-99

Modern Drama:
Plays of the '80s and '90s

Modern Drama:
Plays of the '80s and '90s

introduced by

Graham Whybrow

Top Girls
Caryl Churchill

Hysteria
Terry Johnson

Blasted
Sarah Kane

Shopping and Fucking
Mark Ravenhill

The Beauty Queen of Leenane
Martin McDonagh

Methuen Drama

Methuen Drama

9 10

Methuen Drama
A & C Black Publishers Ltd
36 Soho Square
London W1D 3QY

This collection first published in Great Britain in 2001
by Methuen Publishing Limited as *The Methuen Book of Modern Drama*;
reissued in 2007 as *Modern Drama: Plays of the '80s and '90s*

Top Girls first published by Methuen London in 1982, copyright © 1982,
1984, 1990, 1991 by Caryl Churchill; *Hysteria* first published by Methuen
Drama in 1993, copyright © 1993, 1994 by Terry Johnson; *Blasted* first
published by Methuen Drama in *Frontline Intelligence 2* in 1995, reprinted
with corrections and revisions 2000, copyright © 1995, 2000 Sarah Kane,
2007 Estate of Sarah Kane; *Shopping and Fucking* first published by
Methuen Drama in 1996, copyright © 1996, 1997 by Mark Ravenhill;
The Beauty Queen of Leenane first published by Methuen Drama
in 1996, copyright © 1996 by Martin McDonagh.

Introduction copyright © Graham Whybrow, 2001

The authors and editor have asserted their rights under
the Copyright, Designs and Patents Act, 1988.

A CIP catalogue record for this book
is available from the British Library.

ISBN 978 0 413 76490 4

Typeset by Deltatype Ltd, Birkenhead, Merseyside
Printed and bound in Great Britain by
CPI Cox & Wyman, Reading, Berkshire

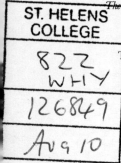
Caution

All rights in these plays are strictly reserved. Application for performance
etc. of *Top Girls*, *Blasted* and *Shopping and Fucking* should be made to
Casarotto Ramsay Ltd, Waverley House, 7–12 Noel Street, London
W1F 8GQ; for *Hysteria* to The Agency, 24 Pottery Lane, London
W11 4LZ; and for *The Beauty Queen of Leenane* to The Rod Hall Agency,
6th Floor, Fairgate House, 78 New Oxford Street, London WC1A 1HB.
No performance may be given unless a licence has been obtained.

Permission to use songs in performance must be secured
from the holders of the songs' copyright.

Contents

Introduction

Modern Drama: Plays of the '80s and '90s is an anthology of
five contemporary plays that have been outstandingly
successful in performance, both nationally and interna-
tionally. The collection includes Caryl Churchill's *Top
Girls*, a landmark play from 1982, and four plays from
the 1990s: Terry Johnson's *Hysteria*, Sarah Kane's
Blasted, Mark Ravenhill's *Shopping and Fucking* and Martin
McDonagh's *The Beauty Queen of Leenane*.

Caryl Churchill is a leading British playwright and the
most consistently inventive in exploring dramatic form.
Since *Top Girls*, she has continued to write imaginatively
conceived and formally challenging plays: from *Fen*
(1983), *Softcops* (1984) and *Serious Money* (1987) through to
The Skriker (1994), *This is a Chair* (1997), *Blue Heart* (1997)
and *Far Away* (2000).

Top Girls is an enduring classic and a play of its time.
It is often remembered for its opening scene, an
exuberant and at times cacophonous party with remarkable women from history and legend. The party
celebrates the spirit and achievements of these women
on the occasion of Marlene's promotion at a recruitment
agency. The play then shifts from celebration to
investigation, moving through the business culture of her
office to the darker side of Marlene's success by
examining her personal choices. The play is informed by
a pivotal moment in the early 1980s, when social and
economic change had liberated women but also fostered
ruthless individualism. The subject finds expressive form
in the play's hybrid structure, reverse chronology and
verbal technique – Churchill's precise notation for
interrupted, overlapping and non-consecutive dialogue

that specifies rhythm and discontinuity for the actors in performance.

Terry Johnson emerged as a playwright in the 1980s, notably with *Insignificance* (1982) and *Unsuitable for Adults* (1984), and he continued through the 1990s with *Imagine Drowning* (1991), *Hysteria* (1993), *Dead Funny* (1994) and *Cleo, Camping, Emmanuelle and Dick* (1997). His plays are flamboyantly conceived, often creating scenarios with characters from popular culture and exploring the gap between the public myth and the private reality. Johnson's plays also explore complex ideas, but these are harnessed to his confident use of theatrical convention and dramatic logic.

Hysteria boldly combines an intellectual thriller with farce. The play explores an ambiguity in Freud's psychoanalysis: if his theory and therapy can recognise the unconscious source of psychological distress, it can also deny that experience as fantasy or wish-fulfilment. As a stage play, this material might have remained an abstract idea about the 'return of the repressed'. Johnson's flair as a playwright is to transform the idea into character and action in a play that is by turns comic, painful, searching, irreverent and abundantly theatrical.

Sarah Kane wrote five full-length plays: *Blasted* (1995), *Phaedra's Love* (1996), *Cleansed* (1998), *Crave* (1998) and the posthumously produced *4.48 Psychosis* (2000). Each play shows the writer making a new departure in exploring dramatic form. Before her tragically early death in 1999, Kane established an international reputation as the most important playwright of her generation.

Blasted is Kane's first full-length play, toughly conceived and tersely written. It opens with an abusive relationship in peacetime England and then explodes into military and human atrocity. *Blasted* thrust the twenty-three-year-old writer into a blaze of notoriety in the press, yet it is now seen as a pioneering contemporary play. Since its first production at the Royal Court's sixty-seat studio, Theatre Upstairs, *Blasted* has been translated into a dozen languages with scores of productions in continental Europe.

Mark Ravenhill's first full-length play, *Shopping and Fucking* (1996), was co-produced by the Royal Court and Out of Joint Theatre Company. It has proved a huge international success, with countless foreign-language productions. He has since written *Faust is Dead* (1997), *Handbag* (1998) and *Some Explicit Polaroids* (1998).

In *Shopping and Fucking*, the characters discover themselves in a world where relationships are reduced to commercial transactions. The search for love, the fear of intimacy, the need to earn: all these impulses inform how they shape their own stories. Ravenhill's talent here is to combine an overview of corrosive capitalism in the 1990s with micro-narratives of characters struggling to define their experience. As the character Robbie says: 'I think we all need stories, we make up stories so that we can get by. And I think a long time ago there were big stories. Stories so big you could live your whole life in them. The Powerful Hands of the Gods and Fate. The Journey to Enlightenment. The March of Socialism. But they all died or the world grew up or grew senile or forgot them, so now we're all making up our own stories. Little stories. But we've each got one.'

Martin McDonagh's first stage play, *The Beauty Queen of Leenane*, was co-produced in 1996 by the Royal Court and Druid Theatre Company. It now forms the first part of McDonagh's 'Leenane Trilogy', together with *A Skull in Connemara* (1997) and *The Lonesome West* (1997). He has since written *The Cripple of Inishmaan* (1997) and *The Lieutenant of Inishmore* (2001). *The Beauty Queen of Leenane* had an extraordinary trajectory for a first play by a twenty-five-year-old writer. The production opened in Ireland at the new Town Hall Theatre in Galway and the next month at the Royal Court Theatre Upstairs in London. It moved to the Royal Court's temporary home at the 600-seat Duke of York's Theatre in the West End, and then transferred to the 900-seat Walter Kerr Theatre on Broadway, where the production won 4 Tony awards and ran for a year. By 2000, McDonagh's plays had been translated into 28 languages and produced in 39 countries, and McDonagh had become the most performed playwright in the USA after Shakespeare.

The Beauty Queen of Leenane seems firmly within the genre of the rural Irish kitchen play, in the tradition of J.M. Synge, John B. Keane and Tom Murphy. However, as a Londoner born of Irish parents, McDonagh writes both within a tradition and against a mythology: the play combines taut storytelling with iconoclastic pastiche. It also includes some heartfelt writing, such as Pato's speech about the ambivalence of exile: 'And when I'm over there in London and working in rain and it's more or less cattle I am, and the young fellas cursing over cards and drunk and sick, and the oul digs over there, all pee-stained mattresses and nothing to do but watch the clock . . . when it's there I am, it's here I wish I was, of course. Who wouldn't? But when it's here I am . . . it isn't *there* I want to be, of course not. But I know it isn't here I want to be either.'

Modern Drama: Plays of the '80s and '90s offers a stimulating introduction to a range of contemporary plays. The collection also offers the opportunity to contrast the plays, to sharpen our sense of what makes them specific and distinct in idea, characterisation, action, story, structure, form, style, method and language. The quality of the plays also shows that modern drama continues to set new challenges. This is a tribute to the playwright as the core artist in the theatre, always searching for a dramatic form that expresses new ways of seeing, thinking and feeling.

Graham Whybrow, March 2001

Top Girls

Caryl Churchill

Caryl Churchill has written for the stage, television and radio. Her stage plays include *Owners* (Royal Court Theatre Upstairs, 1972); *Objections to Sex and Violence* (Royal Court, 1975); *Light Shining in Buckinghamshire* (for Joint Stock, Theatre Upstairs, 1976); *Vinegar Tom* (for Monstrous Regiment, Half Moon and ICA, London, and on tour, 1976); *Traps* (Theatre Upstairs, 1977); *Cloud Nine* (for Joint Stock, Royal Court and on tour, 1979, De Lys Theatre, New York, 1981); *Three More Sleepless Nights* (Soho Poly and Theatre Upstairs, 1980); *Top Girls* (Royal Court, London and Public Theatre, New York, 1982); *Fen* (for Joint Stock, Almeida Theatre and Royal Court, London, and on tour, and Public Theatre, New York, 1983); *Softcops* (RSC in the Pit, 1984); *A Mouthful of Birds*, with David Lan (for Joint Stock, Royal Court and on tour, 1986); *Serious Money* (Royal Court and Wyndhams Theatre, London, 1987); *Icecream* and *Hot Fudge* (Royal Court, London, 1989); *Mad Forest* (Central School of Speech and Drama, London, 1990); *Lives of the Great Poisoners* (Arnolfini, Bristol, 1991); *The Skriker* (Royal National Theatre, 1994); a translation of Seneca's *Thyestes* (Royal Court Theatre Upstairs, 1994); *Blue Heart* (for Out of Joint, Royal Court at the Duke of York's, London, 1997); *This is a Chair* (Royal Court at the Duke of York's, 1997); and *Far Away* (Royal Court Theatre Upstairs, 2000).

Top Girls was first performed at the Royal Court Theatre, London, on 28 August 1982, and transferred to Joe Papp's Public Theatre, New York, later the same year. The cast was as follows:

Marlene	Gwen Taylor
Isabella Bird **Joyce** **Mrs Kidd**	Deborah Findlay
Lady Nijo **Win**	Lindsay Duncan
Dull Gret **Angie**	Carole Hayman
Pope Joan **Louise**	Selina Cadell
Patient Griselda **Nell** **Jeanine**	Lesley Manville
Waitress **Kit** **Shona**	Lou Wakefield

Directed by Max Stafford Clark
Designed by Peter Hartwell

Characters

Isabella Bird *(1831–1904) lived in Edinburgh, travelled extensively between the ages of forty and seventy.*
Lady Nijo *(b.1258), Japanese, was an Emperor's courtesan and later a Buddhist nun who travelled on foot through Japan.*
Dull Gret *is the subject of the Brueghel painting,* Dulle Griet, *in which a woman in an apron and armour leads a crowd of women charging through hell and fighting the devils.*
Pope Joan, *disguised as a man, is thought to have been Pope between 854 and 856.*
Patient Griselda *is the obedient wife whose story is told by Chaucer in 'The Clerk's Tale' of* The Canterbury Tales.

Setting

ACT ONE   Restaurant. Saturday night.
ACT TWO
Scene One: 'Top Girls' Employment agency. Monday
                      morning.
Scene Two: Joyce's backyard. Sunday afternoon.
Scene Three: Employment agency. Monday morning.
ACT THREE Joyce's kitchen. Sunday evening, a year
                      earlier.

Note on layout

A speech usually follows the one immediately before it
BUT:

1: when one character starts speaking before the other has
finished, the point of interruption is marked /.

eg. **Isabella**:   This is the Emperor of Japan? / I once met
the Emperor of Morocco.

    Nijo: In fact he was the ex-Emperor.

2: a character sometimes continues speaking right through
another's speech:

eg. **Isabella**:   When I was forty I thought my life was
over. / Oh I was pitiful. I was

    Nijo: I didn't say I felt it for twenty years. Not
every minute.

    Isabella: sent on a cruise for my health and I felt
even worse. Pains in my bones, pins and
needles . . . *etc.*

3: sometimes a speech follows on from a speech earlier
than the one immediately before it, and continuity is
marked*.

eg. **Griselda**:   I'd seen him riding by, we all had. And
he'd seen me in the fields with the sheep*.

    Isabella: I would have been well suited to minding
sheep.

    Nijo: And Mr Nugent riding by.

    Isabella: Of course not, Nijo, I mean a healthy life
in the open air.

    Joan: *He just rode up while you were minding
the sheep and asked you to marry him?

where 'in the fields with the sheep' is the cue to both 'I
would have been' and 'He just rode up'.

Production note

Top Girls was originally written in three acts and I still find
that structure clearer: Act One, the dinner; Act Two,
Angie's story; Act Three, the year before. But two intervals
do hold things up, so in the original production we made it
two acts with the interval after what is here Act Two, scene
two. Do whichever you prefer.

Caryl Churchill, 1985

Act One

Restaurant. Table set for dinner with white tablecloth. Six places.
Marlene *and* **Waitress**.

Marlene Excellent, yes, table for six. One of them's going to be late but we won't wait. I'd like a bottle of Frascati straight away if you've got one really cold.

The **Waitress** *goes.* **Isabella Bird** *arrives.*

Here we are. Isabella.

Isabella Congratulations, my dear.

Marlene Well, it's a step. It makes for a party. I haven't time for a holiday. I'd like to go somewhere exotic like you but I can't get away. I don't know how you could bear to leave Hawaii. / I'd like to lie in the sun for ever, except of course I

Isabella I did think of settling.

Marlene can't bear sitting still.

Isabella I sent for my sister Hennie to come and join me. I said, Hennie we'll live here for ever and help the natives. You can buy two sirloins of beef for what a pound of chops costs in Edinburgh. And Hennie wrote back, the dear, that yes, she would come to Hawaii if I wished, but I said she had far better stay where she was. Hennie was suited to life in Tobermory.

Marlene Poor Hennie.

Isabella Do you have a sister?

Marlene Yes in fact.

Isabella Hennie was happy. She was good. I did miss its face, my own pet. But I couldn't stay in Scotland. I loathed the constant murk.

Marlene Ah! Nijo!

She sees **Lady Nijo** *arrive. The* **Waitress** *enters with wine.*

Nijo   Marlene!

Marlene   I think a drink while we wait for the others. I think a drink anyway. What a week.

The **Waitress** *pours wine.*

Nijo   It was always the men who used to get so drunk. I'd be one of the maidens, passing the sake.

Isabella   I've had sake. Small hot drink. Quite fortifying after a day in the wet.

Nijo   One night my father proposed three rounds of three cups, which was normal, and then the Emperor should have said three rounds of three cups, but he said three rounds of nine cups, so you can imagine. Then the Emperor passed his sake cup to my father and said, 'Let the wild goose come to me this spring.'

Marlene   Let the what?

Nijo   It's a literary allusion to a tenth-century epic, / His Majesty was very cultured.

Isabella   This is the Emperor of Japan? / I once met the Emperor of Morocco.

Nijo   In fact he was the ex-Emperor.

Marlene   But he wasn't old? / Did you, Isabella?

Nijo   Twenty-nine.

Isabella   Oh it's a long story.

Marlene   Twenty-nine's an excellent age.

Nijo   Well I was only fourteen and I knew he meant something but I didn't know what. He sent me an eight-layered gown and I sent it back. So when the time came I did nothing but cry. My thin gowns were badly ripped. But even that morning when he left / – he'd a green robe with a scarlet lining and

Marlene Are you saying he raped you?

Nijo very heavily embroidered trousers, I already felt different about him. It made me uneasy. No, of course not, Marlene, I belonged to him, it was what I was brought up for from a baby. I soon found I was sad if he stayed away. It was depressing day after day not knowing when he would come. I never enjoyed taking other women to him.

Isabella I certainly never saw my father drunk. He was a clergyman. / And I didn't get married till I was fifty.

The **Waitress** *brings menus.*

Nijo Oh, my father was a very religious man. Just before he died he said to me, 'Serve His Majesty, be respectful, if you lose his favour enter holy orders.'

Marlene But he meant stay in a convent, not go wandering round the country.

Nijo Priests were often vagrants, so why not a nun? You think I shouldn't? / I still did what my father wanted.

Marlene No no, I think you should. / I think it was wonderful.

Dull Gret *arrives.*

Isabella I tried to do what my father wanted.

Marlene Gret, good. Nijo. Gret. / I know Griselda's going to be late, but should we wait for Joan? / Let's get you a drink.

Isabella Hello, Gret! (*Continues to* **Nijo**:) I tried to be a clergyman's daughter. Needlework, music, charitable schemes. I had a tumour removed from my spine and spent a great deal of time on the sofa. I studied the metaphysical poets and hymnology. / I thought I enjoyed intellectual pursuits.

Nijo Ah, you like poetry. I come of a line of eight generations of poets. Father had a poem / in the anthology.

Isabella   My father taught me Latin although I was a girl. / But

Marlene   They didn't have Latin at my school.

Isabella   really I was more suited to manual work. Cooking, washing, mending, riding horses. / Better than reading books,

Nijo   Oh but I'm sure you're very clever.

Isabella   Oh Gret? A rough life in the open air.

Nijo   I can't say I enjoyed my rough life. What I enjoyed most was being the Emperor's favourite / and wearing thin silk.

Isabella   Did you have any horses, Gret?

Gret   Pig.

Pope Joan *arrives.*

Marlene   Oh Joan, thank God, we can order. Do you know everyone? We were just talking about learning Latin and being clever girls. Joan was by way of an infant prodigy. Of course you were. What excited you when you were ten?

Joan   Because angels are without matter they are not individuals. Every angel is a species.

Marlene   There you are.

They laugh. They look at menus.

Isabella   Yes, I forgot all my Latin. But my father was the mainspring of my life and when he died I was so grieved. I'll have the chicken, please, / and the soup.

Nijo   Of course you were grieved. My father was saying his prayers and he dozed off in the sun. So I touched his knee to rouse him. 'I wonder what will happen,' he said, and then he was dead before he finished the sentence. / If he'd died saying

Marlene   What a shock.

Nijo his prayers he would have gone straight to heaven.
/ Waldorf salad.

Joan Death is the return of all creatures to God.

Nijo I shouldn't have woken him.

Joan Damnation only means ignorance of the truth. I was
always attracted by the teachings of John the Scot, though
he was inclined to confuse / God and the world.

Isabella Grief always overwhelmed me at the time.

Marlene What I fancy is a rare steak. Gret?

Isabella I am of course a member of the / Church of
England.*

Gret Potatoes.

Marlene *I haven't been to church for years. / I like
Christmas carols.

Isabella Good works matter more than church
attendance.

Marlene Make that two steaks and a lot of potatoes.
Rare. But I don't do good works either.

Joan Canelloni, please, / and a salad.

Isabella Well, I tried, but oh dear. Hennie did good
works.

Nijo The first half of my life was all sin and the second /
all repentance.*

Marlene Oh what about starters?

Gret Soup.

Joan *And which did you like best?

Marlene Were your travels just a penance? Avocado
vinaigrette. Didn't you / enjoy yourself?

Joan Nothing to start with for me, thank you.

Nijo Yes, but I was very unhappy. / It hurt to remember

Marlene   And the wine list.

Nijo   the past. I think that was repentance.

Marlene   Well I wonder.

Nijo   I might have just been homesick.

Marlene   Or angry.

Nijo   Not angry, no, / why angry?

Gret   Can we have some more bread?

Marlene   Don't you get angry? I get angry.

Nijo   But what about?

Marlene   Yes let's have two more Frascati. And some more bread, please.

The **Waitress** *exits.*

Isabella   I tried to understand Buddhism when I was in Japan but all this birth and death succeeding each other through eternities just filled me with the most profound melancholy. I do like something more active.

Nijo   You couldn't say I was inactive. I walked every day for twenty years.

Isabella   I don't mean walking. / I mean in the head.

Nijo   I vowed to copy five Mahayana sutras. / Do you know how

Marlene   I don't think religious beliefs are something we have in common. Activity yes.

Nijo   long they are? My head was active. / My head ached.

Joan   It's no good being active in heresy.

Isabella   What heresy? She's calling the Church of England / a heresy.

Joan   There are some very attractive / heresies.

Nijo I had never heard of Christianity. Never / heard of it. Barbarians.

Marlene Well I'm not a Christian. / And I'm not a Buddhist.

Isabella You have heard of it?

Marlene We don't all have to believe the same.

Isabella I knew coming to dinner with a pope we should keep off religion.

Joan I always enjoy a theological argument. But I won't try to convert you, I'm not a missionary. Anyway I'm a heresy myself.

Isabella There are some barbaric practices in the east.

Nijo Barbaric?

Isabella Among the lower classes.

Nijo I wouldn't know.

Isabella Well theology always made my head ache.

Marlene Oh good, some food.

The **Waitress** *is bringing the first course.*

Nijo How else could I have left the court if I wasn't a nun? When father died I had only His Majesty. So when I fell out of favour I had nothing. Religion is a kind of nothing / and I dedicated what was left of me to nothing.

Isabella That's what I mean about Buddhism. It doesn't brace.

Marlene Come on, Nijo, have some wine.

Nijo Haven't you ever felt like that? Nothing will ever happen again. I am dead already. You've all felt / like that.

Isabella You thought your life was over but it wasn't.

Joan You wish it was over.

Gret   Sad.

Marlene   Yes, when I first came to London I sometimes
. . . and when I got back from America I did. But only for
a few hours. Not twenty years.

Isabella   When I was forty I thought my life was over. /
Oh I

Nijo   I didn't say I felt it for twenty years. Not every
minute.

Isabella   was pitiful. I was sent on a cruise for my health
and I felt even worse. Pains in my bones, pins and needles
in my hands, swelling behind the ears, and – oh, stupidity.
I shook all over, indefinable terror. And Australia seemed
to me a hideous country, the acacias stank like drains. / I
had a

Nijo   You were homesick.

Isabella   photograph for Hennie but I told her I wouldn't
send it, my hair had fallen out and my clothes were
crooked, I looked completely insane and suicidal.

Nijo   So did I, exactly, dressed as a nun. I was wearing
walking shoes for the first time.

Isabella   I longed to go home, / but home to what?
Houses

Nijo   I longed to go back ten years.

Isabella   are so perfectly dismal.

Marlene   I thought travelling cheered you both up.

Isabella   Oh it did / of course. It was on the trip from

Nijo   I'm not a cheerful person, Marlene. I just laugh a
lot.

Isabella   Australia to the Sandwich Isles, I fell in love
with the sea. There were rats in the cabin and ants in the
food but suddenly it was like a new world. I woke up every
morning happy, knowing there would be nothing to annoy

me. No nervousness. No dressing.

Nijo   Don't you like getting dressed? I adored my clothes. / When I was chosen to give sake to His Majesty's brother,

Marlene   You had prettier colours than Isabella.

Nijo   the Emperor Kameyana, on his formal visit, I wore raw silk pleated trousers and a seven-layered gown in shades of red, and two outer garments, / yellow lined with green and a light

Marlene   Yes, all that silk must have been very . . .

The **Waitress** *starts to clear the first course.*

Joan   I dressed as a boy when I left home.*

Nijo   green jacket. Lady Betto had a five-layered gown in shades of green and purple.

Isabella   *You dressed as a boy?

Marlene   Of course, / for safety.

Joan   It was easy, I was only twelve. Also women weren't / allowed in the library. We wanted to study in Athens.

Marlene   You ran away alone?

Joan   No, not alone, I went with my friend. / He was sixteen

Nijo   Ah, an elopement.

Joan   but I thought I knew more science than he did and almost as much philosophy.

Isabella   Well I always travelled as a lady and I repudiated strongly any suggestion in the press that I was other than feminine.

Marlene   I don't wear trousers in the office. / I could but I don't.

Isabella   There was no great danger to a woman of my age and appearance.

Marlene   And you got away with it, Joan?

Joan   I did then.

The **Waitress** *starts to bring the main course.*

Marlene   And nobody noticed anything?

Joan   They noticed I was a very clever boy. / And when I

Marlene   I couldn't have kept pretending for so long.

Joan   shared a bed with my friend, that was ordinary –
two poor students in a lodging house. I think I forgot I was
pretending.

Isabella   Rocky Mountain Jim, Mr Nugent, showed me
no disrespect. He found it interesting, I think, that I could
make scones and also lasso cattle. Indeed he declared his
love for me, which was most distressing.

Nijo   What did he say? / We always sent poems first.

Marlene   What did you say?

Isabella   I urged him to give up whisky, / but he said it
was too late.

Marlene   Oh Isabella.

Isabella   He had lived alone in the mountains for many
years.

Marlene   But did you – ?

The **Waitress** *goes.*

Isabella   Mr Nugent was a man that any woman might
love but none could marry. I came back to England.

Nijo   Did you write him a poem when you left? / Snow
on the

Marlene   Did you never see him again?

Isabella   No, never.

Nijo   mountains. My sleeves are wet with tears. In

England no tears, no snow.

Isabella Well, I say never. One morning very early in Switzerland, it was a year later, I had a vision of him as I last saw him / in his trapper's clothes with his hair round his face,

Nijo A ghost!

Isabella and that was the day, / I learned later, he died with a

Nijo Ah!

Isabella bullet in his brain. / He just bowed to me and vanished.

Marlene Oh Isabella.

Nijo When your lover dies – One of my lovers died. / The priest Ariake.

Joan My friend died. Have we all got dead lovers?

Marlene Not me, sorry.

Nijo (*to* **Isabella**) I wasn't a nun, I was still at court, but he was a priest, and when he came to me he dedicated his whole life to hell. / He knew that when he died he would fall into one of the three lower realms. And he died, he did die.

Joan (*to* **Marlene**) I'd quarrelled with him over the teachings of John the Scot, who held that our ignorance of God is the same as his ignorance of himself. He only knows what he creates because he creates everything he knows but he himself is above being – do you follow?

Marlene No, but go on.

Nijo I couldn't bear to think / in what shape would he be reborn.*

Joan St Augustine maintained that the Neo-Platonic Ideas are indivisible from God, but I agreed with John that the created

Isabella   *Buddhism is really most uncomfortable.

Joan   world is essences derived from Ideas which derived from God. As Denys the Areopagite said – the pseudo-Denys – first we give God a name, then deny it / then reconcile the

Nijo   In what shape would he return?

Joan   contradiction by looking beyond / those terms –

Marlene   Sorry, what? Denys said what?

Joan   Well we disagreed about it, we quarrelled. And next day he was ill, / I was so annoyed with him, all the time I was

Nijo   Misery in this life and worse in the next, all because of me.

Joan   nursing him I kept going over the arguments in my mind. Matter is not a means of knowing the essence. The source of the species is the Idea. But then I realised he'd never understand my arguments again, and that night he died. John the Scot held that the individual disintegrates / and there is no personal immortality.

Isabella   I wouldn't have you think I was in love with Jim Nugent. It was yearning to save him that I felt.

Marlene (*to* **Joan**)   So what did you do?

Joan   First I decided to stay a man. I was used to it. And I wanted to devote my life to learning. Do you know why I went to Rome? Italian men didn't have beards.

Isabella   The loves of my life were Hennie, my own pet, and my dear husband the doctor, who nursed Hennie in her last illness. I knew it would be terrible when Hennie died but I didn't know how terrible. I felt half of myself had gone. How could I go on my travels without that sweet soul waiting at home for my letters? It was Dr Bishop's devotion to her in her last illness that made me decide to marry him. He and Hennic had the same sweet character. I had not.

Nijo   I thought His Majesty had sweet character because when he found out about Ariake he was so kind. But really it was because he no longer cared for me. One night he even sent me out to a man who had been pursuing me. / He lay awake on the other side of the screens and listened.

Isabella   I did wish marriage had seemed more of a step. I tried very hard to cope with the ordinary drudgery of life. I was ill again with carbuncles on the spine and nervous prostration. I ordered a tricycle, that was my idea of adventure then. And John himself fell ill, with erysipelas and anaemia. I began to love him with my whole heart but it was too late. He was a skeleton with transparent white hands. I wheeled him on various seafronts in a bathchair. And he faded and left me. There was nothing in my life. The doctors said I had gout / and my heart was much affected.

Nijo   There was nothing in my life, nothing, without the Emperor's favour. The Empress had always been my enemy, Marlene, she said I had no right to wear three-layered gowns. / But I was the adopted daughter of my grandfather the Prime Minister. I had been publicly granted permission to wear thin silk.

Joan   There was nothing in my life except my studies. I was obsessed with pursuit of the truth. I taught at the Greek School in Rome, which St Augustine had made famous. I was poor, I worked hard. I spoke apparently brilliantly, I was still very young, I was a stranger; suddenly I was quite famous, I was everyone's favourite. Huge crowds came to hear me. The day after they made me cardinal I fell ill and lay two weeks without speaking, full of terror and regret. / But then I got up

Marlene   Yes, success is very . . .

Joan   determined to go on. I was seized again / with a desperate longing for the absolute.

Isabella   Yes, yes, to go on. I sat in Tobermory among Hennie's flowers and sewed a complete outfit in Jaeger flannel. / I was fifty-six years old.

Nijo   Out of favour but I didn't die. I left on foot, nobody saw me go. For the next twenty years I walked through Japan.

Gret   Walking is good.

The **Waitress** *enters.*

Joan   Pope Leo died and I was chosen. All right then. I would be Pope. I would know God. I would know everything.

Isabella   I determined to leave my grief behind and set off for Tibet.

Marlene   Magnificent all of you. We need some more wine, please, two bottles I think, Griselda isn't even here yet, and I want to drink a toast to you all.

Isabella   To yourself surely, / we're here to celebrate your success.

Nijo   Yes, Marlene.

Joan   Yes, what is it exactly, Marlene?

Marlene   Well it's not Pope but it is managing director.*

Joan   And you find work for people.

Marlene   Yes, an employment agency.

Nijo   *Over all the women you work with. And the men.

Isabella   And very well deserved too. I'm sure it's just the beginning of something extraordinary.

Marlene   Well it's worth a party.

Isabella   To Marlene.*

Marlene   And all of us.

Joan   *Marlene.

Nijo   Marlene.

Gret   Marlene.

Marlene   We've all come a long way. To our courage
and the way we changed our lives and our extraordinary
achievements.

They laugh and drink a toast.

Isabella   Such adventures. We were crossing a mountain
pass at seven thousand feet, the cook was all to pieces, the
muleteers suffered fever and snow blindness. But even
though my spine was agony I managed very well.

Marlene   Wonderful.

Nijo   Once I was ill for four months lying alone at an
inn. Nobody to offer a horse to Buddha. I had to live for
myself, and I did live.

Isabella   Of course you did. It was far worse returning to
Tobermory. I always felt dull when I was stationary. /
That's why I could never stay anywhere.

Nijo   Yes, that's it exactly. New sights. The shrine by the
beach, the moon shining on the sea. The goddess had
vowed to save all living things. /She would even save the
fishes. I was full of hope.

Joan   I had thought the Pope would know everything. I
thought God would speak to me directly. But of course he
knew I was a woman.

Marlene   But nobody else even suspected?

*The **Waitress** brings more wine.*

Joan   In the end I did take a lover again.*

Isabella   In the Vatican?

Gret   *Keep you warm.

Nijo   *Ah, lover.

Marlene   *Good for you.

Joan   He was one of my chamberlains. There are such a

lot of servants when you're a Pope. The food's very good. And I realised I did know the truth. Because whatever the Pope says, that's true.

Nijo   What was he like, the chamberlain?*

Gret   Big cock.

Isabella   Oh Gret.

Marlene   *Did he fancy you when he thought you were a fella?

Nijo   What was he like?

Joan   He could keep a secret.

Marlene   So you did know everything.

Joan   Yes, I enjoyed being Pope. I consecrated bishops and let people kiss my feet. I received the King of England when he came to submit to the Church. Unfortunately there were earthquakes, and some village reported it had rained blood, and in France there was a plague of giant grasshoppers, but I don't think that can have been my fault, do you?*

Laughter.

The grasshoppers fell on the English Channel and were washed up on shore and their bodies rotted and poisoned the air and everyone in those parts died.

Laughter.

Isabella   *Such superstition! I was nearly murdered in China by a howling mob. They thought the barbarians are babies and put them under railway sleepers to make the tracks steady, and ground up their eyes to make the lenses of cameras. / So

Marlene   And you had a camera!

Isabella   they were shouting, 'child-eater, child-eater.' Some people tried to sell girl babies to Europeans for cameras or stew!

Laughter.

Marlene   So apart from the grasshoppers it was a great success.

Joan   Yes, if it hadn't been for the baby I expect I'd have lived to an old age like Theodora of Alexandria, who lived as a monk. She was accused by a girl / who fell in love with her of being the father of her child and –

Nijo   But tell us what happened to your baby. I had some babies.

Marlene   Didn't you think of getting rid of it?

Joan   Wouldn't that be a worse sin than having it? / But a Pope with a child was about as bad as possible.

Marlene   I don't know, you're the Pope.

Joan   But I wouldn't have known how to get rid of it.

Marlene   Other Popes had children, surely.

Joan   They didn't give birth to them.

Nijo   Well you were a woman.

Joan   Exactly and I shouldn't have been a woman. Women, children and lunatics can't be Pope.

Marlene   So the only thing to do / was to get rid of it somehow.

Nijo   You had to have it adopted secretly.

Joan   But I didn't know what was happening. I thought I was getting fatter, but then I was eating more and sitting about, the life of a Pope is quite luxurious. I don't think I'd spoken to a woman since I was twelve. The chamberlain was the one who realised.

Marlene   And by then it was too late.

Joan   Oh I didn't want to pay attention. It was easier to do nothing.

Nijo   But you had to plan for having it. You had to say you were ill and go away.

Joan   That's what I should have done I suppose.

Marlene   Did you want them to find out?

Nijo   I too was often in embarrassing situations, there's no need for a scandal. My first child was His Majesty's, which unfortunately died, but my second was Akebono's. I was seventeen. He was in love with me when I was thirteen, he was very upset when I had to go to the Emperor, it was very romantic, a lot of poems. Now His Majesty hadn't been near me for two months so he thought I was four months pregnant when I was really six, so when I reached the ninth month / I

Joan   I never knew what month it was.

Nijo   announced I was seriously ill, and Akebono announced he had gone on a religious retreat. He held me round the waist and lifted me up as the baby was born. He cut the cord with a short sword, wrapped the baby in white and took it away. It was only a girl but I was sorry to lose it. Then I told the Emperor that the baby had miscarried because of my illness, and there you are. The danger was past.

Joan   But Nijo, I wasn't used to having a woman's body.

Isabella   So what happened?

Joan   I didn't know of course that it was near the time. It was Rogation Day, there was always a procession. I was on the horse dressed in my robes and a cross was carried in front of me, and all the cardinals were following, and all the clergy of Rome, and a huge crowd of people. / We set off from

Marlene   Total Pope.

Joan   St Peter's to go to St John's. I had felt a slight pain earlier, I thought it was something I'd eaten, and then it came back, and came back more often. I thought when this is over I'll go to bed. There were still long gaps when I felt

perfectly all right and I didn't want to attract attention to
myself and spoil the ceremony. Then I suddenly realised
what it must be. I had to last out till I could get home and
hide. Then something changed, my breath started to catch,
I couldn't plan things properly any more. We were in a
little street that goes between St Clement's and the
Colosseum, and I just had to get off the horse and sit down
for a minute. Great waves of pressure were going through
my body, I heard sounds like a cow lowing, they came out
of my mouth. Far away I heard people screaming, 'The
Pope is ill, the Pope is dying.' And the baby just slid out
onto the road.*

Marlene   The cardinals/won't have known where to put
themselves.

Nijo   Oh dear, Joan, what a thing to do! In the street!

Isabella   *How embarrassing.

Gret   In a field, yah.

They are laughing.

Joan   One of the cardinals said, 'The Antichrist!' and fell
over in a faint.

They all laugh.

Marlene   So what did they do? They weren't best
pleased.

Joan   They took me by the feet and dragged me out of
town and stoned me to death.

They stop laughing.

Marlene   Joan, how horrible.

Joan   I don't really remember.

Nijo   And the child died too?

Joan   Oh yes, I think so, yes.

Pause.

The **Waitress** *enters to clear the plates. They start talking quietly.*

Isabella (*to* **Joan**)   I never had any children. I was very fond of horses.

Nijo (*to* **Marlene**)   I saw my daughter once. She was three years old. She wore a plum-red / small-sleeved gown. Akebono's

Isabella   Birdie was my favourite. A little Indian bay mare I rode in the Rocky Mountains.

Nijo   wife had taken the child because her own died. Everyone thought I was just a visitor. She was being brought up carefully so she could be sent to the palace like I was.

Isabella   Legs of iron and always cheerful, and such a pretty face. If a stranger led her she reared up like a bronco.

Nijo   I never saw my third child after he was born, the son of Ariake the priest. Ariake held him on his lap the day he was born and talked to him as if he could understand, and cried. My fourth child was Ariake's too. Ariake died before he was born. I didn't want to see anyone, I stayed alone in the hills. It was a boy again, my third son. But oddly enough I felt nothing for him.

Marlene   How many children did you have, Gret?

Gret   Ten.

Isabella   Whenever I came back to England I felt I had so much to atone for. Hennie and John were so good. I did no good in my life. I spent years in self-gratification. So I hurled myself into committees, I nursed the people of Tobermory in the epidemic of influenza, I lectured the Young Women's Christian Association on Thrift. I talked and talked explaining how the East was corrupt and vicious. My travels must do good to someone beside myself. I wore myself out with good causes.

Marlene   Oh God, why are we all so miserable?

Joan   The procession never went down that street again.

Marlene   They rerouted it specially?

Joan   Yes they had to go all round to avoid it. And they introduced a pierced chair.

Marlene   A pierced chair?

Joan   Yes, a chair made out of solid marble with a hole in the seat / and it was in the Chapel of the Saviour, and after he was

Marlene   You're not serious.

Joan   elected the Pope had to sit in it.

Marlene   And someone looked up his skirts? / Not really?

Isabella   What an extraordinary thing.

Joan   Two of the clergy / made sure he was a man.

Nijo   On their hands and knees!

Marlene   A pierced chair!

Gret   Balls!

Griselda *arrives unnoticed.*

Nijo   Why couldn't he just pull up his robe?

Joan   He had to sit there and look dignified.

Marlene   You could have made all your chamberlains sit in it.*

Gret   Big one, small one.

Nijo   Very useful chair at court.

Isabella   *Or the laird of Tobermory in his kilt.

They are quite drunk. They get the giggles. **Marlene** *notices* **Griselda**.

Marlene   Griselda! / There you are. Do you want to eat?

Griselda   I'm sorry I'm so late. No, no, don't bother.

Marlene   Of course it's no bother. / Have you eaten?

Griselda   No really, I'm not hungry.

Marlene   Well have some pudding.

Griselda   I never eat pudding.

Marlene   Griselda, I hope you're not anorexic. We're having pudding, I am, and getting nice and fat.

Griselda   Oh if everyone is. I don't mind.

Marlene   Now who do you know? This is Joan who was Pope in the ninth century, and Isabella Bird, the Victorian traveller, and Lady Nijo from Japan, Emperor's concubine and Buddhist nun, thirteenth century, nearer your own time, and Gret who was painted by Brueghel. Griselda's in Boccaccio and Petrarch and Chaucer because of her extraordinary marriage. I'd like profiteroles because they're disgusting.

Joan   Zabaglione, please.

Isabella   Apple pie / and cream.

Nijo   What's this?

Marlene   Zabaglione, it's Italian, it's what Joan's having, / it's delicious.

Nijo   A Roman Catholic / dessert? Yes please.

Marlene   Gret?

Gret   Cake.

Griselda   Just cheese and biscuits, thank you.

Marlene   Yes, Griselda's life is like a fairy story, except it starts with marrying the prince.

Griselda   He's only a marquis, Marlene.

Marlene   Well everyone for miles around is his liege and he's absolute lord of life and death and you were the poor

but beautiful peasant girl and he whisked you off. / Near
enough a prince.

Nijo How old were you?

Griselda Fifteen.

Nijo I was brought up in court circles and it was still a
shock. Had you ever seen him before?

Griselda I'd seen him riding by, we all had. And he'd
seen me in the fields with the sheep.*

Isabella I would have been well suited to minding sheep.

Nijo And Mr Nugent riding by.

Isabella Of course not, Nijo, I mean a healthy life in the
open air.

Joan *He just rode up while you were minding the sheep
and asked you to marry him?

Griselda No, no, it was on the wedding day. I was
waiting outside the door to see the procession. Everyone
wanted him to get married so there'd be an heir to look
after us when he died, / and at last he announced a day
for the wedding but

Marlene I don't think Walter wanted to get married. It
is Walter? Yes.

Griselda nobody knew who the bride was, we thought it
must be a foreign princess, we were longing to see her.
Then the carriage stopped outside our cottage and we
couldn't see the bride anywhere. And he came and spoke
to my father.

Nijo And your father told you to serve the Prince.

Griselda My father could hardly speak. The Marquis
said it wasn't an order, I could say no, but if I said yes I
must always obey him in everything.

Marlene That's when you should have suspected.

Griselda But of course a wife must obey her husband. /

And of course I must obey the Marquis.*

Isabella   I swore to obey dear John, of course, but it didn't seem to arise. Naturally I wouldn't have wanted to go abroad while I was married.

Marlene   *Then why bother to mention it at all? He'd got a thing about it, that's why.

Griselda   I'd rather obey the Marquis than a boy from the village.

Marlene   Yes, that's a point.

Joan   I never obeyed anyone. They all obeyed me.

Nijo   And what did you wear? He didn't make you get married in your own clothes? That would be perverse.*

Marlene   Oh, you wait.

Griselda   *He had ladies with him who undressed me and they had a white silk dress and jewels for my hair.

Marlene   And at first he seemed perfectly normal?

Griselda   Marlene, you're always so critical of him. / Of course he was normal, he was very kind.

Marlene   But Griselda, come on, he took your baby.

Griselda   Walter found it hard to believe I loved him. He couldn't believe I would always obey him. He had to prove it.

Marlene   I don't think Walter likes women.

Griselda   I'm sure he loved me, Marlene, all the time.

Marlene   He just had a funny way / of showing it.

Griselda   It was hard for him too.

Joan   How do you mean he took away your baby?

Nijo   Was it a boy?

Griselda   No, the first one was a girl.

Nijo Even so it's hard when they take it away. Did you see it at all?

Griselda Oh yes, she was six weeks old.

Nijo Much better to do it straight away.

Isabella But why did your husband take the child?

Griselda He said all the people hated me because I was just one of them. And now I had a child they were restless. So he had to get rid of the child to keep them quiet. But he said he wouldn't snatch her, I had to agree and obey and give her up. So when I was feeding her a man came in and took her away. I thought he was going to kill her even before he was out of the room.

Marlene But you let him take her? You didn't struggle?

Griselda I asked him to give her back so I could kiss her. And I asked him to bury her where no animals could dig her up. / It

Isabella Oh my dear.

Griselda was Walter's child to do what he liked with.*

Marlene Walter was bonkers.

Gret Bastard.

Isabella *But surely, murder.

Griselda I had promised.

Marlene I can't stand this. I'm going for a pee.

Marlene *goes out. The* **Waitress** *brings dessert.*

Nijo No, I understand. Of course you had to, he was your life. And were you in favour after that?

Griselda Oh yes, we were very happy together. We never spoke about what had happened.

Isabella I can see you were doing what you thought was your duty. But didn't it make you ill?

Griselda   No, I was very well, thank you.

Nijo   And you had another child?

Griselda   Not for four years, but then I did, yes, a boy.

Nijo   Ah a boy. / So it all ended happily.

Griselda   Yes he was pleased. I kept my son till he was
two years old. A peasant's grandson. It made the people
angry. Walter explained.

Isabella   But surely he wouldn't kill his children / just
because –

Griselda   Oh it wasn't true. Walter would never give in
to the people. He wanted to see if I loved him enough.

Joan   He killed his children / to see if you loved him
enough?

Nijo   Was it easier the second time or harder?

Griselda   It was always easy because I always knew I
would do what he said.

Pause. They start to eat.

Isabella   I hope you didn't have any more children.

Griselda   Oh no, no more. It was twelve years till he
tested me again.

Isabella   So whatever did he do this time? / My poor
John, I never loved him enough, and he would never have
dreamt . . .

Griselda   He sent me away. He said the people wanted
him to marry someone else who'd give him an heir and
he'd got special permission from the Pope. So I said I'd go
home to my father. I came with nothing / so I went with
nothing. I

Nijo   Better to leave if your master doesn't want you.

Griselda   took off my clothes. He let me keep a slip so
he wouldn't be shamed. And I walked home barefoot. My

father came out in tears. Everyone was crying except me.

Nijo   At least your father wasn't dead. / I had nobody.

Isabella   Well it can be a relief to come home. I loved to see Hennie's sweet face again.

Griselda   Oh yes, I was perfectly content. And quite soon he sent for me again.

Joan   I don't think I would have gone.

Griselda   But he told me to come. I had to obey him. He wanted me to help prepare his wedding. He was getting married to a young girl from France / and nobody except me knew how to arrange things the way he liked them.

Nijo   It's always hard taking him another woman.

Marlene *comes back.*

Joan   I didn't live a woman's life. I don't understand it.

Griselda   The girl was sixteen and far more beautiful than me. I could see why he loved her. / She had her younger brother with her as a page.

The **Waitress** *enters.*

Marlene   Oh God, I can't bear it. I want some coffee. Six coffees. Six brandies. / Double brandies. Straightaway.

Griselda   They all went in to the feast I'd prepared. And he stayed behind and put his arms round me and kissed me. / I felt half asleep with the shock.

Nijo   Oh, like a dream.

Marlene   And he said, 'This is your daughter and your son.'

Griselda   Yes.

Joan   What?

Nijo   Oh. Oh I see. You got them back.

Isabella   I did think it was remarkably barbaric to kill them but you learn not to say anything. So he had them brought up secretly I suppose.

Marlene   Walter's a monster. Weren't you angry? What did you do?

Griselda   Well I fainted. Then I cried and kissed the children. / Everyone was making a fuss of me.

Nijo   But did you feel anything for them?

Griselda   What?

Nijo   Did you feel anything for the children?

Griselda   Of course, I loved them.

Joan   So you forgave him and lived with him?

Griselda   He suffered so much all those years.

Isabella   Hennie had the same sweet nature.

Nijo   So they dressed you again?

Griselda   Cloth of gold.

Joan   I can't forgive anything.

Marlene   You really are exceptional, Griselda.

Nijo   Nobody gave me back my children.

Nijo *cries. The* **Waitress** *brings brandies.*

Isabella   I can never be like Hennie. I was always so busy in England, a kind of business I detested. The very presence of people exhausted my emotional reserves. I could not be like Hennie however I tried. I tried and was as ill as could be. The doctor suggested a steel net to support my head, the weight of my own head was too much for my diseased spine. / It is dangerous to put oneself in depressing circumstances. Why should I do it?

Joan   Don't cry.

Nijo   My father and the Emperor both died in the autumn. So much pain.

Joan Yes, but don't cry.

Nijo They wouldn't let me into the palace when he was dying. I hid in the room with his coffin, then I couldn't find where I'd left my shoes, I ran after the funeral procession in bare feet, I couldn't keep up. When I got there it was over, a few wisps of smoke in the sky, that's all that was left of him. What I want to know is, if I'd still been at court, would I have been allowed to wear full mourning?

Marlene I'm sure you would.

Nijo Why do you say that? You don't know anything about it. Would I have been allowed to wear full mourning?

Isabella How can people live in this dim pale island and wear our hideous clothes? I cannot and will not live the life of a lady.

Nijo I'll tell you something that made me angry. I was eighteen, at the Full Moon Ceremony. They make a special rice gruel and stir it with their sticks, and then they beat their women across the loins so they'll have sons and not daughters. So the Emperor beat us all / very hard as usual – that's not it,

Marlene What a sod.

Nijo Marlene, that's normal, what made us angry, he told his attendants they could beat us too. Well they had a wonderful time. / So Lady Genki and I made a plan, and the ladies all hid

*The **Waitress** has entered with coffees.*

Marlene I'd like another brandy please. Better make it six.

Nijo in his rooms, and Lady Mashimizu stood guard with a stick at the door, and when His Majesty came in Genki seized him and I beat him till he cried out and promised he would never order anyone to hit us again. Afterwards there was a terrible fuss. The nobles were horrified. 'We wouldn't even dream of stepping on Your Majesty's shadow.' And I had hit him with a stick. Yes, I hit him with a stick.

Joan   Suave, mari magno turbantibus aequora ventis, e terra magnum alterius spectare laborem; non quia vexari quemquamst iucunda voluptas, sed quibus ipse malis careas quia cernere suave est. Suave etiam belli certamina magna tueri per campos instructa tua sine parte pericli. Sed nil dulcius est, bene quam munita tenere edita doctrina sapientum templa serena, / despicere unde queas alios passimque videre errare atque viam palantis quaerere vitae,

Griselda   I do think – I do wonder – it would have been nicer if Walter hadn't had to.

Isabella   Why should I? Why should I?

Marlene   Of course not.

Nijo   I hit him with a stick.

Joan   certare ingenio, contendere nobilitate, noctes atque dies niti praestante labore ad summas emergere opes retumque potiri. O miseras / hominum mentis, o pectora caeca!*

Isabella   Oh miseras!

Nijo   *Pectora caeca.

Joan   qualibus in tenebris vitae quantisque periclis degitur hoc aevi quodcumquest! / nonne videre nil aliud sibi naturam latrare, nisi utqui corpore seiunctus dolor absit, mente fruatur

Joan *subsides.*

Gret   We come into hell through a big mouth. Hell's black and red. / It's like the village where I come from. There's a river and

Marlene (*to* **Joan**) Shut up, pet.

Isabella Listen, she's been to hell.

Gret a bridge and houses. There's places on fire like
when the soldiers come. There's a big devil sat on a roof
with a big hole in his arse and he's scooping stuff out of it
with a big ladle and it's falling down on us, and it's money,
so a lot of the women stop and get some. But most of us is
fighting the devils. There's lots of little devils, our size, and
we get them down all right and give them a beating.
There's lots of funny creatures round your feet, you don't
like to look, like rats and lizards, and nasty things, a bum
with a face, and fish with legs, and faces on things that
don't have faces on. But they don't hurt, you just keep
going. Well we'd had worse, you see, we'd had the
Spanish. We'd all had family killed. My big son die on a
wheel. Birds eat him. My baby, a soldier run her through
with a sword. I'd had enough, I was mad, I hate the
bastards. I come out my front door that morning and shout
till my neighbours come out and I said, 'Come on, we're
going where the evil come from and pay the bastards out.'
And they all come out just as they was / from baking or
washing in their

Nijo All the ladies come.

Gret aprons, and we push down the street and the
ground opens up and we go through a big mouth into a
street just like ours but in hell. I've got a sword in my
hand from somewhere and I fill a basket with gold cups
they drink out of down there. You just keep running on
and fighting / you didn't stop for nothing. Oh we give
them devils such a beating.

Nijo Take that, take that.

Joan Something something something mortisque timores
tum vacuum pectus – damn.
Quod si ridicula –
something something on and on and on and something
splendorem purpureai.

Isabella I thought I would have a last jaunt up the west river in China. Why not? But the doctors were so very grave. I just went to Morocco. The sea was so wild I had to be landed by ship's crane in a coal bucket. / My horse was a terror to me a

Gret Coal bucket, good.

Joan nos in luce timemus
something
terrorem.

Isabella powerful black charger.

Nijo *is laughing and crying.* **Joan** *gets up and is sick in a corner.* **Marlene** *is drinking* **Isabella**'s *brandy.*

Isabella So off I went to visit the Berber sheikhs in full blue trousers and great brass spurs. I was the only European woman ever to have seen the Emperor of Morocco. I was seventy years old. What lengths to go to for a last chance of joy. I knew my return of vigour was only temporary, but how marvellous while it lasted.

Act Two

Scene One

Employment Agency. **Marlene** *and* **Jeanine**.

Marlene Right, Jeanine, you are Jeanine, aren't you? Let's have a look. Os and As. / No As, all those Os you probably

Jeanine Six Os.

Marlene could have got an A. / Speeds, not brilliant, not too bad.

Jeanine I wanted to go to work.

Marlene Well, Jeanine, what's your present job like?

Jeanine I'm a secretary.

Marlene Secretary or typist?

Jeanine I did start as a typist but the last six months I've been a secretary.

Marlene To?

Jeanine To three of them, really, they share me. There's Mr Ashford, he's the office manager, and Mr Philby / is sales, and –

Marlene Quite a small place?

Jeanine A bit small.

Marlene Friendly?

Jeanine Oh it's friendly enough.

Marlene Prospects?

Jeanine I don't think so, that's the trouble. Miss Lewis is secretary to the managing director and she's been there for ever, and Mrs Bradford/ is –

Marlene So you want a job with better prospects?

Jeanine I want a change.

Marlene So you'll take anything comparable?

Jeanine No, I do want prospects. I want more money.

Marlene You're getting – ?

Jeanine Hundred.

Marlene It's not bad you know. You're what? Twenty?

Jeanine I'm saving to get married.

Marlene Does that mean you don't want a long-term job, Jeanine?

Jeanine I might do.

Marlene Because where do the prospects come in? No kids for a bit?

Jeanine Oh no, not kids, not yet.

Marlene So you won't tell them you're getting married?

Jeanine Had I better not?

Marlene It would probably help.

Jeanine I'm not wearing a ring. We thought we wouldn't spend on a ring.

Marlene Saves taking it off.

Jeanine I wouldn't take it off.

Marlene There's no need to mention it when you go for an interview. / Now, Jeanine, do you have a feel for any particular

Jeanine But what if they ask?

Marlene kind of company?

Jeanine I thought advertising.

Marlene People often do think advertising. I have got a

few vacancies but I think they're looking for something
glossier.

Jeanine   You mean how I dress? / I can dress different. I

Marlene   I mean experience.

Jeanine   dress like this on purpose for where I am now.

Marlene   I have a marketing department here of a
knitwear manufacturer. / Marketing is near enough
advertising. Secretary

Jeanine   Knitwear?

Marlene   to the marketing manager, he's thirty-five,
married, I've sent him a girl before and she was happy, left
to have a baby, you won't want to mention marriage there.
He's very fair I think, good at his job, you won't have to
nurse him along. Hundred and ten, so that's better than
you're doing now.

Jeanine   I don't know.

Marlene   I've a fairly small concern here, father and two
sons, you'd have more say potentially, secretarial and
reception duties, only a hundred but the job's going to
grow with the concern and then you'll be in at the top
with new girls coming in underneath you.

Jeanine   What is it they do?

Marlene   Lampshades. / This would be my first choice
for you.

Jeanine   Just lampshades?

Marlene   There's plenty of different kinds of lampshade.
So we'll send you there, shall we, and the knitwear second
choice. Are you free to go for an interview any day they
call you?

Jeanine   I'd like to travel.

Marlene   We don't have any foreign clients. You'd have
to go elsewhere.

Jeanine Yes I know. I don't really . . . I just mean . . .

Marlene Does your fiancé want to travel?

Jeanine I'd like a job where I was here in London and with him and everything but now and then – I expect it's silly. Are there jobs like that?

Marlene There's personal assistant to a top executive in a multinational. If that's the idea you need to be planning ahead. Is that where you want to be in ten years?

Jeanine I might not be alive in ten years.

Marlene Yes but you will be. You'll have children.

Jeanine I can't think about ten years.

Marlene You haven't got the speeds anyway. So I'll send you to these two shall I? You haven't been to any other agency? Just so we don't get crossed wires. Now, Jeanine, I want you to get one of these jobs, all right? If I send you that means I'm putting myself on the line for you. Your presentation's OK, you look fine, just be confident and go in there convinced that this is the best job for you and you're the best person for the job. If you don't believe it they won't believe it.

Jeanine Do you believe it?

Marlene I think you could make me believe it if you put your mind to it.

Jeanine Yes, all right.

Scene Two

Joyce's *backyard. The house with back door is upstage. Downstage a shelter made of junk, made by children. Two girls,* **Angie** *and* **Kit**, *are in it, squashed together.* **Angie** *is sixteen,* **Kit** *is twelve. They cannot be seen from the house.* **Joyce** *calls from the house.*

Joyce Angie. Angie, are you out there?

Silence. They keep still and wait. When nothing else happens they relax.

Angie Wish she was dead.

Kit Wanna watch *The Exterminator*?

Angie You're sitting on my leg.

Kit There's nothing on telly. We can have an ice cream. Angie?

Angie Shall I tell you something?

Kit Do you wanna watch *The Exterminator*?

Angie It's X, innit.

Kit I can get into Xs.

Angie Shall I tell you something?

Kit We'll go to something else. We'll go to Ipswich. What's on the Odeon?

Angie She won't let me, will she?

Kit Don't tell her.

Angie I've no money.

Kit I'll pay.

Angie She'll moan though, won't she?

Kit I'll ask her for you if you like.

Angie I've no money, I don't want you to pay.

Kit I'll ask her.

Angie She don't like you.

Kit I still got three pounds birthday money. Did she say she don't like me? I'll go by myself then.

Angie Your mum don't let you. I got to take you.

Kit She won't know.

Angie You'd be scared who'd sit next to you.

Kit   No I wouldn't.
She does like me anyway.
Tell me then.

Angie   Tell you what?

Kit   It's you she doesn't like.

Angie   Well I don't like her so tough shit.

Joyce (*off*)   Angie. Angie. Angie. I know you're out there.
I'm not coming out after you. You come in here.

Silence. Nothing happens.

Angie   Last night when I was in bed. I been thinking
yesterday could I make things move. You know, make
things move by thinking about them without touching them.
Last night I was in bed and suddenly a picture fell down
off the wall.

Kit   What picture?

Angie   My gran, that picture. Not the poster. The
photograph in the frame.

Kit   Had you done something to make it fall down?

Angie   I must have done.

Kit   But were you thinking about it?

Angie   Not about it, but about something.

Kit   I don't think that's very good.

Angie   You know the kitten?

Kit   Which one?

Angie   There only is one. The dead one.

Kit   What about it?

Angie   I heard it last night.

Kit   Where?

Angie   Out here. In the dark. What if I left you here in the dark all night?

Kit   You couldn't. I'd go home.

Angie   You couldn't.

Kit   I'd / go home.

Angie   No you couldn't, not if I said.

Kit   I could.

Angie   Then you wouldn't see anything. You'd just be ignorant.

Kit   I can see in the daytime.

Angie   No you can't. You can't hear it in the daytime.

Kit   I don't want to hear it.

Angie   You're scared that's all.

Kit   I'm not scared of anything.

Angie   You're scared of blood.

Kit   It's not the same kitten anyway. You just heard an old cat, / you just heard some old cat.

Angie   You don't know what I heard. Or what I saw. You don't know nothing because you're a baby.

Kit   You're sitting on me.

Angie   Mind my hair / you silly cunt.

Kit   Stupid fucking cow, I hate you.

Angie   I don't care if you do.

Kit   You're horrible.

Angie   I'm going to kill my mother and you're going to watch.

Kit   I'm not playing.

Angie   You're scared of blood.

Kit *puts her hand under her dress, brings it out with blood on her finger.*

Kit   There, see, I got my own blood, so.

Angie *takes* **Kit***'s hand and licks her finger.*

Angie   Now I'm a cannibal. I might turn into a vampire now.

Kit   That picture wasn't nailed up right.

Angie   You'll have to do that when I get mine.

Kit   I don't have to.

Angie   You're scared.

Kit   I'll do it, I might do it. I don't have to just because you say. I'll be sick on you.

Angie   I don't care if you are sick on me, I don't mind sick. I don't mind blood. If I don't get away from here I'm going to die.

Kit   I'm going home.

Angie   You can't go through the house. She'll see you.

Kit   I won't tell her.

Angie   Oh great, fine.

Kit   I'll say I was by myself. I'll tell her you're at my house and I'm going there to get you.

Angie   She knows I'm here, stupid.

Kit   Then why can't I go through the house?

Angie   Because I said not.

Kit   My mum don't like you anyway.

Angie   I don't want her to like me. She's a slag.

Kit   She is not.

Angie   She does it with everyone.

Kit   She does not.

Angie You don't even know what it is.

Kit Yes I do.

Angie Tell me then.

Kit We get it all at school, cleverclogs. It's on television. You haven't done it.

Angie How do you know?

Kit Because I know you haven't.

Angie You know wrong then because I have.

Kit Who with?

Angie I'm not telling you / who with.

Kit You haven't anyway.

Angie How do you know?

Kit Who with?

Angie I'm not telling you.

Kit You said you told me everything.

Angie I was lying wasn't I?

Kit Who with? You can't tell me who with because / you never –

Angie Sh.

Joyce *has come out of the house. She stops halfway across the yard and listens. They listen.*

Joyce You there, Angie? Kit? You there, Kitty? Want a cup of tea? I've got some chocolate biscuits. Come on now I'll put the kettle on. Want a choccy bicky, Angie?

They all listen and wait.

Fucking rotten little cunt. You can stay there and die. I'll lock the back door.

They all wait.

Joyce *goes back to the house.*

Angie *and* **Kit** *sit in silence for a while.*

Kit   When there's a war, where's the safest place?

Angie   Nowhere.

Kit   New Zealand is, my mum said. Your skin's burned right off. Shall we go to New Zealand?

Angie   I'm not staying here.

Kit   Shall we go to New Zealand?

Angie   You're not old enough.

Kit   You're not old enough.

Angie   I'm old enough to get married.

Kit   You don't want to get married.

Angie   No but I'm old enough.

Kit   I'd find out where they were going to drop it and stand right in the place.

Angie   You couldn't find out.

Kit   Better than walking round with your skin dragging on the ground. Eugh. / Would you like walking round with your skin dragging on the ground?

Angie   You couldn't find out, stupid, it's a secret.

Kit   Where are you going?

Angie   I'm not telling you.

Kit   Why?

Angie   It's a secret.

Kit   But you tell me all your secrets.

Angie   Not the true secrets.

Kit   Yes you do.

Angie   No I don't.

Kit   I want to go somewhere away from the war.

Angie   Just forget the war.

Kit I can't.

Angie You have to. It's so boring.

Kit I'll remember it at night.

Angie I'm going to do something else anyway.

Kit What? Angie, come on. Angie.

Angie It's a true secret.

Kit It can't be worse than the kitten. And killing your mother. And the war.

Angie Well I'm not telling you so you can die for all I care.

Kit My mother says there's something wrong with you playing with someone my age. She says why haven't you got friends your own age. People your own age know there's something funny about you. She says you're a bad influence. She says she's going to speak to your mother.

Angie *twists* **Kit***'s arm till she cries out.*

Angie Say you're a liar.

Kit She said it not me.

Angie Say you eat shit.

Kit You can't make me.

Angie *lets go.*

Angie I don't care anyway. I'm leaving.

Kit Go on then.

Angie You'll all wake up one morning and find I've gone.

Kit Good.

Angie I'm not telling you when.

Kit Go on then.

Angie I'm sorry I hurt you.

Kit   I'm tired.

Angie   Do you like me?

Kit   I don't know.

Angie   You do like me.

Kit   I'm going home.

Kit *gets up.*

Angie   No you're not.

Kit   I'm tired.

Angie   She'll see you.

Kit   She'll give me a chocolate biscuit.

Angie   Kitty.

Kit   Tell me where you're going.

Angie   Sit down.

Kit *sits in the hut again.*

Kit   Go on then.

Angie   Swear?

Kit   Swear.

Angie   I'm going to London. To see my aunt.

Kit   And what?

Angie   That's it.

Kit   I see my aunt all the time.

Angie   I don't see my aunt.

Kit   What's so special?

Angie   It is special. She's special.

Kit   Why?

Angie   She is.

Kit Why?

Angie She is.

Kit Why?

Angie My mother hates her.

Kit Why?

Angie Because she does.

Kit Perhaps she's not very nice.

Angie She is nice.

Kit How do you know?

Angie Because I know her.

Kit You said you never see her.

Angie I saw her last year. You saw her.

Kit Did I?

Angie Never mind.

Kit I remember her. That aunt. What's so special?

Angie She gets people jobs.

Kit What's so special?

Angie I think I'm my aunt's child. I think my mother's really my aunt.

Kit Why?

Angie Because she goes to America, now shut up.

Kit I've been to London.

Angie Now give us a cuddle and shut up because I'm sick.

Kit You're sitting on my arm.

Silence. **Joyce** *comes out and comes up to them quietly.*

Joyce Come on.

Kit   Oh hello.

Joyce   Time you went home.

Kit   We want to go to the Odeon.

Joyce   What time?

Kit   Don't know.

Joyce   What's on?

Kit   Don't know.

Joyce   Don't know much do you?

Kit   That all right then?

Joyce   Angie's got to clean her room first.

Angie   No I don't.

Joyce   Yes you do, it's a pigsty.

Angie   Well I'm not.

Joyce   Then you're not going. I don't care.

Angie   Well I am going.

Joyce   You've no money, have you?

Angie   Kit's paying anyway.

Joyce   No she's not.

Kit   I'll help you with your room.

Joyce   That's nice.

Angie   No you won't. You wait here.

Kit   Hurry then.

Angie   I'm not hurrying. You just wait.

Angie *goes into the house. Silence*

Joyce   I don't know.

Silence.

How's school then?

Kit   All right.

Joyce   What are you now? Third year?

Kit   Second year.

Joyce   Your mum says you're good at English.

Silence.

Maybe Angie should've stayed on.

Kit   She didn't like it.

Joyce   I didn't like it. And look at me. If your face fits at school it's going to fit other places too. It wouldn't make no difference to Angie. She's not going to get a job when jobs are hard to get. I'd be sorry for anyone in charge of her. She'd better get married. I don't know who'd have her, mind. She's one of those girls might never leave home. What do you want to be when you grow up, Kit?

Kit   Physicist.

Joyce   What?

Kit   Nuclear physicist.

Joyce   Whatever for?

Kit   I could, I'm clever.

Joyce   I know you're clever, pet.

Silence.

I'll make a cup of tea.

Silence.

Looks like it's going to rain.

Silence.

Don't you have friends your own age?

Kit   Yes.

Joyce   Well then.

Kit   I'm old for my age.

Joyce   And Angie's simple is she? She's not simple.

Kit   I love Angie.

Joyce   She's clever in her own way.

Kit   You can't stop me.

Joyce   I don't want to.

Kit   You can't, so.

Joyce   Don't be cheeky, Kitty. She's always kind to little children.

Kit   She's coming so you better leave me alone.

Angie comes out. She has changed into an old best dress, slightly small for her.

Joyce   What you put that on for? Have you done your room? You can't clean your room in that.

Angie   I looked in the cupboard and it was there.

Joyce   Of course it was there, it's meant to be there. Is that why it was a surprise, finding something in the right place? I should think she's surprised, wouldn't you, Kit, to find something in her room in the right place.

Angie   I decided to wear it.

Joyce   Not today, why? To clean your room? You're not going to the pictures till you've done your room. You can put your dress on after if you like.

Angie picks up a brick.

Joyce   Have you done your room? You're not getting out of it, you know.

Kit   Angie, let's go.

Joyce   She's not going till she's done her room.

Kit   It's starting to rain.

Joyce   Come on, come on then. Hurry and do your room, Angie, and then you can go to the cinema with Kit.

Oh it's wet, come on. We'll look up the time in the paper. Does your mother know, Kit, it's going to be a late night for you, isn't it? Hurry up, Angie. You'll spoil your dress. You make me sick.

Joyce *and* **Kit** *run in.*

Angie *stays where she is. Sound of rain.*

Kit *comes out of the house and shouts.*

Kit   Angie. Angie, come on, you'll get wet.

Kit *comes back to* **Angie**.

Angie   I put on this dress to kill my mother.

Kit   I suppose you thought you'd do it with a brick.

Angie   You can kill people with a brick.

Kit   Well you didn't, so.

Scene Three

Office of 'Top Girls' Employment Agency. Three desks and a small interviewing area. Monday morning. **Win** *and* **Nell** *have just arrived for work.*

Nell   Coffee coffee coffee coffee / coffee.

Win   The roses were smashing. / Mermaid.

Nell   Ohhh.

Win   Iceberg. He taught me all their names.

Nell *has some coffee now.*

Nell   Ah. Now then.

Win   He has one of the finest rose gardens in West Sussex. He exhibits.

Nell   He what?

Win   His wife was visiting her mother. It was like living together.

Nell   Crafty, you never said.

Win   He rang on Saturday morning.

Nell   Lucky you were free.

Win   That's what I told him.

Nell   Did you hell.

Win   Have you ever seen a really beautiful rose garden?

Nell   I don't like flowers. / I like swimming pools.

Win   Marilyn. Esther's Baby. They're all called after birds.

Nell   Our friend's late. Celebrating all weekend I bet you.

Win   I'd call a rose Elvis. Or John Conteh.

Nell   Is Howard in yet?

Win   If he is he'll be bleeping us with a problem.

Nell   Howard can just hang onto himself.

Win   Howard's really cut up.

Nell   Howard thinks because he's a fella the job was his as of right. Our Marlene's got far more balls than Howard and that's that.

Win   Poor little bugger.

Nell   He'll live.

Win   He'll move on.

Nell   I wouldn't mind a change of air myself.

Win   Serious?

Nell   I've never been a staying-put lady. Pastures new.

Win   So who's the pirate?

Nell   There's nothing definite.

Win   Inquiries?

Nell   There's always inquiries. I'd think I'd got bad breath if there stopped being inquiries. Most of them can't afford me. Or you.

Win I'm all right for the time being. Unless I go to Australia.

Nell There's not a lot of room upward.

Win Marlene's filled it up.

Nell Good luck to her. Unless there's some prospects moneywise.

Win You can but ask.

Nell Can always but ask.

Win So what have we got? I've got a Mr Holden I saw last week.

Nell Any use?

Win Pushy. Bit of a cowboy.

Nell Good-looker?

Win Good dresser.

Nell High-flyer?

Win That's his general idea certainly but I'm not sure he's got it up there.

Nell Prestel wants six high-flyers and I've only seen two and a half.

Win He's making a bomb on the road but he thinks it's time for an office. I sent him to IBM but he didn't get it.

Nell Prestel's on the road.

Win He's not overbright.

Nell Can he handle an office?

Win Provided his secretary can punctuate he should go far.

Nell Bear Prestel in mind then, I might put my head round the door. I've got that poor little nerd I should never have said I could help. Tender heart me.

Win Tender like old boots. How old?

Nell Yes well forty-five.

Win Say no more.

Nell He knows his place, he's not after calling himself a manager, he's just a poor little bod wants a better commission and a bit of sunshine.

Win Don't we all.

Nell He's just got to relocate. He's got a bungalow in Dymchurch.

Win And his wife says.

Nell The lady wife wouldn't care to relocate. She's going through the change.

Win It's his funeral, don't waste your time.

Nell I don't waste a lot.

Win Good weekend you?

Nell You could say.

Win Which one?

Nell One Friday, one Saturday.

Win Aye aye.

Nell Sunday night I watched telly.

Win Which of them do you like best really?

Nell Sunday was best, I liked the Ovaltine.

Win Holden, Barker, Gardner, Duke.

Nell I've a lady here thinks she can sell.

Win Taking her on?

Nell She's had some jobs.

Win Services?

Nell No, quite heavy stuff, electric.

Win   Tough bird like us.

Nell   We could do with a few more here.

Win   There's nothing going here.

Nell   No but I always want the tough ones when I see them. Hang onto them.

Win   I think we're plenty.

Nell   Derek asked me to marry him again.

Win   He doesn't know when he's beaten.

Nell   I told him I'm not going to play house, not even in Ascot.

Win   Mind you, you could play house.

Nell   If I chose to play house I would play house ace.

Win   You could marry him and go on working.

Nell   I could go on working and not marry him.

Marlene *arrives.*

Marlene   Morning, ladies.

Win *and* **Nell** *cheer and whistle.*

Marlene   Mind my head.

Nell   Coffee coffee coffee.

Win   We're tactfully not mentioning you're late.

Marlene   Fucking tube.

Win   We've heard that one.

Nell   We've used that one.

Win   It's the top executive doesn't come in as early as the poor working girl.

Marlene   Pass the sugar and shut your face, pet.

Win   Well I'm delighted.

Nell   Howard's looking sick.

Win   Howard is sick. He's got ulcers and heart. He told me.

Nell   He'll have to stop then won't he?

Win   Stop what?

Nell   Smoking, drinking, shouting. Working.

Win   Well, working.

Nell   We're just looking through the day.

Marlene   I'm doing some of Pam's ladies. They've been piling up while she's away.

Nell   Half a dozen little girls and an arts graduate who can't type.

Win   I spent the whole weekend at his place in Sussex.

Nell   She fancies his rose garden.

Win   I had to lie down in the back of the car so the neighbours wouldn't see me go in.

Nell   You're kidding.

Win   It was funny.

Nell   Fuck that for a joke.

Win   It was funny.

Marlene   Anyway they'd see you in the garden.

Win   The garden has extremely high walls.

Nell   I think I'll tell the wife.

Win   Like hell.

Nell   She might leave him and you could have the rose garden.

Win   The minute it's not a secret I'm out on my ear.

Nell   Don't know why you bother.

Win   Bit of fun.

Nell   I think it's time you went to Australia.

Win   I think it's pushy Mr Holden time.

Nell   If you've any really pretty bastards, Marlene, I want some for Prestel.

Marlene   I might have one this afternoon. This morning it's all Pam's secretarial.

Nell   Not long now and you'll be upstairs watching over us all.

Marlene   Do you feel bad about it?

Nell   I don't like coming second.

Marlene   Who does?

Win   We'd rather it was you than Howard. We're glad for you, aren't we, Nell.

Nell   Oh yes. Aces.

Interview
Win *and* **Louise**.

Win   Now, Louise, hello, I have your details here. You've been very loyal to the one job I see.

Louise   Yes I have.

Win   Twenty-one years is a long time in one place.

Louise   I feel it is. I feel it's time to move on.

Win   And you are what age now?

Louise   I'm in my early forties.

Win   Exactly?

Louise   Forty-six.

Win   It's not necessarily a handicap, well it is of course we have to face that, but it's not necessarily a disabling handicap, experience does count for something.

Louise   I hope so.

Win   Now between ourselves is there any trouble, any reason why you're leaving that wouldn't appear on the form?

Louise   Nothing like that.

Win   Like what?

Louise   Nothing at all.

Win   No long-term understandings come to a sudden end, making for an insupportable atmosphere?

Louise   I've always completely avoided anything like that at all.

Win   No personality clashes with your immediate superiors or inferiors?

Louise   I've always taken care to get on very well with everyone.

Win   I only ask because it can affect the reference and it also affects your motivation, I want to be quite clear why you're moving on. So I take it the job itself no longer satisfies you. Is it the money?

Louise   It's partly the money. It's not so much the money.

Win   Nine thousand is very respectable. Have you dependants?

Louise   No, no dependants. My mother died.

Win   So why are you making a change?

Louise   Other people make changes.

Win   But why are you, now, after spending most of your life in the one place?

Louise   There you are, I've lived for that company, I've given my life really you could say because I haven't had a great deal of social life, I've worked in the evenings. I

haven't had office entanglements for the very reason you
just mentioned and if you are committed to your work you
don't move in many other circles. I had management status
from the age of twenty-seven and you'll appreciate what
that means. I've built up a department. And there it is, it
works extremely well, and I feel I'm stuck there. I've spent
twenty years in middle management. I've seen young men
who I trained go on, in my own company or elsewhere, to
higher things. Nobody notices me, I don't expect it, I don't
attract attention by making mistakes, everybody takes it for
granted that my work is perfect. They will notice me when
I go, they will be sorry I think to lose me, they will offer
me more money of course, I will refuse. They will see
when I've gone what I was doing for them.

Win If they offer you more money you won't stay?

Louise No I won't.

Win Are you the only woman?

Louise Apart from the girls of course, yes. There was
one, she was my assistant, it was the only time I took on a
young woman assistant, I always had my doubts. I don't
care greatly for working with women, I think I pass as a
man at work. But I did take on this young woman, her
qualifications were excellent, and she did well, she got a
department of her own, and left the company for a
competitor where she's now on the board and good luck to
her. She has a different style, she's a new kind of attractive
well-dressed – I don't mean I don't dress properly. But
there is a kind of woman who is thirty now who grew up
in a different climate. They are not so careful. They take
themselves for granted. I have had to justify my existence
every minute, and I have done so, I have proved – well.

Win Let's face it, vacancies are going to be ones where
you'll be in competition with younger men. And there are
companies that will value your experience enough you'll be
in with a chance. There are also fields that are easier for a
woman, there is a cosmetic company here where your
experience might be relevant. It's eight and a half, I don't

know if that appeals.

Louise I've proved I can earn money. It's more important to get away. I feel it's now or never. I sometimes / think –

Win You shouldn't talk too much at an interview.

Louise I don't. I don't normally talk about myself. I know very well how to handle myself in an office situation. I only talk to you because it seems to me this is different, it's your job to understand me, surely. You asked the questions.

Win I think I understand you sufficiently.

Louise Well good, that's good.

Win Do you drink?

Louise Certainly not. I'm not a teetotaller, I think that's very suspect, it's seen as being an alcoholic if you're teetotal. What do you mean? I don't drink. Why?

Win I drink.

Louise I don't.

Win Good for you.

Main office
Marlene *and* **Angie**.

Angie *arrives.*

Angie Hello.

Marlene Have you an appointment?

Angie It's me. I've come.

Marlene What? It's not Angie?

Angie It was hard to find this place. I got lost.

Marlene How did you get past the receptionist? The girl on the desk, didn't she try to stop you?

Angie   What desk?

Marlene   Never mind.

Angie   I just walked in. I was looking for you.

Marlene   Well you found me.

Angie   Yes.

Marlene   So where's your mum? Are you up in town for the day?

Angie   Not really.

Marlene   Sit down. Do you feel all right?

Angie   Yes thank you.

Marlene   So where's Joyce?

Angie   She's at home.

Marlene   Did you come up on a school trip then?

Angie   I've left school.

Marlene   Did you come up with a friend?

Angie   No. There's just me.

Marlene   You came up by yourself, that's fun. What have you been doing? Shopping? Tower of London?

Angie   No. I just come here. I come to you.

Marlene   That's very nice of you to think of paying your aunty a visit. There's not many nieces make that the first port of call. Would you like a cup of coffee?

Angie   No thank you.

Marlene   Tea, orange?

Angie   No thank you.

Marlene   Do you feel all right?

Angie   Yes thank you.

Marlene   Are you tired from the journey?

Angie Yes, I'm tired from the journey.

Marlene You sit there for a bit then. How's Joyce?

Angie She's all right.

Marlene Same as ever.

Angie Oh yes.

Marlene Unfortunately you've picked a day when I'm rather busy, if there's ever a day when I'm not, or I'd take you out to lunch and we'd go to Madame Tussaud's. We could go shopping. What time do you have to be back? Have you got a day return?

Angie No.

Marlene So what train are you going back on?

Angie I came on the bus.

Marlene So what bus are you going back on? Are you staying the night?

Angie Yes.

Marlene Who are you staying with? Do you want me to put you up for the night, is that it?

Angie Yes please.

Marlene I haven't got a spare bed.

Angie I can sleep on the floor.

Marlene You can sleep on the sofa.

Angie Yes please.

Marlene I do think Joyce might have phoned me. It's like her.

Angie This is where you work is it?

Marlene It's where I have been working the last two years but I'm going to move into another office.

Angie It's lovely.

Marlene My new office is nicer than this. There's just the one big desk in it for me.

Angie Can I see it?

Marlene Not now, no, there's someone else in it now. But he's leaving at the end of next week and I'm going to do his job.

Angie Is that good?

Marlene Yes, it's very good.

Angie Are you going to be in charge?

Marlene Yes I am.

Angie I knew you would be.

Marlene How did you know?

Angie I knew you'd be in charge of everything.

Marlene Not quite everything.

Angie You will be.

Marlene Well we'll see.

Angie Can I see it next week then?

Marlene Will you still be here next week?

Angie Yes.

Marlene Don't you have to go home?

Angie No.

Marlene Why not?

Angie It's all right.

Marlene Is it all right?

Angie Yes, don't worry about it.

Marlene Does Joyce know where you are?

Angie Yes of course she does.

Marlene Well does she?

Angie Don't worry about it.

Marlene How long are you planning to stay with me then?

Angie You know when you came to see us last year?

Marlene Yes, that was nice wasn't it?

Angie That was the best day of my whole life.

Marlene So how long are you planning to stay?

Angie Don't you want me?

Marlene Yes yes, I just wondered.

Angie I won't stay if you don't want me.

Marlene No, of course you can stay.

Angie I'll sleep on the floor. I won't be any bother.

Marlene Don't get upset.

Angie I'm not. I'm not. Don't worry about it.

Mrs Kidd *comes in.*

Mrs Kidd Excuse me.

Marlene Yes.

Mrs Kidd Excuse me.

Marlene Can I help you?

Mrs Kidd Excuse me bursting in on you like this but I have to talk to you.

Marlene I am engaged at the moment. / If you could go to reception –

Mrs Kidd I'm Rosemary Kidd, Howard's wife, you don't recognise me but we did meet, I remember you of course / but you wouldn't –

Marlene Yes of course, Mrs Kidd, I'm sorry, we did

meet. Howard's about somewhere I expect, have you
looked in his office?

Mrs Kidd   Howard's not about, no. I'm afraid it's you
I've come to see if I could have a minute or two.

Marlene   I do have an appointment in five minutes.

Mrs Kidd   This won't take five minutes. I'm very sorry.
It is a matter of some urgency.

Marlene   Well of course. What can I do for you?

Mrs Kidd   I just wanted a chat, an informal chat. It's not
something I can simply – I'm sorry if I'm interrupting your
work. I know office work isn't like housework / which is all
interruptions.

Marlene   No no, this is my niece. Angie. Mrs Kidd.

Mrs Kidd   Very pleased to meet you.

Angie   Very well thank you.

Mrs Kidd   Howard's not in today.

Marlene   Isn't he?

Mrs Kidd   He's feeling poorly.

Marlene   I didn't know. I'm sorry to hear that.

Mrs Kidd   The fact is he's in a state of shock. About
what's happened.

Marlene   What has happened?

Mrs Kidd   You should know if anyone. I'm referring to
you being appointed managing director instead of Howard.
He hasn't been at all well all weekend. He hasn't slept for
three nights. I haven't slept.

Marlene   I'm sorry to hear that, Mrs Kidd. Has he
thought of taking sleeping pills?

Mrs Kidd   It's very hard when someone has worked all
these years.

Marlene Business life is full of little setbacks. I'm sure Howard knows that. He'll bounce back in a day or two. We all bounce back.

Mrs Kidd If you could see him you'd know what I'm talking about. What's it going to do to him working for a woman? I think if it was a man he'd get over it as something normal.

Marlene I think he's going to have to get over it.

Mrs Kidd It's me that bears the brunt. I'm not the one that's been promoted. I put him first every inch of the way. And now what do I get? You women this, you women that. It's not my fault. You're going to have to be very careful how you handle him. He's very hurt.

Marlene Naturally I'll be tactful and pleasant to him, you don't start pushing someone round. I'll consult him over any decisions affecting his department. But that's no different, Mrs Kidd, from any of my other colleagues.

Mrs Kidd I think it is different, because he's a man.

Marlene I'm not quite sure why you came to see me.

Mrs Kidd I had to do something.

Marlene Well you've done it, you've seen me. I think that's probably all we've time for. I'm sorry he's been taking it out on you. He really is a shit, Howard.

Mrs Kidd But he's got a family to support. He's got three children. It's only fair.

Marlene Are you suggesting I give up the job to him then?

Mrs Kidd It had crossed my mind if you were unavailable after all for some reason, he would be the natural second choice I think, don't you? I'm not asking.

Marlene Good.

Mrs Kidd You mustn't tell him I came. He's very proud.

Marlene   If he doesn't like what's happening here he can go and work somewhere else.

Mrs Kidd   Is that a threat?

Marlene   I'm sorry but I do have some work to do.

Mrs Kidd   It's not that easy, a man of Howard's age. You don't care. I thought he was going too far but he's right. You're one of these ballbreakers / that's what you are. You'll end up

Marlene   I'm sorry but I do have some work to do.

Mrs Kidd   miserable and lonely. You're not natural.

Marlene   Could you please piss off?

Mrs Kidd   I thought if I saw you at least I'd be doing something.

Mrs Kidd *goes.*

Marlene   I've got to go and do some work now. Will you come back later?

Angie   I think you were wonderful.

Marlene   I've got to go and do some work now.

Angie   You told her to piss off.

Marlene   Will you come back later?

Angie   Can't I stay here?

Marlene   Don't you want to go sightseeing?

Angie   I'd rather stay here.

Marlene   You can stay here I suppose, if it's not boring.

Angie   It's where I most want to be in the world.

Marlene   I'll see you later then.

Marlene *goes.*

Angie *sits at* **Win**'s *desk.*

Interview
Nell *and* **Shona**.

Nell Is this right? You are Shona?

Shona Yeh.

Nell It says here you're twenty-nine.

Shona Yeh.

Nell Too many late nights, me. So you've been where you are for four years, Shona, you're earning six basic and three commission. So what's the problem?

Shona No problem.

Nell Why do you want a change?

Shona Just a change.

Nell Change of product, change of area?

Shona Both.

Nell But you're happy on the road?

Shona I like driving.

Nell You're not after management status?

Shona I would like management status.

Nell You'd be interested in titular management status but not come off the road?

Shona I want to be on the road, yeh.

Nell So how many calls have you been making a day?

Shona Six.

Nell And what proportion of those are successful?

Shona Six.

Nell That's hard to believe.

Shona Four.

Nell You find it easy to get the initial interest, do you?

Shona Oh yeh, I get plenty of initial interest.

Nell And what about closing?

Shona I close, don't I?

Nell Because that's what an employer is going to have doubts about with a lady as I needn't tell you, whether she's got the guts to push through to a closing situation. They think we're too nice. They think we listen to the buyer's doubts. They think we consider his needs and his feelings.

Shona I never consider people's feelings.

Nell I was selling for six years, I can sell anything, I've sold in three continents, and I'm jolly as they come but I'm not very nice.

Shona I'm not very nice.

Nell What sort of time do you have on the road with the other reps? Get on all right? Handle the chat?

Shona I get on. Keep myself to myself.

Nell Fairly much of a loner are you?

Shona Sometimes.

Nell So what field are you interested in?

Shona Computers.

Nell That's a top field as you know and you'll be up against some very slick fellas there, there's some very pretty boys in computers, it's an American-style field.

Shona That's why I want to do it.

Nell Video systems appeal? That's a high-flying situation.

Shona Video systems appeal OK.

Nell Because Prestel have half a dozen vacancies I'm

looking to fill at the moment. We're talking in the area of ten to fifteen thousand here and upwards.

Shona   Sounds OK.

Nell   I've half a mind to go for it myself. But it's good money here if you've got the top clients. Could you fancy it do you think?

Shona   Work here?

Nell   I'm not in a position to offer, there's nothing officially going just now, but we're always on the lookout. There's not that many of us. We could keep in touch.

Shona   I like driving.

Nell   So the Prestel appeals?

Shona   Yeh.

Nell   What about ties?

Shona   No ties.

Nell   So relocation wouldn't be a problem.

Shona   No problem.

Nell   So just fill me in a bit more could you about what you've been doing.

Shona   What I've been doing. It's all down there.

Nell   The bare facts are down here but I've got to present you to an employer.

Shona   I'm twenty-nine years old.

Nell   So it says here.

Shona   We look young. Youngness runs in the family in our family.

Nell   So just describe your present job for me.

Shona   My present job at present. I have a car. I have a Porsche. I go up the M1 a lot. Burn up the M1 a lot.

Straight up the M1 in the fast lane to where the clients
are, Staffordshire, Yorkshire, I do a lot in Yorkshire. I'm
selling electric things. Like dishwashers, washing machines,
stainless-steel tubs are a feature and the reliability of the
programme. After-sales service, we offer a very good after-
sales service, spare parts, plenty of spare parts. And fridges,
I sell a lot of fridges specially in the summer. People want
to buy fridges in the summer because of the heat melting
the butter and you get fed up standing the milk in a basin
of cold water with a cloth over, stands to reason people
don't want to do that in this day and age. So I sell a lot of
them. Big ones with big freezers. Big freezers. And I stay in
hotels at night when I'm away from home. On my expense
account. I stay in various hotels. They know me, the ones I
go to. I check in, have a bath, have a shower. Then I go
down to the bar, have a gin and tonic, have a chat. Then
I go into the dining room and have dinner. I usually have
fillet steak and mushrooms, I like mushrooms. I like smoked
salmon very much. I like having a salad on the side. Green
salad. I don't like tomatoes.

Nell   Christ what a waste of time.

Shona   Beg your pardon?

Nell   Not a word of this is true is it?

Shona   How do you mean?

Nell   You just filled in the form with a pack of lies.

Shona   Not exactly.

Nell   How old are you?

Shona   Twenty-nine.

Nell   Nineteen?

Shona   Twenty-one.

Nell   And what jobs have you done? Have you done any?

Shona   I could though, I bet you.

Main office

Angie *sitting as before.*

Win *comes in.*

Win Who's sitting in my chair?

Angie What? Sorry.

Win Who's been eating my porridge?

Angie What?

Win It's all right, I saw Marlene. Angie isn't it? I'm Win. And I'm not going out for lunch because I'm knackered. I'm going to set me down here and have a yoghurt. Do you like yoghurt?

Angie No.

Win That's good because I've only got one. Are you hungry?

Angie No.

Win There's a cafe on the corner.

Angie No thank you. Do you work here?

Win How did you guess?

Angie Because you look as if you might work here and you're sitting at the desk. Have you always worked here?

Win No I was headhunted. That means I was working for another outfit like this and this lot came and offered me more money. I broke my contract, there was a hell of a stink. There's not many top ladies about. Your aunty's a smashing bird.

Angie Yes I know.

Win Fan are you? Fan of your aunty's?

Angie Do you think I could work here?

Win Not at the moment.

Angie How do I start?

Win What can you do?

Angie I don't know. Nothing.

Win Type?

Angie Not very well. The letters jump up when I do capitals. I was going to do a CSE in commerce but I didn't.

Win What have you got?

Angie What?

Win CSEs, Os.

Angie Nothing, none of that. Did you do all that?

Win Oh yes, all that, and a science degree funnily enough. I started out doing medical research but there's no money in it. I thought I'd go abroad. Did you know they sell Coca-Cola in Russia and Pepsi-Cola in China? You don't have to be qualified as much as you might think. Men are awful bullshitters, they like to make out jobs are harder than they are. Any job I ever did I started doing it better than the rest of the crowd and they didn't like it. So I'd get unpopular and I'd have a drink to cheer myself up. I lived with a fella and supported him for four years, he couldn't get work. After that I went to California. I like the sunshine. Americans know how to live. This country's too slow. Then I went to Mexico, still in sales, but it's no country for a single lady. I came home, went bonkers for a bit, thought I was five different people, got over that all right, the psychiatrist said I was perfectly sane and highly intelligent. Got married in a moment of weakness and he's inside now, he's been inside four years, and I've not been to see him too much this last year. I like this better than sales, I'm not really that aggressive. I started thinking sales was a good job if you want to meet people, but you're meeting people that don't want to meet you. It's no good if you like being liked. Here your clients want to meet you because you're the one doing them some good. They hope.

Angie *has fallen asleep.* **Nell** *comes in.*

Nell   You're talking to yourself, sunshine.

Win   So what's new?

Nell   Who is this?

Win   Marlene's little niece.

Nell   What's she got, brother, sister? She never talks about her family.

Win   I was telling her my life story.

Nell   Violins?

Win   No, success story.

Nell   You've heard Howard's had a heart attack?

Win   No, when?

Nell   I heard just now. He hadn't come in, he was at home, he's gone to hospital. He's not dead. His wife was here, she rushed off in a cab.

Win   Too much butter, too much smoke. We must send him some flowers.

Marlene *comes in.*

Win   You've heard about Howard?

Marlene   Poor sod.

Nell   Lucky he didn't get the job if that's what his health's like.

Marlene   Is she asleep?

Win   She wants to work here.

Marlene   Packer in Tesco more like.

Win   She's a nice kid. Isn't she?

Marlene   She's a bit thick. She's a bit funny.

Win   She thinks you're wonderful.

Marlene   She's not going to make it.

Act Three

A year earlier. Sunday evening. **Joyce***'s kitchen.* **Joyce**, **Angie**, **Marlene**. **Marlene** *is taking presents out of a bright carrier bag.* **Angie** *has already opened a box of chocolates.*

Marlene Just a few little things. / I've no memory for

Joyce There's no need.

Marlene birthdays have I, and Christmas seems to slip by. So I think I owe Angie a few presents.

Joyce What do you say?

Angie Thank you very much. Thank you very much, Aunty Marlene.

She opens a present. It is the dress from Act One, new.

Angie Oh look, Mum, isn't it lovely?

Marlene I don't know if it's the right size. She's grown up since I saw her. / I knew she was always tall for her age.

Angie Isn't it lovely?

Joyce She's a big lump.

Marlene Hold it up, Angie, let's see.

Angie I'll put it on, shall I?

Marlene Yes, try it on.

Joyce Go on to your room then, we don't want / a strip show thank you.

Angie Of course I'm going to my room, what do you think? Look, Mum, here's something for you. Open it, go on. What is it? Can I open it for you?

Joyce Yes, you open it, pet.

Angie Don't you want to open it yourself? / Go on.

Joyce I don't mind, you can do it.

Angie It's something hard. It's – what is it? A bottle. Drink is it? No, it's what? Perfume, look. What a lot. Open it, look, let's smell it. Oh it's strong. It's lovely. Put it on me. How do you do it? Put it on me.

Joyce You're too young.

Angie I can play wearing it like dressing up.

Joyce And you're too old for that. Here, give it here, I'll do it, you'll tip the whole bottle over yourself / and we'll have you smelling all summer.

Angie Put it on you. Do I smell? Put it on Aunty too. Put it on Aunty too. Let's all smell.

Marlene I didn't know what you'd like.

Joyce There's no danger I'd have it already, / that's one thing.

Angie Now we all smell the same.

Marlene It's a bit of nonsense.

Joyce It's very kind of you, Marlene, you shouldn't.

Angie Now. I'll put on the dress and then we'll see.

Angie goes.

Joyce You've caught me on the hop with the place in a mess. / If you'd let me know you was coming I'd have got

Marlene That doesn't matter.

Joyce something in to eat. We had our dinner dinnertime. We're just going to have a cup of tea. You could have an egg.

Marlene No, I'm not hungry. Tea's fine.

Joyce I don't expect you take sugar.

Marlene Why not?

Joyce You take care of yourself.

Marlene How do you mean you didn't know I was coming?

Joyce You could have written. I know we're not on the phone but we're not completely in the dark ages, / we do have a postman.

Marlene But you asked me to come.

Joyce How did I ask you to come?

Marlene Angie said when she phoned up.

Joyce Angie phoned up, did she?

Marlene Was it just Angie's idea?

Joyce What did she say?

Marlene She said you wanted me to come and see you. / It was a couple of weeks ago. How was I to know that's a

Joyce Ha.

Marlene ridiculous idea? My diary's always full a couple of weeks ahead so we fixed it for this weekend. I was meant to get here earlier but I was held up. She gave me messages from you.

Joyce Didn't you wonder why I didn't phone you myself?

Marlene She said you didn't like using the phone. You're shy on the phone and can't use it. I don't know what you're like, do I.

Joyce Are there people who can't use the phone?

Marlene I expect so.

Joyce I haven't met any.

Marlene Why should I think she was lying?

Joyce Because she's like what she's like.

Marlene How do I know / what she's like?

Joyce It's not my fault you don't know what she's like.

You never come and see her.

Marlene   Well I have now / and you don't seem over the moon.*

Joyce   Good.
*Well I'd have got a cake if she'd told me.

Pause.

Marlene   I did wonder why you wanted to see me.

Joyce   I didn't want to see you.

Marlene   Yes, I know. Shall I go?

Joyce   I don't mind seeing you.

Marlene   Great, I feel really welcome.

Joyce   You can come and see Angie any time you like, I'm not stopping you. / You know where we are. You're the

Marlene   Ta ever so.

Joyce   one went away, not me. I'm right here where I was.
And will be a few years yet I shouldn't wonder.

Marlene   All right. All right.

Joyce *gives* **Marlene** *a cup of tea.*

Joyce   Tea.

Marlene   Sugar?

Joyce *passes* **Marlene** *the sugar.*

Marlene   It's very quiet down here.

Joyce   I expect you'd notice it.

Marlene   The air smells different too.

Joyce   That's the scent.

Marlene   No, I mean walking down the lane.

Joyce   What sort of air you get in London then?

Angie *comes in, wearing the dress. It fits.*

Marlene   Oh, very pretty. / You do look pretty, Angie.

Joyce   That fits all right.

Marlene   Do you like the colour?

Angie   Beautiful. Beautiful.

Joyce   You better take it off, / you'll get it dirty.

Angie   I want to wear it. I want to wear it.

Marlene   It is for wearing after all. You can't just hang it up and look at it.

Angie   I love it.

Joyce   Well if you must you must.

Angie   If someone asks me what's my favourite colour I'll tell them it's this. Thank you very much, Aunty Marlene.

Marlene   You didn't tell your mum you asked me down.

Angie   I wanted it to be a surprise.

Joyce   I'll give you a surprise / one of these days.

Angie   I thought you'd like to see her. She hasn't been here since I was nine. People do see their aunts.

Marlene   Is it that long? Doesn't time fly?

Angie   I wanted to.

Joyce   I'm not cross.

Angie   Are you glad?

Joyce   I smell nicer anyhow, don't I?

Kit *comes in without saying anything, as if she lived there.*

Marlene   I think it was a good idea, Angie, about time. We are sisters after all. It's a pity to let that go.

Joyce   This is Kitty, / who lives up the road. This is Angie's Aunty Marlene.

Kit　What's that?

Angie　It's a present. Do you like it?

Kit　It's all right. / Are you coming out?*

Marlene　Hello, Kitty.

Angie　*No.

Kit　What's that smell?

Angie　It's a present.

Kit　It's horrible. Come on.*

Marlene　Have a chocolate.

Angie　*No, I'm busy.

Kit　Coming out later?

Angie　No.

Kit (*to* **Marlene**)　Hello.

Kit *goes without a chocolate.*

Joyce　She's a little girl Angie sometimes plays with because she's the only child lives really close. She's like a little sister to her really. Angie's good with little children.

Marlene　Do you want to work with children, Angie? / Be a teacher or a nursery nurse?

Joyce　I don't think she's ever thought of it.

Marlene　What do you want to do?

Joyce　She hasn't an idea in her head what she wants to do. / Lucky to get anything.

Marlene　Angie?

Joyce　She's not clever like you.

Pause.

Marlene　I'm not clever, just pushy.

Joyce   True enough.

Marlene *takes a bottle of whisky out of the bag.*

Joyce   I don't drink spirits.

Angie   You do at Christmas.

Joyce   It's not Christmas, is it?

Angie   It's better than Christmas.

Marlene   Glasses?

Joyce   Just a small one then.

Marlene   Do you want some, Angie?

Angie   I can't, can I?

Joyce   Taste it if you want. You won't like it.

Marlene   We got drunk together the night your grandfather died.

Joyce   We did not get drunk.

Marlene   I got drunk. You were just overcome with grief.

Joyce   I still keep up the grave with flowers.

Marlene   Do you really?

Joyce   Why wouldn't I?

Marlene   Have you seen Mother?

Joyce   Of course I've seen Mother.

Marlene   I mean lately.

Joyce   Of course I've seen her lately, I go every Thursday.

Marlene (*to* **Angie**)   Do you remember your grandfather?

Angie   He got me out of the bath one night in a towel.

Marlene   Did he? I don't think he ever gave me a bath. Did he give you a bath, Joyce? He probably got soft in his old age. Did you like him?

Angie   Yes of course.

Marlene   Why?

Angie   What?

Marlene   So what's the news? How's Mrs Paisley? Still going crazily? / And Dorothy. What happened to Dorothy?*

Angie   Who's Mrs Paisley?

Joyce   *She went to Canada.

Marlene   Did she? What to do?

Joyce   I don't know. She just went to Canada.

Marlene   Well / good for her.

Angie   Mr Connolly killed his wife.

Marlene   What, Connolly at Whitegates?

Angie   They found her body in the garden. / Under the cabbages.

Marlene   He was always so proper.

Joyce   Stuck-up git. Connolly. Best lawyer money could buy but he couldn't get out of it. She was carrying on with Matthew.

Marlene   How old's Matthew then?

Joyce   Twenty-one. / He's got a motorbike.

Marlene   I think he's about six.

Angie   How can he be six? He's six years older than me. / If he was six I'd be nothing, I'd be just born this minute.

Joyce   Your aunty knows that, she's just being silly. She means it's so long since she's been here she's forgotten about Matthew.

Angie   You were here for my birthday when I was nine. I had a pink cake. Kit was only five then, she was four, she hadn't started school yet. She could read already when she went to school. You remember my birthday? / You remember me?

Marlene Yes, I remember the cake.

Angie You remember me?

Marlene Yes, I remember you.

Angie And Mum and Dad was there, and Kit was.

Marlene Yes, how is your dad? Where is he tonight? Up the pub?

Joyce No, he's not here.

Marlene I can see he's not here.

Joyce He moved out.

Marlene What? When did he? / Just recently?*

Angie Didn't you know that? You don't know much.

Joyce *No, it must be three years ago. Don't be rude, Angie.

Angie I'm not, am I, Aunty? What else don't you know?

Joyce You was in America or somewhere. You sent a postcard.

Angie I've got that in my room. It's the Grand Canyon. Do you want to see it? Shall I get it? I can get it for you.

Marlene Yes, all right.

Angie *goes.*

Joyce You could be married with twins for all I know. You must have affairs and break up and I don't need to know about any of that so I don't see what the fuss is about.

Marlene What fuss?

Angie *comes back with the postcard.*

Angie 'Driving across the states for a new job in LA. It's a long way but the car goes very fast. It's very hot. Wish you were here. Love from Aunty Marlene.'

Joyce   Did you make a lot of money?

Marlene   I spent a lot.

Angie   I want to go to America. Will you take me?

Joyce   She's not going to America, she's been to America, stupid.

Angie   She might go again, stupid. It's not something you do once. People who go keep going all the time, back and forth on jets. They go on Concorde and Laker and get jet lag. Will you take me?

Marlene   I'm not planning a trip.

Angie   Will you let me know?

Joyce   Angie, / you're getting silly.

Angie   I want to be American.

Joyce   It's time you were in bed.

Angie   No it's not. / I don't have to go to bed at all tonight.

Joyce   School in the morning.

Angie   I'll wake up.

Joyce   Come on now, you know how you get.

Angie   How do I get? / I don't get anyhow.

Joyce   Angie.
Are you staying the night?

Marlene   Yes, if that's all right. / I'll see you in the morning.

Angie   You can have my bed. I'll sleep on the sofa.

Joyce   You will not, you'll sleep in your bed. / Think I can't

Angie   Mum.

Joyce   see through that? I can just see you going to sleep
/ with us talking.

Angie   I would, I would go to sleep, I'd love that.

Joyce   I'm going to get cross, Angie.

Angie   I want to show her something.

Joyce   Then bed.

Angie   It's a secret.

Joyce   Then I expect it's in your room so off you go.
Give us a shout when you're ready for bed and your
aunty'll be up and see you.

Angie   Will you?

Marlene   Yes of course.

Angie *goes.*

Silence.

Marlene   It's cold tonight.

Joyce   Will you be all right on the sofa? You can / have
my bed.

Marlene   The sofa's fine.

Joyce   Yes the forecast said rain tonight but it's held off.

Marlene   I was going to walk down to the estuary but
I've left it a bit late. Is it just the same?

Joyce   They cut down the hedges a few years back. Is
that since you were here?

Marlene   But it's not changed down the end, all the
mud? And the reeds? We used to pick them when they
were bigger than us. Are there still lapwings?

Joyce   You get strangers walking there on a Sunday. I
expect they're looking at the mud and the lapwings, yes.

Marlene   You could have left.

Joyce   Who says I wanted to leave?

Marlene   Stop getting at me then, you're really boring.

Joyce   How could I have left?

Marlene   Did you want to?

Joyce   I said how, / how could I?

Marlene   If you'd wanted to you'd have done it.

Joyce   Christ.

Marlene   Are we getting drunk?

Joyce   Do you want something to eat?

Marlene   No, I'm getting drunk.

Joyce   Funny time to visit, Sunday evening.

Marlene   I came this morning. I spent the day.

Angie (*off*)   Aunty! Aunty Marlene!

Marlene   I'd better go.

Joyce   Go on then.

Marlene   All right.

Angie (*off*)   Aunty! Can you hear me? I'm ready.

Marlene *goes.* **Joyce** *goes on sitting.* **Marlene** *comes back.*

Joyce   So what's the secret?

Marlene   It's a secret.

Joyce   I know what it is anyway.

Marlene   I bet you don't. You always said that.

Joyce   It's her exercise book.

Marlene   Yes, but you don't know what's in it.

Joyce   It's some game, some secret society she has with Kit.

Marlene   You don't know the password. You don't know the code.

Joyce You're really in it, aren't you. Can you do the handshake?

Marlene She didn't mention a handshake.

Joyce I thought they'd have a special handshake. She spends hours writing that but she's useless at school. She copies things out of books about black magic, and politicians out of the paper. It's a bit childish.

Marlene I think it's a plot to take over the world.

Joyce She's been in the remedial class the last two years.

Marlene I came up this morning and spent the day in Ipswich. I went to see Mother.

Joyce Did she recognise you?

Marlene Are you trying to be funny?

Joyce No, she does wander.

Marlene She wasn't wandering at all, she was very lucid thank you.

Joyce You were very lucky then.

Marlene Fucking awful life she's had.

Joyce Don't tell me.

Marlene Fucking waste.

Joyce Don't talk to me.

Marlene Why shouldn't I talk? Why shouldn't I talk to you? / Isn't she my mother too?

Joyce Look, you've left, you've gone away, / we can do without you.

Marlene I left home, so what, I left home. People do leave home / it is normal.

Joyce We understand that, we can do without you.

Marlene   We weren't happy. Were you happy?

Joyce   Don't come back.

Marlene   So it's just your mother, is it, your child, you never wanted me round, / you were jealous of me because I was the

Joyce   Here we go.

Marlene   little one and I was clever.

Joyce   I'm not clever enough for all this psychology / if that's what it is.

Marlene   Why can't I visit my own family / without all this?*

Joyce   Aah.
Just don't go on about Mum's life when you haven't been to see her for how many years. / I go and see her every week.

Marlene   It's up to me.
*Then don't go and see her every week.

Joyce   Somebody has to.

Marlene   No they don't. / Why do they?

Joyce   How would I feel if I didn't go?

Marlene   A lot better.

Joyce   I hope you feel better.

Marlene   It's up to me.

Joyce   You couldn't get out of here fast enough.

Marlene   Of course I couldn't get out of here fast enough. What was I going to do? Marry a dairyman who'd come home pissed? / Don't you fucking this fucking that fucking bitch

Joyce   Christ.

Marlene   fucking tell me what to fucking do fucking.

Joyce   I don't know how you could leave your own child.

Marlene   You were quick enough to take her.

Joyce   What does that mean?

Marlene   You were quick enough to take her.

Joyce   Or what? Have her put in a home? Have some stranger / take her would you rather?

Marlene   You couldn't have one so you took mine.

Joyce   I didn't know that then.

Marlene   Like hell, / married three years.

Joyce   I didn't know that. Plenty of people / take that long.

Marlene   Well it turned out lucky for you, didn't it?

Joyce   Turned out all right for you by the look of you. You'd be getting a few less thousand a year.

Marlene   Not necessarily.

Joyce   You'd be stuck here / like you said.

Marlene   I could have taken her with me.

Joyce   You didn't want to take her with you. It's no good coming back now, Marlene, / and saying –

Marlene   I know a managing director who's got two children, she breastfeeds in the boardroom, she pays a hundred pounds a week on domestic help alone and she can afford that because she's an extremely high-powered lady earning a great deal of money.

Joyce   So what's that got to do with you at the age of seventeen?

Marlene   Just because you were married and had somewhere to live –

Joyce   You could have lived at home. / Or live with me

Marlene   Don't be stupid.

Joyce   and Frank. / You said you weren't keeping it. You

Marlene   You never suggested.

Joyce   shouldn't have had it / if you wasn't going to keep it.

Marlene   Here we go.

Joyce   You was the most stupid, / for someone so clever you was the most stupid, get yourself pregnant, not go to the doctor, not tell.

Marlene   You wanted it, you said you were glad, I remember the day, you said I'm glad you never got rid of it, I'll look after it, you said that down by the river. So what are you saying, sunshine, you don't want her?

Joyce   Course I'm not saying that.

Marlene   Because I'll take her, / wake her up and pack now.

Joyce   You wouldn't know how to begin to look after her.

Marlene   Don't you want her?

Joyce   Course I do, she's my child.

Marlene   Then what are you going on about / why did I have her?

Joyce   You said I got her off you / when you didn't –

Marlene   I said you were lucky / the way it –

Joyce   Have a child now if you want one. You're not old.

Marlene   I might do.

Joyce   Good.

Pause.

Marlene   I've been on the pill so long / I'm probably sterile.

Joyce   Listen, when Angie was six months I did get pregnant and I lost it because I was so tired looking after your fucking baby / because she cried so much – yes I did tell

Marlene   You never told me.

Joyce   you – / and the doctor said if I'd sat down all day with

Marlene   Well I forgot.

Joyce   my feet up I'd've kept it / and that's the only chance I ever had because after that –

Marlene   I've had two abortions, are you interested? Shall I tell you about them? Well I won't, it's boring, it wasn't a problem. I don't like messy talk about blood / and what a bad

Joyce   If I hadn't had your baby. The doctor said.

Marlene   time we all had. I don't want a baby. I don't want to talk about gynaecology.

Joyce   Then stop trying to get Angie off of me.

Marlene   I come down here after six years. All night you've been saying I don't come often enough. If I don't come for another six years she'll be twenty-one, will that be OK?

Joyce   That'll be fine, yes, six years would suit me fine.

Pause.

Marlene   I was afraid of this.
I only came because I thought you wanted . . .
I just want . . .

Marlene *cries.*

Joyce   Don't grizzle, Marlene, for God's sake.
Marly? Come on, pet. Love you really.
Fucking stop it, will you?

Marlene   No, let me cry. I like it.

They laugh, **Marlene** *begins to stop crying.*

I knew I'd cry if I wasn't careful.

Joyce   Everyone's always crying in this house. Nobody takes any notice.

Marlene   You've been wonderful looking after Angie.

Joyce   Don't get carried away.

Marlene   I can't write letters but I do think of you.

Joyce   You're getting drunk. I'm going to make some tea.

Marlene   Love you.

Joyce *gets up to make tea.*

Joyce   I can see why you'd want to leave. It's a dump here.

Marlene   So what's this about you and Frank?

Joyce   He was always carrying on, wasn't he? And if I wanted to go out in the evening he'd go mad, even if it was nothing, a class, I was going to go to an evening class. So he had this girlfriend, only twenty-two poor cow, and I said go on, off you go, hoppit. I don't think he even likes her.

Marlene   So what about money?

Joyce   I've always said I don't want your money.

Marlene   No, does he send you money?

Joyce   I've got four different cleaning jobs. Adds up. There's not a lot round here.

Marlene   Does Angie miss him?

Joyce   She doesn't say.

Marlene   Does she see him?

Joyce   He was never that fond of her to be honest.

Marlene   He tried to kiss me once. When you were engaged.

Joyce Did you fancy him?

Marlene No, he looked like a fish.

Joyce He was lovely then.

Marlene Ugh.

Joyce Well I fancied him. For about three years.

Marlene Have you got someone else?

Joyce There's not a lot round here. Mind you, the minute you're on your own, you'd be amazed how your friends' husbands drop by. I'd sooner do without.

Marlene I don't see why you couldn't take my money.

Joyce I do, so don't bother about it.

Marlene Only got to ask.

Joyce So what about you? Good job?

Marlene Good for a laugh. / Got back from the US of A a bit

Joyce Good for more than a laugh I should think.

Marlene wiped out and slotted into this speedy employment agency and still there.

Joyce You can always find yourself work then.

Marlene That's right.

Joyce And men?

Marlene Oh there's always men.

Joyce No one special?

Marlene There's fellas who like to be seen with a high-flying lady. Shows they've got something really good in their pants. But they can't take the day to day. They're waiting for me to turn into the little woman. Or maybe I'm just horrible of course.

Joyce Who needs them?

Marlene   Who needs them? Well I do. But I need
adventures more. So on on into the sunset. I think the
eighties are going to be stupendous.

Joyce   Who for?

Marlene   For me. / I think I'm going up up up.

Joyce   Oh for you. Yes, I'm sure they will.

Marlene   And for the country, come to that. Get the
economy back on its feet and whoosh. She's a tough lady,
Maggie. I'd give her a job. / She just needs to hang in
there. This country

Joyce   You voted for them, did you?

Marlene   needs to stop whining. / Monetarism is not
stupid.

Joyce   Drink your tea and shut up, pet.

Marlene   It takes time, determination. No more slop. /
And

Joyce   Well I think they're filthy bastards.

Marlene   who's got to drive it on? First woman prime
minister. Terrifico. Aces. Right on. / You must admit.
Certainly gets my vote.

Joyce   What good's first woman if it's her? I suppose
you'd have liked Hitler if he was a woman. Ms Hitler. Got
a lot done, Hitlerina. / Great adventures.

Marlene   Bosses still walking on the workers' faces? Still
Dadda's little parrot? Haven't you learned to think for
yourself? I believe in the individual. Look at me.

Joyce   I am looking at you.

Marlene   Come on, Joyce, we're not going to quarrel
over politics.

Joyce   We are though.

Marlene   Forget I mentioned it. Not a word about the

slimy unions will cross my lips.

Pause.

Joyce You say Mother had a wasted life.

Marlene Yes I do. Married to that bastard.

Joyce What sort of life did he have? / Working in the fields like

Marlene Violent life?

Joyce an animal. / Why wouldn't he want a drink?

Marlene Come off it.

Joyce You want a drink. He couldn't afford whisky.

Marlene I don't want to talk about him.

Joyce You started, I was talking about her. She had a rotten life because she had nothing. She went hungry.

Marlene She was hungry because he drank the money. / He used to hit her.

Joyce It's not all down to him. / Their lives were rubbish. They

Marlene She didn't hit him.

Joyce were treated like rubbish. He's dead and she'll die soon and what sort of life / did they have?

Marlene I saw him one night. I came down.

Joyce Do you think I didn't? / They didn't get to America and

Marlene I still have dreams.

Joyce drive across it in a fast car. / Bad nights, they had bad days.

Marlene America, America, you're jealous. / I had to get out,

Joyce Jealous?

Marlene   I knew when I was thirteen, out of their house, out of them, never let that happen to me, / never let him, make my own way, out.

Joyce   Jealous of what you've done, you're ashamed of me if I came to your office, your smart friends, wouldn't you, I'm ashamed of you, think of nothing but yourself, you've got on, nothing's changed for most people / has it?

Marlene   I hate the working class / which is what you're going

Joyce   Yes you do.

Marlene   to go on about now, it doesn't exist any more, it means lazy and stupid. / I don't like the way they talk. I don't

Joyce   Come on, now we're getting it.

Marlene   like beer guts and football vomit and saucy tits / and brothers and sisters –

Joyce   I spit when I see a Rolls-Royce, scratch it with my ring / Mercedes it was.

Marlene   Oh very mature –

Joyce   I hate the cows I work for / and their dirty dishes with blanquette of fucking veau.

Marlene   and I will not be pulled down to their level by a flying picket and I won't be sent to Siberia / or a loony bin

Joyce   No, you'll be on a yacht, you'll be head of Coca-Cola and you wait, the eighties is going to be stupendous all right because we'll get you lot off our backs –

Marlene   just because I'm original. And I support Reagan even if he is a lousy movie star because the reds are swarming up his map and I want to be free in a free world –

Joyce   What? / What?

Marlene   I know what I mean / by that – not shut up
here.

Joyce   So don't be round here when it happens because if
someone's kicking you I'll just laugh.

Silence.

Marlene   I don't mean anything personal. I don't believe
in class. Anyone can do anything if they've got what it
takes.

Joyce   And if they haven't?

Marlene   If they're stupid or lazy or frightened, I'm not
going to help them get a job, why should I?

Joyce   What about Angie?

Marlene   What about Angie?

Joyce   She's stupid, lazy and frightened, so what about
her?

Marlene   You run her down too much. She'll be all
right.

Joyce   I don't expect so, no. I expect her children will say
what a wasted life she had. If she has children. Because
nothing's changed and it won't with them in.

Marlene   Them, them. / Us and them?

Joyce   And you're one of them.

Marlene   And you're us, wonderful us, and Angie's us /
and Mum and Dad's us.

Joyce   Yes, that's right, and you're them.

Marlene   Come on, Joyce, what a night. You've got what
it takes.

Joyce   I know I have.

Marlene   I didn't really mean all that.

Joyce   I did.

Marlene   But we're friends anyway.

Joyce   I don't think so, no.

Marlene   Well it's lovely to be out in the country. I really must make the effort to come more often.
I want to go to sleep.
I want to go to sleep.

Joyce *gets blankets for the sofa.*

Joyce   Goodnight then. I hope you'll be warm enough.

Marlene   Goodnight. Joyce –

Joyce   No, pet. Sorry.

Joyce *goes.* **Marlene** *sits wrapped in a blanket and has another drink.* **Angie** *comes in.*

Angie   Mum?

Marlene   Angie? What's the matter?

Angie   Mum?

Marlene   No, she's gone to bed. It's Aunty Marlene.

Angie   Frightening.

Marlene   Did you have a bad dream? What happened in it? Well you're awake now, aren't you, pet?

Angie   Frightening.

Hysteria

or Fragments of an Analysis of an Obsessional Neurosis

Terry Johnson

Terry Johnson's plays include *Amabel* (Bush, London, 1979); *Days Here So Dark* (Paines Plough at the Tricycle, London, 1981); *Insignificance* (Royal Court, London, 1982 and filmed by Nicolas Roeg, 1985); *Cries from the Mammal House* (Open Heart Enterprises with the Royal Court, London, 1984); *Unsuitable for Adults* (Bush, London, 1984); *Tuesday's Child*, written with Kate Lock (Theatre Royal, Stratford East, 1985); *Imagine Drowning* (Hampstead Theatre, London, 1991); *Hysteria* (Royal Court, London, 1993; Duke of York's Theatre as part of the Royal Court Classics season, 1995); *Dead Funny* (Hampstead Theatre, 1994), an adaptation of Edward Ravenscroft's *The London Cuckolds* (Royal National Theatre, 1998), *Cleo, Camping, Emmanuelle and Dick* (Royal National Theatre, 1998) and an adaptation of *The Graduate* (The Gielgud Theatre, London, 2000).

For Marion

Hysteria was first performed at the Royal Court Theatre, London, on 26 August 1993. The cast was as follows:

Sigmund Freud   Henry Goodman
Jessica   Phoebe Nicholls
Abraham Yahuda   David de Keyser
Salvador Dali   Tim Potter

Directed by Phyllida Lloyd
Designed by Mark Thompson
Lighting by Rick Fisher
Sound by Paul Arditti

Characters

Sigmund Freud, *an energetic old man with startling eyebrows. He has cancer of the jaw, but this should only affect his speech at the end of the play.*
Jessica, *a woman in her late twenties or early thirties.*
Abraham Yahuda, *a large man in his sixties. An even greater weight and status than Freud.*
Salvador Dali, *a small or tall Spaniard with a strange moustache and a talent for painting.*

The style of playing varies as Freud's last thoughts, recent memories and suppressed anxieties dictate the action.

Depending on the resources of the theatre, other actors may make a brief appearance in Act Two.

Setting

1938

Sigmund Freud's study at 20 Maresfield Gardens, Hampstead, London. A large, high-ceilinged room plastered in pastel-blue. The room is furnished richly: dark oaks and mahogany.

US, french windows lead to a narrow porch, and beyond, a well-kept garden.

USR, the door to a closet. SR, a large desk. DSR, a wood-burning stove.

Along the wall SL, an armless analysis couch covered with a rich Moroccan rug and half a dozen cushions. On the wall above, another beautiful rug. Just beyond the head of the couch, a comfortable tub chair.

DSL, the door to the rest of the house.

There are bookshelves holding fine embossed volumes, and every available surface holds antiquities from Ancient Greece, Rome, Egypt and the Orient. The vast majority of these are small human figures in pottery, wood and bronze.

The setting should be naturalistically rendered to contrast with the design challenge towards the end of Act Two.

Act One

Scene One

A shaft of light rises to isolate **Freud** *asleep in the tub seat. His eyes open and he stares steadily at a large dark* **Figure** *downstage. (In fact* **Yahuda**, *but featureless, a primordial, paternal presence.)*

The **Figure**'s *hands move under the sharp glare of an anglepoise lamp. A hypodermic syringe and a phial glint as he fills one from the other.*

He approaches **Freud** *and as he does, we hear the growing sound of human turmoil; people shoving, shouting, hundreds of people, a sense of urgency, even panic.*

The **Figure** *dwarfs* **Freud**. *We are aware now of the enormous, paralysing tension in* **Freud**. *An unbearable pain has met an immovable object.*

The **Figure** *injects* **Freud**. *A train engine whistles, then the sound of a steam train pulling out of a station washes over the voices and obliterates the hubbub ... shouts of departure make way for the powerful, demanding noise of the train.*

Freud *suddenly relaxes as the morphine hits. The train noise becomes a gentle, reassuring clatter, like a lullaby.*

The **Figure** *leaves. The lights slowly change, the train subsides.*

Freud's *study. Night. Rain beyond the windows.*

Freud asleep in the tub chair. Wakes and looks at his watch. A long silence.

Freud If you are waiting for me to break the silence you will be deeply disappointed. The silence is yours alone, and is far more eloquent than you imagine.

He turns in his chair and looks towards the couch. Double-takes when he sees there is no one on it. Looks around the room. Opens the door, peers out, closes the door. Goes to his desk. Hesitantly presses the buzzer on an unfamiliar Bakelite intercom.

Freud   Anna?

Anna   (*a voice pulled from sleep*)   Yes, Father?

Freud   She's gone.

Anna   Who, Father?

Freud   Where's she gone?

Anna   Where's who gone?

Freud   It's um . . .

Looks at his watch.

Anna   What is it?

Freud   Ten to.

Anna   It's ten to five. It's the middle of the night.

Freud   There was a girl.

Anna   Have you slept yet?

Freud   I had a patient.

Anna   Maybe you dreamed her.

Freud   I don't dream patients, I dream surgeons and publishers.

Anna   Go to bed, Father.

Freud   The nights are valuable.

Anna   Yahuda will be here for lunch, and you've an appointment with Mr Dali immediately after.

Freud   I'll sleep in the morning. What's this thing?

In front of his face hangs an electric light pull; a four-foot cord with a brass knob on the end.

Anna   What thing?

Freud   This thing hanging here in front of me. This thing in my hand.

Anna   Um . . .

Freud   It's just dangling here. It's got a nob on the end.

Anna   Mm hm?

Freud   What is it?

Anna   I've ... no idea.

Freud   What am I supposed to do with it?

Anna   Shall I call the nurse?

Freud   Shall I give it a pull?

Anna   No, just ... leave it alone, Father.

He pulls it. The lights go out.

Freud *Scheisse!*

Anna   Father?

Freud   The lights have gone out.

Anna   Oh ... that!

Freud   Damn thing.

Anna   It's a light pull.

Freud   I know what it is; what's it doing here?

Anna   Ernst put it up this afternoon.

Freud   I can't see a thing.

A crash of falling objects.

Anna   Father?

Freud   I hate the dark.

Anna   You should be asleep.

Freud   I know what's in it.

Anna   You need more, not less, as time passes.

Freud   The body maybe. The mind more than ever craves ...

He switches on the light.

Freud   Illumination.

Anna   Shall I come down?

Freud   No, I'm fine.

Anna   Goodnight then.

Freud   Goodnight.

He switches off the intercom. Some of the antique figures on his desk have been knocked over; he rights them. He picks up his pen to write. Nothing comes. He gets up and lies on the couch.

I have been preparing, somewhat unsuccessfully, for my death which Yahuda would have me believe is imminent. I am inclined to agree with his diagnosis, but this morbid preparation is . . . difficult. I have never liked waiting for trains; standing on the platform looking back down the track: never a glance, of course, in the direction of one's destination. Like all the trains I ever caught, this one is running late. And so I wait. I rearrange the luggage at my feet; I unfold and refold my newspaper, failing to find anything of interest, even though the headlines roar. And over and over I mentally rehearse the panic of boarding, check my watch with the clock, grow anxious and inexplicably . . . impatient. I prepare and prepare and yet remain unprepared, because when the train arrives there is never time to button the jacket or check the ticket or even say a meaningful goodbye. So until my inevitably fraught departure, all I can do is wait, and rearrange the luggage.

His eyes have closed.

A pause, then a figure appears through the rain and stops outside the french windows. **Jessica** *is sopping wet and initially appears waif-like. She wears a thin mackintosh. Her hair hangs dripping to her shoulders.*

She taps on the glass. **Freud** *opens his eyes. She taps again. He rises, disorientated, and discovers the source of the noise. She smiles.*

Freud   Go away. Go away. This is a private house, not Madame Tussaud's. I admit I found it flattering when I arrived, this English passion for standing and staring, but I'd rather be melted down, thank you, than have any more thumbnails surreptitiously pressed into my flesh, so please . . . go away! Oh very well, stay where you are, catch your death for all I care. What do you want?

He goes to his intercom. She raps frantically. He doesn't press the buzzer. She speaks. We don't hear her through the glass.

Jessica   I have to speak to you.

Freud   What?

Jessica   I have to speak to you.

Freud   I can't hear you. Go away.

Very matter-of-fact, she takes out a cut-throat razor and holds it to her wrist.

Jessica   I have to speak to you.

Freud *looks away. Thinks. Then goes to the french windows and unlocks them. He steps back. She enters.*

Freud   Stop there! Stop.

She stops. Closes the razor. Offers it to him. He takes it and secures it in a drawer.

Jessica   I wasn't sure you'd let me in.

Freud   You're sopping wet.

Jessica   It's raining.

Freud   That rug is from Persia.

Jessica   You told me to stop.

Freud   Get off the rug.

She steps forward.

Freud   No closer. Step sideways. To the left. Stand there.

Jessica   Here?

Freud   Good.

Jessica   Good.

Freud   How did you get into the garden?

Jessica   I climbed. Where the elm rests on the wall.

Freud   I'll have a tree surgeon to it first thing in the morning.

Jessica   Grazed my knee; look.

Freud   What are you, some sort of insomniac student?

Jessica   No.

Freud   You want me to read something you wrote?

Jessica   No.

Freud   Are you inebriated, irresponsible, rich? Is this a dare?

Jessica   No.

Freud   Do you know who I am?

Jessica   Oh yes.

Freud   Then what do you want?

Jessica   I don't know. I haven't yet decided.

Freud   Who are you?

Jessica   Don't you recognise me?

Freud   It feels as though I should.

Jessica   Yes, you should.

Freud   We've met?

Jessica   No, never.

Freud   Please. It's late. Who are you?

Jessica   I am your Anima, Professor Freud.

Freud   My what?

Jessica   It's a psychological term denoting the denied

female element of the male psyche.

Freud   I know what it is.

Jessica   Denied but desired.

Freud   Damn nonsense, that's what it is. Did *he* send you?

Jessica   Who?

Freud   The Lunatic. Jung the crackpot, friend of the gods?

Jessica   No.

Freud   He did, didn't he? This is his feeble idea of a practical joke.

Jessica   No one sent me.

Freud   Due to my advancing years I am quite prepared to come up against the odd figment of my own imagination, but I have no time for flesh-and-blood imposters. And I certainly refuse to confront aspects of my personality I did not even propose! Anima is tosh. Archetypes are a theatrical diversion!

Jessica   I've not read much Jung.

Freud   Not much is too much. How long have you been in the garden?

Jessica   All night. Watching the house. The lights going out. Then one last light, illuminating you.

Freud   Perhaps you should sit. Judging from your behaviour so far you are either dangerously impulsive or pathologically unhappy.

Jessica   That's true.

Freud   Which?

Jessica   Both, I think. I have inverted morbid tendencies, I know. And a great deal of free-floating anxiety desperate for someone to land on. I am mildly dysfunctional, yes.

Freud   You have recently been in analysis?

Jessica   No, I've recently been in a library.

Freud   What do you want of me?

Jessica   Later.

Freud   There is no later. If you are looking for a doctor, I'm afraid I have to disappoint you. I cannot take any more patients. Those I see now will soon be abandoned. I cannot add to my unfinished business.

Jessica   What if I were desperate?

Freud   There would be no point; I could never conclude. I will give you the name of a good man.

Jessica   No.

Freud   My health deteriorates daily. There are others now more able than I . . .

Jessica   No. It's you I must see.

Freud   Then you must be disappointed. I shall call someone to show you out.

Jessica   Don't do that.

Freud   It's very late. I'm an old man.

Jessica   What's wrong with your mouth?

Freud   With this half, nothing. The other half I left in Vienna.

Jessica   How careless of you.

Freud   It's in a jar of formaldehyde. The surgery was drastic, but advisable.

Jessica   I think I'd rather die than have a piece of me removed.

Freud   Cancer cells develop a passionate urge to replicate. They abandon any concern for the function of their familial organ and strike out to conquer foreign tissue. They undermine the natural state, absorb and conquer! They are the National Socialists of human meat; best left, I felt, in

Austria. Now, you must go.

Jessica   It's still raining.

Freud   How could you possibly get any wetter? Please.

Jessica   I'm cold.

Freud   I'm not unsympathetic, but if you want to get warm, get home.

Jessica   I have no home.

Freud   I must insist. This is improper.

Jessica   I'll show you improper.

She takes off her coat.

Freud   What are you doing?

She takes off her dress.

Please, I am perfectly aware you wish to gain my attention but this is highly inappropriate. I shall call my daughter.

Jessica   And how will you explain me?

Freud   There is nothing to explain.

Jessica   Naked and screaming?

Freud   She will understand.

Jessica   But will the inhabitants of West Hampstead?

Freud   Now stop this. Your behaviour is totally unacceptable!

Jessica   My behaviour, Professor Freud, is as you first diagnosed. It is desperate, as am I!

She goes into the garden, still undressing.

Freud   Come back inside!

Jessica   Do I start screaming or will you give me an hour of your precious time?

Freud   I will not be blackmailed. Come out of the rain.

Jessica   No. I shall stand here until I'm too wet to think. Too cold to care.

Thunder.

Freud *takes her coat and pursues her. Brings her back inside, wrapped.*

Freud   Sit.

He moves a chair nearer the stove and ushers her into it.

Jessica   Thank you. I'm sorry.

She cries.

Freud   I shall try to help. But could we please remember this is my study, not some boulevard farce.

Jessica   This isn't your study. Your study was in Vienna.

Freud   Who are you?

Jessica   Is it the same?

Freud   Almost. In the Bergasse it wasn't as simple to walk out into the garden.

Jessica   Why?

Freud   I was on the second floor. And there were many more books.

Jessica   More?

Freud   I had to choose between books and the survivors.

Jessica   Who?

Freud   The figures.

Jessica   They're beautiful.

Freud   And were buried, unseen, for centuries. It would have been criminal to inter them again. It felt bad enough cramming them into rail crates for transportation. Each of them is quite unique but packed in side by side, they lose their individual identities. Wrapped in newsprint they become . . . faceless.

Jessica   Are you in pain?

Freud   Yes. Are you?

Jessica   Oh yes.

Freud   Intermittent?

Jessica   Constant. I thought there were drugs.

Freud   I prefer to think in pain than dream in oblivion.

Jessica   I dream in pain.

Freud   I cannot take you on. I have no . . . time. You understand.

Jessica   It won't take long.

Freud   Would that were true.

Jessica   It won't. I know what's wrong with me.

Freud   Self-analysis is rarely successful.

Jessica   You did it.

Freud   I had the advantage of being me.

Jessica   And you were all you had to go on. I've read your books. All of them.

Freud   Have you really?

Jessica   Yes.

Freud   Understand much?

Jessica   Most.

Freud   Hmph.

Jessica   I didn't much enjoy *Jokes and Their Relationship to the Unconscious*. If you were going to analyse jokes you might have chosen a couple that were funny. I suspect you've no sense of humour.

Freud   Nonsense. Only last week I was taken to the theatre and I laughed three or four times.

Jessica   What at?

Freud   I believe it was called *Rookery Nook*.

Jessica   Doesn't prove you've a sense of humour; proves you've a complete lack of taste.

Freud   It had a seductive logic, and displayed all the splendid, ha!, anal obsessions of the English.

Jessica   Frankly, some of your concepts are funnier than your jokes.

Freud   For instance?

Jessica   Penis envy, for instance. How in a thousand years of civilised thought anyone could imagine a penis an object of envy is beyond me. Those I have seen erect and bobbing seem positively mortified at their own enthusiasm. The only one I ever saw flaccid looked like something that had fallen out of its shell. Euugh! Why would anyone envy a squidgy single-minded probiscus that thinks it's God's special gift to those without.

Freud   You say you've done no analysis?

Jessica   None.

Freud   I think you should begin as soon as possible.

She lies on the couch.

But not with me. Tomorrow afternoon I will refer you. Until then, you must let me sleep.

Jessica   I'll be fine.

Freud   You can't stay here.

Jessica   Don't pretend you're not curious, Professor. You're longing to know what brought me here. There's nothing you'd like better than to see me barefoot in the head.

Freud   You are mistaken.

Jessica   Please.

Freud   If I were to listen to anything you had to say, I would do so only because you are obviously disturbed, and only on the understanding that what we were doing was an assessment pending a referral.

Jessica   All right.

Freud   Very well.

He sits at the head of the couch.

Jessica   How do we start?

Pause.

I can't see you.

Pause. She twists around. He looks at her with a well-practised neutral expression.

That's the point, is it? That's part of it?

She lies back. Pause.

And silence? Is that part of it too? It is, isn't it? How many minutes of silence must you have endured?

Sunrise happens; a shaft of red light and a burst of birdsong.

I don't know how to begin. I was born in Vienna twenty-nine years ago. I am an only child. My mother was beautiful, my father was the owner of a small printworks and a temple elder. We lived in a tall, narrow house. It had four floors but not many more rooms; a strange house, as if built by a child, an unsteady tower of wooden bricks. My father had a bad hip; he couldn't climb stairs. He had a room made up in what was the parlour. This was his room, at the bottom of the house. Anyway, I grew. I grew up, as you can see.

Freud *makes a note.*

Jessica   You made a note, I heard you scribble.

She twists around.

Jessica What did you write, what did I say?

She gets the same neutral expression.

I see. Well anyway, here I am. Should I talk about now or then? Past or present? Both, I know, I'm sure, but which end should I begin?

She rubs briefly at the top of her breast, as if removing a splash of wine. A hysterical manifestation.

Why am I here? I'm here because I was sent. I wouldn't have come of my own accord. I have been married two years and my husband is concerned for me. I would find it flattering if it were not. . . . He worries about my appetite, which is small, but does not concern me. I eat no more than I desire. My husband also wishes I spent more time outdoors; I prefer it inside. It is merely a preference, not an illness. So that's why I'm here. It is desired that I eat like a horse and live like one too, in a field if possible. If you could turn me into a horse my husband would be overjoyed.

She rubs.

What has he told you?

She gags.

Freud Would you like some water?

Jessica No thank you. Don't stand up. I don't like the outdoors, and I don't need three enormous meals a day.

Freud How long have you felt this way?

Jessica A year. Maybe longer. Yes. Nearly two. It's always longer than I remember.

Freud When did it start?

Jessica It developed. Nothing sudden, nothing . . .

She rubs. Shakes her stiff fingers.

One just becomes happier staying indoors, and less
interested in the taste of food. Really, I wouldn't be here at
all if it weren't for my wretched husband.

Freud   What is wrong with your hand?

Jessica   Didn't he tell you? The fingers of my hand. My
hand has been examined by specialists; neither could
explain the problem with my fingers.

Freud   What is the problem?

Jessica   We thought arthritis, but we're assured otherwise.
These three fingers have grown stiff, you see. They bend at
the joints but will not move apart. The hand still functions.
I can use it. But it looks so ... reptilian. It is intensely
frustrating.

Freud   And there is no physiological impairment?

Jessica   None, I'm assured.

She gags, then rubs.

I'm sorry. Don't stand up. Well? Can you help me?

Freud   No. I cannot.

Jessica   I'm sorry?

Freud   It is now certainly time for me to go to my bed.

Jessica   That was hardly a full consultation, Professor;
we're barely beyond the symptoms.

Freud   I am as aware of the symptoms as you. And I am
aware of the aetiology of your hysterical paralysis, as well
as the traumatic triggers of your anorexia and agoraphobia.

Jessica   So soon?

Freud   I know these things not because your compulsive
behaviour is unconvincing or because I am capable of
completing an analysis in less than ten minutes, but because
I published the facts of this case thirty years ago, and you
no doubt, judging by your excellent knowledge of them,

read it only recently. Now I am very tired, both of your games and of this evening . . .

Jessica   Please, don't call anyone.

Freud   Either you leave, this instant, or I'll wake the house.

Jessica   It was a stupid thing to do. I'm sorry.

Freud   What do you take me for?

Jessica   It's a case history that interests me, that's all.

Freud   So you are a student?

Jessica   Yes. Yes, I am.

Freud   Then your methods of study are most unorthodox.

Jessica   May we discuss the case of Rebecca S?

Freud   Certainly not. You disturb me, you attempt to deceive me . . .

Jessica   Did I?

Freud   What?

Jessica   Deceive you?

Freud   Not for very long.

Jessica   I did though, didn't I? The gagging and the . . .

She rubs.

Was that how she . . . ?

Freud   I was very explicit in my descriptions. You were very accurate in your impersonation.

Jessica   Spooky.

Freud   Now if you've had your fun . . .

Jessica   Listen. I know I'm a fool. But Rebecca means a lot to me. She's the basis of my thesis. Please.

Freud   You have an incredible nerve. I responded in

good faith to your hysterical dishonesty. Had you chosen a less deceitful path to my door we may have had something to discuss. As it is you have forfeited any right to my time and attention. This is my final word. Now you may go into the garden and scream or dance with the spring fairies, I care not.

Jessica   What would Dr Jung say if he heard you mention fairies?

Freud   He'd probably take me down the path and attempt to introduce us. Now go home.

Jessica   I have no home.

Freud   Enough.

Jessica   Please . . .

Freud   Not one more word.

Jessica   I'll go then.

Freud   Good.

Jessica   Could I ask one thing of you?

Freud   One thing.

Jessica   Could you lend me a pair of wellingtons?

Freud   Wellingtons.

Jessica   My feet are freezing. No, it's too much to ask. I'm sorry; I'll be fine.

Freud   Wait there.

Jessica   No really, I couldn't.

Freud   It's a small price.

Jessica   A pair of socks would be heaven; those thick sort of woolly ones.

Freud *leaves.*

Jessica*'s manner changes. She goes to the filing cabinet and rifles through it. A door noise off. She pulls out a maroon file and hurries.*

She opens the french windows wide, then hides in the closet.

Freud *returns, with boots and walking socks, to find her gone. Stands at the french windows for a while, until his confusion turns to philosophical acceptance. He closes the windows and leaves his study, switching off the light.*

Jessica *comes out of the closet. Turns on the anglepoise. Takes a journal out of her coat pocket, and carefully puts it on the desk.*

She opens the file, finds flimsy carbon copies of correspondence.

Settles down to work her way through the correspondence; a concentrated, obsessive search . . .

Lights fade.

Scene Two

Late afternoon. **Jessica** *has gone, as have the wellingtons. The room is reasonably tidy.*

Door opens and in marches **Yahuda**, *an elderly Jewish doctor. He clutches a visiting bag and a bound document.* **Freud** *follows.*

Yahuda   No, no, no. I'm not here to debate with you. No one in your family, no friend, colleague or critic has ever convinced you you were wrong about anything. I'm quite happy to be argued into my grave, but I'm not about to be argued into yours. I did you the courtesy of reading this . . . babble, now will you do me the courtesy of listening.

Yahuda *stops at a chessboard in play and takes a move he's already prepared.*

Freud   I had wondered at your silence during lunch.

Yahuda   Being polite has given me indigestion. We are both old men.

Freud   Time is short.

Yahuda   I shall allow your ill health to temper my anger, but not to lessen my resolve. I shall not leave this room until you have agreed not to publish this work.

Freud   My friend . . .

Yahuda   That remains to be seen.

Freud   I see.

Yahuda   The first paragraph made my blood run cold. 'If Moses was an Egyptian . . .'

Freud   If.

Yahuda   You do not mean the if, Freud. None of your ifs are questions; all your ifs are excuses for the outrageous statements they precede. Your proposal is that the man who gave us the word of God, the founder of the Jewish nation, was an Egyptian aristocrat.

Freud   A simple reading of the facts . . .

Yahuda   You deny his origins . . .

Freud   Any intelligent analysis . . .

Yahuda   You undermine the core of the myth!

Freud   Myth, precisely.

Yahuda   The symbolic expression . . .

Freud   The reflection of an inner desire . . .

Yahuda   Of a basic truth . . .

Freud   A perversion of truth, an attempt to satisfy . . .

Yahuda   Moses was a Jew! Moses was chosen! If Moses was not a Jew, then we were not chosen! He was a Jew as I am a Jew. And you?

Freud   I have never denied, ever denied . . .

Yahuda   Well, deny Moses and you deny us! At this time, of all times.

Freud   Yes.

Yahuda   When the little we have is being wrenched from us.

Freud   I know.

Yahuda   At this most terrible hour . . .

Freud   I take away our best man.

Yahuda   This is dreadful stuff. It is irreligious, unforgivably ill-timed, badly-argued piffle.

Freud   But apart from that, what did you think?

Yahuda   There can be no discussion. You may not publish.

Freud *takes a move on the chessboard.*

Freud   Yahuda, you are a scholar. A believer I know, but a scholar all the same. And you do not believe that the Red Sea parted . . .

Yahuda   The this and that of the event . . .

Freud   Or that a babe floated down a river in a basket . . .

Yahuda   Are lost in the mist, the history. The mystery . . .

Freud   A babe in a basket would have drowned as sure as our nation on the ocean floor.

Yahuda   The myth, Freud.

Freud   You know these things for what they are.

Yahuda   The myth is what's important.

Freud   Have you been talking to the lunatic?

Yahuda   Remove the essence of the myth and you undermine the foundation of our faith; you lead us to an agnostic hell. As indeed you seem intent on doing. Here. Right here. 'The undeniable power of faith can be explained away like any other neurotic compulsion.' 'Religion is the neurosis of humanity.'

Freud   It's not a new idea.

Yahuda   You presume to find no evidence of God but in the heads of men. In the imaginings of desperate minds. And what is a mind, according to your people? Sparks in the brain.

Freud   And a little history.

Yahuda   Well, God is more than meat and electricity. Or the suffering of a child. Or the arrogance of a traitor Jew.

Freud   What alternative are you suggesting? That I censor my last thoughts, have them held in trust against a day when some other man, as he surely will, reaches the same conclusions and is told; well, there was someone else in darker times who thought the same as you. No, God is no more light in this darkness than a candle in a hurricane; eventually he will be snuffed out. But if one man's denial can explode him then that tiny conflagration would be a light far brighter than the guttering hopes he kindles in us. The death of God would light us not to hell or heaven, but to ourselves. Imagine. That we begin to believe in ourselves.

Yahuda   Damn yourself if you must.

Freud   I have to publish.

Yahuda   But remember one thing.

Freud   What?

Yahuda   You are not the only Jew who will die this year.

The pain **Freud** *has been suppressing overwhelms him. He fights and defeats it.*

Yahuda   Sigmund? Are you in pain?

Freud   Most uncalled for.

Yahuda   I shall examine you.

Freud   We both know what you'll find.

Yahuda   Fetch a towel. A man in your condition should

be making peace with his God and his fellow man. Not
denying one and outraging the other.

Freud *goes to the closet.*

Freud I have spent my life standing up for unpleasant
truths . . .

He opens the closet. An arm comes out and gives him a towel.

Thank you.

He closes the door.

. . . But it has never been my desire to offend . . .

Stops. Realises. Looks back.

Yahuda   Know this, Freud. Unless you reconsider, you
lose my friendship.

Freud   Good God.

Yahuda   Harsh, I know, but there it is.

Freud   Get out.

Yahuda   No need to be offensive.

Freud   No, not you.

Yahuda   Then who?

Freud   What?

Yahuda   You said, 'Get out!'

Freud   Indeed. Get out . . . your things. Get your things
out of your bag. And please, examine me.

Freud *sits and positions an anglepoise over his mouth.* **Yahuda**
takes an instrument from his bag, and peers into **Freud***'s mouth.*

Yahuda   Be certain of one thing; there is precious little I
would not do to prevent your publishing. If you had the
clap I'd hang the Hippocratic oath and seriously consider
blackmail. But not you of course. Guiltless. Half a century
of meddling in other people's passions, countless female
patients lying there in front of you, and never a whisper of

impropriety. No scantily clad secrets in your closet, more's the pity. Oh, for a scandalous lever to prize you off your pedestal.

Freud Ont ee ihiculoh.

Yahuda What?

Freud Nothing.

Yahuda That certain things are hidden from us . . .

Freud Ot?

Yahuda Does not deny their existence.

Freud Ot hings?

Yahuda The minds of men, the face of God. You devote yourself to one invisible thing yet refuse to contemplate the other.

Finishes the examination.

It's as you thought.

Freud Inoperable?

Yahuda It's very deep now. I'm sorry.

Freud No, if I had a God to thank, I would.

Freud *grimaces.*

Yahuda That's me prodding around. A pressure bandage?

Freud Thank you.

Yahuda *removes from his bag a bicycle pump, a puncture repair outfit and an inner tube.*

Freud What do you intend doing with that?

Yahuda Mend my bike. Of course . . . Two centigrams of morphine . . .

Freud No.

Yahuda Just the one?

Freud   Absolutely not.

Yahuda   Sooner or later.

Freud   No.

Yahuda *ties the bandage tight around* **Freud**'s *jaw, with a bow on the top of his head.*

Yahuda   It's hard watching even a stubborn irreligious fool like you make his way to a self-defined oblivion.

Freud   I cannot end with an act of disavowal.

Yahuda   Then end in silence.

Yahuda *moves to the closet.*

Freud   No!

Yahuda   What?

Freud   Don't go in there.

Yahuda   I need to wash my hands.

Freud   Please. Use the one across the hall. This we use now as a closet. So much correspondence, so many books . . .

Yahuda   Hmmph.

He heads for the door. Stops on his way to examine the chessboard. Almost takes a move, but stops himself.

You think everyone but you is a complete fool.

Exits.

Freud *rushes to the closet and flings open the door.*

Freud   You said you were going, I thought you were gone.

Jessica *appears wearing her raincoat and wellingtons.*

Jessica   Get rid of your visitor, Professor. We have work to do.

Freud   We have no such thing. I have other appointments.

Jessica   Cancel them.

Freud   I said I would arrange a referral.

Jessica *goes back into the closet.*

Freud   Would you please come out of there! Very well, you give me no choice . . .

He steps towards the closet.
The raincoat hits him full in the face.

Freud   My God.

Yahuda *enters through the other door.*

Freud *closes the closet door.*

Yahuda   I left my bike in the garden. I'll fix the puncture then I'll be off.

Freud   Good.

Yahuda   And you've another visitor; some Spanish idiot with a ridiculous moustache. Dilly, Dally?

Freud   Dali.

Yahuda   Doolally by the look of him.

Freud   The painter.

Yahuda   Really? If you want a physician's advice, you're not up to it. You should be resting, not entertaining foreigners.

Freud   A favour for a friend.

Yahuda   Whose is that? (*Raincoat.*)

Freud   Mine.

Yahuda   Is it raining?

Freud   Usually.

Yahuda   Looks all right to me.

Freud   The forecast was ominous.

Yahuda   Indoor storms imminent?

Freud   Yes. No. A possibility of flash flooding.

Yahuda   Damn. I'll bring my bike inside.

Freud   No.

Yahuda   I can't mend it in the rain.

Freud   It's not raining.

Yahuda   You said it was just about to.

Freud   No, I said there was the possibility of some weather. They weren't precise as to which sort.

Yahuda   Looks awfully small for you.

Freud   It shrank.

Yahuda   When the last flash flood came thundering through your study, I suppose?

Freud   Why don't you bring your bike through and mend it in the hall?

Yahuda   As you wish. Though upstairs might be best.

Freud   Upstairs?

Yahuda   To eliminate any danger of sudden drowning.

Yahuda *exits though the windows.* **Freud** *opens the closet to return the coat.*

Freud   Now please, I must insist that you come out of the closet.

Jessica   Whatever you say . . .

Freud   No. I mean, stay where you are, put your clothes back on and then . . .

A wellington boot flies out, which he catches.

Please. You must modify this behaviour immediately.
This is a childish and ineffectual form of protest

since I haven't a clue what you're protesting *about*.

Jessica's *arm appears from the closet. Between her fingers, a letter of* **Freud**'s. *He moves until it's in front of his face, and starts to read it.*

Freud   I don't understand.

She stuffs the letter right down into the boot. **Yahuda** *re-enters pushing his bike and walking on one heel.*

Freud *closes the closet.*

Yahuda   You're overrun by snails; they're all over the path. I've trodden on half a dozen.

Freud   Please, the rug.

Yahuda   Could you take this for a second?

He hands the bike to **Freud**. *It is covered in snails and has a hot-water bottle tied to the handlebars.*

Where's your bootscraper?

Freud   We don't have a bootscraper.

Yahuda   This is England, for heaven's sake.

Freud   And every bootscraper I encounter sends me flying into or out of someone's bloody conservatory!

Yahuda   I'll find a stick or something. (*A crunch.*) There goes another one!

Yahuda *exits.*

Freud *puts the wellington on the floor and uses his free hand in an attempt to retrieve the carbon copy.*

Yahuda (*off*)   What the devil? Freud! What's this?

Freud *rises, his arm inside the boot.*

Yahuda *re-enters, hopping. He has only one shoe on.*

Freud   What's what!

Yahuda   I don't know what you call the damn things. It

was in the middle of your lawn.

Standing on one leg, he holds up **Jessica**'s *slip. It falls in front of him.*

Dali (*off*)   No no no! Is all right! I see myself!

A sharp knock on the other door. Enter **Dali**. *A surprised pause, then sheer delight.*

Dali   So. Is true. What Dali merely dreams, you live!!

Freud   I can assure you there's a perfectly rational explanation.

Dali   He does not wish to hear it.

Freud   Who?

Dali   Dali.

Freud   Of course. Tell your Mr Dali I shall see him in just a few minutes.

Dali   But he is here.

Freud   I'm aware of that.

Yahuda   And there's more of it, underwear and all sorts.

Freud   It must have blown off the line. I'll be a few minutes.

Dali   No, but he is here.

Yahuda   There is no line.

Freud   I know he's here, I heard you the first time. Ask him to wait a few minutes.

Yahuda   Whose is it?

Dali   But wait he cannot. He is here.

Freud   Look dammit . . .

Dali   I am he.

Freud   Oh, I see.

Yahuda   I'll put it on the compost.

Freud   No! Give it to me.

Yahuda   It's not yours, is it?

Freud   Yes. No. It's . . . my daughter's.

Yahuda   Anna's? At her age she should be dressing for warmth.

He drapes the slip over **Freud**'*s arm and turns.*

Freud   You are he.

Dali   And he is honoured.

A crunch.

Yahuda   Oh shit. There goes another one.

Yahuda *exits on his heel.*

Dali *rises, sits, pulls out a pad.*

Dali   You will not object?

Freud   What?

Dali   A first impression.

Freud   Ah.

Dali *sketches.*

Freud   It's not my bike. And my physician has piles, thus the . . . (*Hot-water bottle.*) As for the snails . . .

Dali   Dali is passionate with snails.

Freud   For, you mean.

Dali   For, with, Dali's passions knows no bounds.

Freud   They just . . . took a liking to the bike, I suppose.

Dali   You have a head like a snail.

Freud   Thank you very much.

Yahuda *re-enters with a clean shoe and more clothing.*

Yahuda   You want the rest?

Freud   Yahuda, this is um . . .

Dali   Dali.

Yahuda   We met in the hall. Has Anna lost a lot of weight in the last week?

Dali   You suffer from piles.

Yahuda   How extraordinarily acute of you.

Dali   Dali suffers also.

Yahuda   I know; I've seen your pictures.

Dali   You do not like the work of Dali?

Yahuda   You want a frank answer?

Dali   Always.

Yahuda   I find your work explicitly obscene, deliberately obtuse, tasteless, puerile and very unpleasant to look at.

Dali   What is not to like in this?

Yahuda   I think I'll leave you to it, Freud.

Dali   This is the man; the only man who can fully appreciate the genius of Dali's spontaneous method of irrational cognition and his critical interpretative association of delusional phenomena. Wait.

Exits.

Yahuda   You want some advice?

Freud   What?

Yahuda   Don't let him get on the couch.

Dali *enters with a finished canvas.* Metamorphosis of Narcissus.

Dali   Is for you. Now you tell me. Look closely, and tell me . . . from what does Dali suffer?

Freud   Eyesight?

Dali   Is true. This man is genius.

Yahuda   Excuse me, I have an operation to perform.

Freud   Please, don't feel you have to . . .

Yahuda   No, no. I'm sure you two have much to discuss. Here.

Offers **Freud** *a bundle of underwear.*

Freud   Thank you.

Yahuda   I'm damned if I can imagine her in them. In fact I'm grateful I can't imagine her in them. I'll see you when he's gone.

Exit **Yahuda** *with his bike.* **Dali** *resumes his sketch.*

Freud   I'd really rather you didn't.

Dali   A thought, an idea from your head, it belongs to you. But your image belongs to Dali. Please.

Freud   I must insist. Put your pencil away.

Dali   You neither do not like the work of Dali?

Freud   Not if I am to be the subject. If I'd known this was your intention . . .

Dali   Please. Dali has no intentions, only intent.

He puts his pad down.

I have come to salute you . . .

Freud   Please don't bother.

Dali   . . . on behalf of all true disciples of the critical–paranoiac school of paint.

Freud   Who are they?

Dali   Dali. He is the only true disciples.

Freud   I see.

Dali   You are held in great esteem. We, by which I mean Dali and I, are engaged in a great struggle to drag up the monstrous from the safety of our dreams and commit to the canvas. It is you who have inspired this.

Freud I am most flattered.

Dali You say to dream, and there to search which is what I do. You say paranoia it transform reality to conform with the unconscious obsession, yes? So Dali gazes; is turned to stone, but and an egg. Narcissus flowers from the egg. Desiring to be reborn he only gazes at himself and dreams of death. Life in this state is as unlikely as a flower from an egg. Expressed with masterly technique and ingenious illusion of course, and this is what Dali does, and only him. Would you like me to hang him?

Freud Oh please, don't bother yourself.

Dali Is no bother. Is an honour. I put it here.

Freud That's a Picasso.

Dali Picasso is Spanish. (*Removes painting.*) So is Dali.

Freud You like Picasso?

Dali Picasso is genius. (*Tosses painting.*) So is Dali.

Freud I much admire *Guernica.*

Dali Picasso is Communist.

Freud Yes.

Dali Neither is Dali.

Freud You'll have to forgive me for being frank. I am in a certain amount of pain.

Dali Divine.

Freud Distracting. It's been a pleasure to meet you.

Dali No. Dali cannot go. Not so soon. Let me describe to you the painting I have just completed. It is called ... *Dream Caused By The Flight Of A Bee. Around A Pomegranate One Second Before Waking Up.* It depicts the splitting of a pomegranate and the emergence of a large gold fish. From the mouth of the fish leaps a tiger. From the mouth of the tiger leaps ... another tiger. From the mouth of this tiger, a rifle with fixed bayonet about to pierce the white flesh of a naked girl, narrowly misses her armpit. Beyond all this a white elephant with impossible legs carries past a monument of ice.

Pause.

Dali You have to see it for yourself, really.

Freud Again, forgive my lack of courtesy ...

Dali Please, have none.

Freud Very well. I have always thought the surrealist movement a conspiracy of complete fools. But as you had the audacity to elect me some sort of patron saint, I thought it only polite to meet you. I now find I lack the energy even to be polite.

Dali Excellent! Dali has no concern for your health, no desire to be liked, and no manners. Creatures who live in the shell, Dali eats. Until the moment he dies, he does as he please. And he refuses to leave.

Freud I don't think I've ever met a more complete example of a Spaniard.

Dali Do you mind if I examine your room?

Freud Yes.

Dali But I must.

Dali *looks around the room. Very nosy. Almost opens closet.*

Freud I suppose the war has brought you to England?

Dali In Spain until one week ago, Dali paint and is contemptuous of the Fascist machine rolling towards. Then he thinks: no, this is all getting too historical for Dali. Immediately the desire to leave is enormous, and acted upon immediately.

Freud Have you any idea when the desire to leave here

might become at all substantial?

Dali When Dali, being here with you, no longer feels real to Dali.

Freud Shouldn't take too long then?

Dali Please. Your life is almost over. Don't waste your precious time trying to analyse Dali; he is completely sane. In fact, the only one.

*He finds a snail on **Freud**'s desk. Unsticks it, pulls it from its shell and eats it.*

It's not good. What sort of snail is this?

Freud English garden.

Swallows it.

Dali Is tasteless. Typical English.

Freud *looks for and finds another snail, which he deposits in a wastepaper bin. This becomes a running joke.* **Dali** *continues to look around, arrives at the closet and opens the door.* **Freud** *looks up.*

Freud N ... er ...

Dali *looks inside the closet and turns to stone. He closes the door, goes to **Freud** at the desk. Leans on the desk. Opens his mouth, closes it. Goes back to the closet. Opens it, goes inside, closes door behind him. A muffled blow, a cry and a crash.* **Dali** *emerges holding his genitals. Unable to speak for some time.*

Dali The girl in your closet.

Freud Yes?

Dali A hallucination, no?

Freud No? I mean, girl? What girl?

Dali In the closet.

Freud There's a girl in my closet?

Dali Naked girl.

Freud Nonsense. She must be a figment of your unique imagination.

Dali   She kick me in the phallus.

Freud   An impressive hallucinatory sensation.

Dali   I have pain in the testicle.

Freud   Hysterical.

Dali   No, is not funny.

Freud   Obviously you are at the peak of your imaginative powers.

Dali   You think?

Freud *leads him to the door.*

Freud   Your fantasies have grown so undeniable, they push through the fabric of reality. It is imperative you return home and paint at once.

Dali   A naked girl in the closet of Freud with the hooves of a stallion; is good.

Freud   Visionary.

Dali   I shall dedicate to you.

Freud   Thank you, goodbye.

Dali   The pain is transformed; is divine.

Freud   So good to have met you.

Dali   The honour, it is Dali's. I owe you my life.

Freud   An unintentional gift, I assure you.

Dali   Goodbye!

He leaves. **Freud** *grabs the clothing and has his hand on the closet door handle when* **Dali** *re-enters.*

Dali   No, no, no, no, no! I cannot leave.

Freud *hides the clothing behind his back*

Freud   Please, be firm in your retholution. Resolution.

Dali   Dali is firm in his trousers. His pain has transformed, his member tumescent. Dali is obsessed. The vision in the closet must be his. He must look again.

Freud   No.

Enter **Yahuda**. **Freud** *spins.*

Yahuda   Anna's? I think not. Give them to me.

Freud   The what?

Yahuda   The flimsies.

Freud   I don't have them.

But **Dali** *can see them, and pounces.*

Dali   Ahah! The garments of the Goddess.

He takes the bundle and buries his face.

Yahuda   Has he met your daughter?

Dali   She is a feast; you smell.

Yahuda *takes the bundle.*

Yahuda   I'll do no such thing. Freud, there's about enough silk here to cover Anna's left shin. I intend to confront her with these.

Freud   Ah.

He heads for the door.

Yahuda   And you'd better hope for a positive identification.

Freud   No, Yahuda . . . !

Dali   She fill my senses!

He throws off his jacket, grabs his pad, and opens the closet.

Freud   No!

Freud *rushes for the closet,* **Yahuda** *escapes. Closet door closes behind* **Dali** *before* **Freud** *can get there. He rushes to the other door, but it closes behind* **Yahuda**.

A pause. **Freud** *eyes the closet. Vague Spanish mumblings from within.*

Freud *approaches the door, curious. Puts his ear to it. As he straightens, the door flies open, hitting him on the jaw.* **Dali** *hurtles out, trips and lands spectacularly, out for the count.*

Jessica (*off*) I am a defenceless woman and refuse to be intimidated by amorous Spaniards!

Freud His arousal is entirely your responsibility.

Jessica A woman has the right to sit naked in a cupboard without being propositioned.

Freud I would defend your right, but not your choice of cupboard. Should this man sadly regain consciousness, I can give you no guarantee of his behaviour unless you get dressed.

Jessica Very well; give me my clothes.

Freud Ah.

Jessica (*off*) What does that mean? Ah?

Freud I have temporarily mislaid them.

Jessica Then you'll have to take me as I come.

Freud No! Wait. Here.

Throws her **Dali**'*s jacket.*

Jessica Thank you.

Freud All right?

Jessica Well, I don't think I'll get into the royal enclosure.

Freud Please, stay hidden.

Jessica If you swear to give me a hearing.

Freud All right, I swear.

Jessica When?

Freud   When Yahuda's gone. I'll give two knocks.

He closes the door. It opens again.

Jessica   It's bloody cold in here; I want more clothes.

Freud   All right! All right! I'll get you some. Just wait quietly.

Freud *closes the door on her again. Lifts* **Dali***'s head, looks in his eyes. Drops his head and starts to remove his trousers.*

Enter **Yahuda**.

Yahuda   She's never seen them in her life.

He sees **Freud** *and* **Dali***. Pause.*

Yahuda   You and I have to have a serious chat.

Freud   I was just . . . removing his trousers.

Yahuda   So I see. He appears to be unconscious.

Freud   Exactly. He began hyperventilating and fainted. I'm loosening his clothing.

Yahuda   He breathes through his backside as well, does he?

Freud   He was complaining of abdominal pains.

Yahuda   Really?

Yahuda*'s professionalism takes over. He examines* **Dali***.*

Freud   Most definitely. Indigestion maybe, but perhaps something very serious. Hopefully a ruptured appendix.

Yahuda   Hopefully!?

Freud   Well I mean, something worth you rushing him to hospital for, but of course hopefully not, touch wood.

Raps twice on the nearest bit of wood, which happens to be the closet door.

Jessica *comes out of the closet.* **Freud** *steers her back in and closes the door, stubbing her elbow.*

Jessica Ow.

Freud Ow. That was the sound he made, just before he collapsed.

Yahuda *rises.*

Dali Owwww.

Yahuda This man has suffered a blow to the head.

Freud Yes. He's very tall. On his way to the garden, he hit his head on the top of the doorframe.

Yahuda As he fainted?

Freud Yes.

Yahuda Which?

Freud Both.

Yahuda That's not possible.

Freud Yes it is. He was standing on the filing cabinet, fainted, and hit his head on the way down.

Yahuda What was he doing on the filing cabinet?

Freud I don't know. I wasn't here. I was already in the garden.

Yahuda Doing what?

Freud Chasing a swan.

Yahuda Where did that come from?

Freud I haven't the faintest idea. But it could have been the swan that entered the room very aggressively and forced Dali to retreat to the filing cabinet where he fainted in terror.

Yahuda This is utter nonsense.

Freud The answer is a sponge cake.

Yahuda What?

Freud Nothing.

Yahuda Freud, you've finally lost your marbles. Sixty years of clinical smut has taken its toll. Cross-dressing, violent tendencies and attempted sodomy . . . I'll keep it quiet of course, but I don't think you'll be publishing much else.

Freud That is slanderous! What proof have you?

Dali Owww.

Yahuda I'll get my bag. When he regains consciousness I shall find out exactly what's been going on here.

Yahuda *exits.*

Freud *close to panic. Knocks on the closet. Lifts* **Dali** *by the ankles. The closet door remains closed.* **Freud** *drops* **Dali** *and knocks again. Lifts* **Dali** *by the ankles. The door remains closed.* **Freud** *goes to the door.*

Freud Open the damn door.

The door opens. He gets **Dali** *by the ankles and slides him towards the closet.*

Freud I gave the signal.

Jessica You hurt my elbow.

Freud Two knocks is the signal.

Jessica That's what you did, and I came out and look at my elbow.

Freud Not one knock, not three knocks; two knocks.

Jessica I'm not having him in here.

Freud He's been rendered harmless. Just a few minutes, please.

Jessica Added to those you already owe me.

Closes door as **Yahuda** *enters.*

Pause.

Yahuda Where is he?

Freud   He left.

Yahuda   He what?

Freud   Through the garden, went over the wall. What a morning. You were right; I should be resting.

Yahuda   He was only half-conscious.

Freud   Self-induced trance; he uses it to paint.

Yahuda   Rubbish.

Freud   Exactly. No, you're right. It's rubbish. He was faking. Practical joke. Spanish, of course. Bike all right?

Yahuda   What about the underwear?

Freud   What?

Yahuda   This stuff.

Pulls it from his pocket.

Freud   Ah.

Yahuda   Well?

Freud   What did I say last time?

Yahuda   You said it was your daughter's.

Freud   Utter nonsense. She's far too . . .

Yahuda   I completely concur.

Freud   But she's hoping to lose weight. These are a sort of incentive to diet.

Yahuda   What sort of a fool do you take me for?

Freud   Yahuda . . . The truth of the matter is . . . You may laugh, but er . . . you may not even believe it, but er . . . Well . . . The Spanish lunatic came early this morning; we had given him permission to paint in the garden. He brought with him a young lady, a professional model . . .

Yahuda   It's common knowledge Dali only ever paints his wife.

Freud   His wife. She was his wife. The model was. His
wife the model. He set up his easel, she unfortunately
disrobed. If we had known, it goes without saying ... They
were discovered shortly before you arrived. To save you
any embarrassment they were hurried indoors and Dali
made a pretence of arriving after you.

Yahuda   She's Russian, isn't she?

Freud   Wh ... er?

Yahuda   Dali's wife.

Freud   She's er ... is she? Is. Russian, yes.

Yahuda   Where is she now?

Freud   Oh, she ... she left. Much earlier.

Yahuda   What was she wearing?

Freud   Um ... I give up. What was she wearing?

Yahuda   Well not these, for a start.

Freud   Well no, but I lent her a jacket and ... my
wellingtons.

Yahuda *eyes the wellington.*

Freud   She only took one.

Yahuda   I see. And then presumably she hopped half
naked all the way down the Finchley Road?

Freud   No, she hopped across the lawn to the laburnum
bush beneath which she had previously concealed her
clothes. Then she left.

Yahuda   No one passed me.

Freud   Ah, no; they climbed over the wall.

Yahuda   What on earth for?

Freud   They um, they're in training. They intend to
climb a mountain together in the spring. A small

Himalayan one. They're very adventurous and very in love.

Yahuda   If you say so.

Freud   Yes?

Yahuda   I'm sure the Himalayas are knee-deep in fornicating Spaniards. Not to mention naked Russians looking for their wellington boots.

Freud   Well, apparently so.

Pause.

Yahuda   All right, I believe you.

Freud   You do?

Yahuda   I'd believe anything of the Godless avant-garde.

Freud *collapses with relief.*

Yahuda   There's only one more thing you need to explain.

Freud   Yes?

Yahuda *wanders to the closet. Raps it once with his knuckles. His hand waves through the air as if to rap again,* **Freud** *stiffens, but the hand becomes an accusing finger.*

Yahuda   What's in the closet?

Freud   Absolutely nothing.

Yahuda   Don't give me that; you've been buzzing around it like a blowfly.

Freud *joins him at the closet.*

Freud   Papers, papers, a life's work . . .

Yahuda   Open it up.

Freud   I've mislaid the key.

Yahuda   Open this door.

He raps twice. **Freud** *instantly adds a third rap. Grins inanely.*

Yahuda *frowns, suspicious. Raps twice again.* **Freud** *adds a third rap.*

Yahuda *raps once.* **Freud** *raps twice.*

Yahuda *dummies a rap.* **Freud** *raps twice, then hurriedly adds one.*

Yahuda   What in God's name is wrong with you?

Freud *is desperately trying to remember the count.*

Yahuda *raps again, once, and strides away.* **Freud** *in complete confusion adds another one, and also walks away. Then stops dead.*

Freud *Scheisse.*

The closet opens. **Jessica***, dressed in* **Dali***'s clothes, walks out. Sees* **Yahuda***'s back. As she turns, so does he; she attempts to return to the closet.*

Yahuda   Ahah! Stop where you are!

She stops.

Over the wall is he, Freud?

He closes the closet to cut off her escape. She keeps her back to him.

All right, you bohemian buffoon; what have you got to say for yourself?

Jessica *shrugs.*

Yahuda   Don't give me any of your continental gestures. Just please inform me what sort of a relationship you have with this man.

Another shrug.

Yahuda   Turn around dammit and face me like a man.

Jessica *fiddles with her hair.*

Yahuda   I swear he's got shorter.

Jessica *turns round. She's attempted to fashion herself a moustache. A pause.*

Yahuda   All right, Freud; over to you. Let's hear it.

Freud   Um . . .

Jessica   Dr Yahuda, the truth is . . .

Freud   You wish to speak to me!

Jessica   That's true.

Freud   So in order for our conversation to happen, you did not leave with your husband.

Jessica   Who?

Freud   Dali; your husband. Because you wished to speak to me.

Jessica   That's right. I didn't go with my husband Dali, Dali my husband because . . . (*Dreadful Spanish accent.*) . . . I thtayed behind to thpeak to Profethor Freud which ith why I wath thitting in the clothet.

Freud   Besides; you'd had a row.

Jessica   Ith correct.

Freud   And you hit him on the head.

Jessica   Thith ith true.

Yahuda   With a swan, presumably?

Jessica   *Que?*

Yahuda   May I ask you a personal question?

Jessica   Thertainly.

Yahuda   What country do you come from?

Jessica   Thpain, of courth.

Freud, *behind* **Yahuda** *now, gestures frantically.*

Jessica   Not thpain? No, I hate thpain. Spain. Spain? Plagh!

Yahuda   So?

Jessica   Sssso ... I come from ...

Freud *tries to look like Lenin.*

Jessica   A very important city um ... near Mount Rushmore. No, no. Only joking.

Freud *holds up an umbrella and with his curved arm, tries to make a hammer and sickle.*

Jessica   It rains a lot. Where I come from. England, it's ... no.

He stands in a Russian sort of way.

The people where I come from are very rugged because it rains so much.

He slow marches.

In fact many of them are dead.

He tries the same thing again, but more exaggerated.

Turkey? No. I'm just having you on. If you seriously want to know, um ...

Freud *stabs at his head with a finger, impersonating Trotsky's death.*

Jessica   Where I come from ... they're all mad. The entire country is completely barmy. France! It's France! I'm French! No, I'm not, what a stupid thing to say.

She's losing her patience with **Freud**, *he's losing his with her. He stands with his finger on his head.*

Mars. I come from Mars.

Freud *does a Russian dance.*

Jessica   Or Russia, I don't give a t ... Russia! Russia? I come from Russia. That's where I come from. Russia.

Yahuda   Really?

Jessica   Oh yes. It's very warm for October, isn't it? Precious little snow.

Yahuda   You don't sound Russian.

Jessica   Oh ... *Vy mozhete skazat' mnye chuke proiti k zimnemu dvortcu? Dva kilograma svekly i butylku vodki. Da zdravstvuyet velikii Sovetskii Soyuz!* (Can you tell me the way to the Winter Palace? I would like half a pound of beetroot and a bottle of vodka, please. Long live the glorious USSR!)

Freud   Oh, bravo.

Yahuda   All right, I give up.

Freud   That was brilliant.

Yahuda   But you came close, Freud, so be warned; I may be willing to suspend my disbelief this far, but not one step further.

Deli *comes out of the closet in his underwear.*

Dali   Excuse me please. Dali does not remove his clothings.

Freud   I can explain this.

Dali   Pretty girls remove their clothings for Dali, not versa vice!

Freud   In fact I can, I can explain this.

Yahuda   Freud, will you tell me why on earth you are consorting with these lunatics?

Freud   Patients, Yahuda.

Yahuda   I've been patient long enough!

Freud   No, these are my patients.

Yahuda   Patients?

Freud   My last patients. A couple of mild cases to occupy my mind until ...

Yahuda   I see. Well, you always were one for a challenge, weren't you? Now it all falls into place.

Freud You are a generous and understanding man.

Yahuda Not at all. I'd better leave you to it then. Good afternoon.

Freud Good afternoon.

Yahuda I'll be back of course.

Freud Mmm?

Yahuda You know what for.

Freud *discerns something sinister in these parting words as* **Yahuda** *exits.*

Dali In London the first thing I visit is the famous West End and I see *Look for the Nookie* or somesuch . . .

Freud *Rookery Nook.*

Dali Is so. And I think no; is ridiculous. But in England is like this, and is great fun. So Dali chase you through french windows, round the garden, back through front door, yes?

Jessica No, I don't think so.

Dali You want to kick him again in the reproductives?

Jessica No.

Dali Please.

Jessica I didn't come here for this.

Dali What is this?

Jessica This pathetic farce.

She takes her clothes and goes back into the closet.

Dali Oh. But then you will pose for Dali, yes?

Jessica No.

Dali You think Dali try to seduce you is not true. Dali does not touch. His only passion is to *look*.

Jessica Well, he can look elsewhere.

Dali Your armpit, it is divine. I must make unto it the graven image!

Jessica *emerges, buttoning her dress.*

Dali Where have you hidden it?

Jessica Under my arm. Professor Freud, I wish to continue the analysis.

Freud Whose?

Jessica The one we began.

Freud What is the point? It was concluded years ago.

Jessica Humour me.

Freud The details of the case are fully documented.

Jessica But they're not. Not in your own notes.

She produces a small book.

Jessica This journal belonged to the patient you called Rebecca S. Her real name was Miriam Stein. This is the journal she kept of her work with you.

Freud So?

Jessica I'd like us to read it.

Freud To what end?

Jessica I've simplified what she remembered of the sessions, and selected the most apposite passages. Please; read with me.

Freud I have neither the time nor the inclination.

Dali Please.

Jessica What?

Dali *waves some money at her.*

Dali To consider my request a professional proposition.

Jessica Go to hell.

Dali Is a substantial sum.

Jessica   Please.

Freud   It's out of the question.

Jessica   Why?

Dali   Name your price.

Jessica   I'm not for sale.

Dali   The armpit only. My Venus.

He kisses her hand ...

Jessica   Why not?

Freud   It would be a pointless exercise.

... and lifts her arm for a peek.

Jessica   Get off!

Dali   On my knees.

Jessica   Pointless?

Dali   You see; he begs.

Jessica   Are you sure?

Freud   I will have nothing to do with it.

Dali   Dali will do anything you ask.

Jessica   Can you read English?

Dali   Dali is perfect English. Not have got you ears?

Jessica   Very well. Read the passages underlined.

Dali   *Que?*

Freud   Look, I really must insist ...

Dali   What for is this?

Jessica   We are going to reconstruct one of the Professor's case histories. You sit here. When we are finished you may have fifteen minutes to do what you will with my armpit.

Dali   Is a deal. I am to be the fraud of the great Freud, yes?

Dali *sits in the tub seat.*

Freud   No. I will not tolerate this.

Dali   Ah.

Jessica   What anxieties are prompting your objections, Professor? Read the passages marked with an F.

Dali   But if the Professor object to this worm presuming to embody him then this Dali cannot possibly . . .

Jessica *puts her hand behind her head.*

Dali   . . . refuse you, my darling, and to hell with this man and his beard also.

Freud   Very well, if you insist. Get it over with.

Jessica   From the top of the page.

Dali   So. 'As you speak to me you will notice ideas will occur that you feel are not important, are nonsensical, not necessary to mention. But these disconnected things are the things you *must* mention.' Dali knows this; he has read this from the book. 'You must say whatever goes through your mind. Leave nothing unsaid, especially that which is unpleasant to say.' Maestro.

Jessica   Concentrate.

Dali   Of course.

Jessica   It's a warm day. I had difficulty getting here. The cab driver was reluctant to raise the canopy, and I cannot travel in an open cab.

Dali   She knows this; is word-perfect.

Jessica   Shut up. Instead of persuading the cabbie, my husband berated me. I had to insist quite firmly, which has made me a little anxious.

She rubs her breast.

Jessica I wish I hadn't come. I don't like leaving the house.

Dali *rubs his nipple exotically.*

Jessica Your line.

Dali *Que?*

Jessica What are you doing?

Dali Is what it says here. I was gently rubbing my breast.

Jessica Not your breast, my breast.

Dali You rub the breast of the patient? Is not in the published works you did this.

He reaches out, she slaps his hand.

Jessica She was rubbing her own breast.

Dali *Que?* Oh, *si.*

Jessica You see?

Dali *Si.*

Jessica 'I' is me.

Dali *Que?*

Jessica 'I' is me.

Dali *Si.* Is obvious, but very bad English.

Freud Listen . . .

Jessica Can we get on!

Dali *Si, si.* So . . .

Jessica I don't like leaving the house. I feel safer inside.

Dali 'I notice you are rubbing your breast.'

Jessica Am I?

Dali 'Yes.'

Jessica I hadn't noticed.

Dali   'Continue.'

Jessica   Walking across a field or a town square is a
nightmare. I want to stick to the hedge or the edge of the
wall, but even then there's this constant possibility . . . A
wicker basket. Just came into my head. Is that the sort of
thing?

Dali   Is good, no? Apologise. 'Continue.'

Jessica   When I was young we had a wicker basket; I
used to play ships in it. It was a picnic basket. I don't
know why I've thought of this, but . . . my mother reading
to us, the story of Chicken Little. A piece of the sky falls
on his head. Bits of the sky falling. I hate the sky, the way
the clouds scud. Looking through my grandmother's
window. There's a birdcage next to me with a canary. It's
got some sort of disease; its beak is being eaten away.

Gags.

Something I've just remembered, God it was horrible, and
I'd forgotten all about it. I'm lying in my grandmother's
garden. I'm an adult, I'm nineteen and she's told me to
wait for something spectacular. I remember this now. She
said if I lay still I'd get a spectacular surprise. And I'm full
of anticipation, waiting for her to bring out a cake or
something and suddenly . . .

She rubs.

The air is full of birds. Starlings. Not just a few dozen but
thousands. A black cloud of starlings. A tattered sky and
those horrible birds just . . .

She gags.

I run inside. I'm really angry with her. And the starlings
roost in trees all round the house and I sit curled up in a
cold dark study in a leather chair and listen to the noise
and I am terrified. Some of them swoop to the windowsill.
My heart races. I'm scared of the starlings. I'm frightened
of the birds.

Dali *applauds.*

Jessica   Don't do that.

Dali   It says this. 'There was applause.'

Jessica *takes the journal.*

Jessica   'There was a pause.'

Dali   I see, *si. Si.*

Pause.

In this pause you think maybe I light a cigar?

Jessica   No.

Dali   No, *si.*

Jessica   I don't know why but I'm thinking now of a flame, a small, a candle flame . . . and it's burning *upside down.* I don't understand that. A heavy sky. Leaden. I'm afraid of the sky. No I'm not. It's not the sky, is it? It's that a bird might fly, might pass overhead. Not all those starlings, something far worse; one bird in a blue sky. That's what frightens me. The *possibility* of a bird.

She rubs.

Freud   Are you finished?

Jessica   No. Later in that same first session, they discuss her eating disorder and she free-associates around food and meals. I haven't learned this bit. Give it to me.

She reads.

'Knife, fork and spoon should be lined up just so. A knife should never be put into the mouth . . . all these rules my father had. Preparing for a picnic . . . the basket! Being allowed to boil the eggs.' And eventually . . . here it is.

Freud   Look . . .

Dali   Please . . . shhh.

Jessica 'I am about seven years old. I am at the table. My father is giving a dinner party and I have begged to attend. I am on my absolutely best behaviour. The candles are lit and the mahogany shines. I have spooned my soup from the far side of the bowl and I have not spilt a drop. The meat is carved and the vegetables passed. My mother is proud of me. At this point in the analysis I burst into tears and was unable to continue for some time. Dr Freud waited silently. Eventually I was able to recall the rest of the dinner party. I ask my mother to pass the salt. My father disapproves of my using condiments, but I am on my honour to act as an adult. I tip the salt cellar, but nothing comes out. The salt is damp. I shake the salt cellar, only once, and the silver top flies off. Salt pours in a thick quick flow all over my plate, all over my food, and flicks down the table as I try to stop the flow. The guests turn as one to look at me. Some laugh. I feel the most unbearable humiliation. My ears burn. My mother brushes some of the salt into her hand with a napkin, but the food is ruined. So I pick up my knife and fork and I eat it. I pretend it does not taste disgusting. I eat until my mouth is dry, my gums are stinging. Tears of shame and embarrassment spilling and rolling down my cheek. I run upstairs and vomit. Put myself to bed, the bed is cold. I listen miserably to the guests leaving, then my father throws open the door and shouts that I am clumsy, unworthy, a stupid child. I lie in the dark afterwards wondering why he hates me so.' You then announced that the session must come to a close. Then asked, in passing, how often she had intercourse with her husband. She refused to answer. She was pressured to do so.

Freud Where is this leading? What is your point?

Jessica I need to take this step by step. We shall leap to another session; the sixth.

Dali Is great shame. I miss any good bits?

Jessica This is a really good bit.

Freud No. You have told me nothing I do not know.

Dali   But is getting to the really good bit.

Freud   I refuse to participate any further.

Jessica   We're almost there.

Freud   Please. Leave.

She opens a desk drawer and pulls out her razor.

Jessica   I'm sorry but I have to finish this. Help me finish it.

Dali   Please. I say something?

Jessica   Yes?

Dali   Goodbye.

Jessica   Stay where you are.

Dali   Just here?

Jessica   Just there.

Dali   Is good. Is very nice just here. No need to move at all, never.

Freud   Put that down.

Jessica   Let me do what I have to do and then I swear, I'll disappear.

Freud   Very well, but give me the razor.

Jessica   No.

Dali   Is good to give it to him. Is better to keep it, though. Boy, it's really nice just here, isn't it?

Jessica   Sit down. By this time her anorexia has been suspended. She's eating again, quite well. The gagging has greatly reduced; she has successfully related the gagging to the taste of salt, real or imagined, and thus to the trauma of the dinner party. From there.

Dali   'I wish you to concentrate on your fear of birds. What thoughts come to you?'

Jessica   The smell of leather. Mahogany. A candle flame.
Of course, at the dinner party the candle flames were
reflected in the polished wood. They were upside down.

Dali   'What of the birds?'

Jessica   Oh, birds, eggs, boiled eggs ... the picnic basket.
I'm sick to death of that picnic bask ...

Dali   'A pause.'

Jessica   I'm eating a boiled egg at a picnic. My whole
family is there. My father has refused to undo his collar. It
is very hot. He offers me salt in which to dip my egg. I of
course decline. I'm in my late teens by now, I think of
myself as very demure. I am dressed in white. And there
are friends of the family there. This is more than a ... It
was my father's birthday! I feel good towards him. I feel he
likes me now. He gives me the odd stiff smile. I wish we
were alone; I'm sure we could talk together now. I wish we
were alone. A long way off a child is crying. I take a bite
of the egg. My father calls my name. Miriam. No! I look
up and smile and no!

She cries out in disgust. Rubs violently. Gags.

Dali   'Relax.'

The fit continues.

Dali   'You are here, you are safe. He embraces her.'

The fit continues.

Dali   Is your line.

Freud   He embraces her!

Dali   Oh, *si*. Sorry. Is allowed?

Freud   Yes, is allowed.

Dali *embraces her. She passes out, a silent pause, wakes with a
scream.*

Jessica   No! It's all over me; my dress, my breast.

Dali   What is this?

Jessica   A bird, a filthy bird. A streak of white, a sudden flash of green, it's warm and wet and it's on my breast. An unspeakable mess; it's bird excrement.

She calms down.

Jessica   Without thinking, I wipe at the stuff with my fingers. It makes it worse. It's fluid and pungent, it's everywhere, but especially on my beautiful new ... breast. And all over my fingers. My father, thankfully, looks away embarrassed. He pretends he saw nothing. I clean up as best I can but my dress is stained and however much I try to clean them, all afternoon my fingers feel ... sticky. Stuck together. All the way home, I hide my hand. All the way home I can smell it. And my father, all the way home, never once looks at me.

Pause.

Jessica   Is that how it was? Her fit?

Dali   Was magnificent.

Jessica   Is that how it was?

Freud   Similar.

Jessica   And did you embrace her?

Freud   Yes.

Jessica   She says ... (*Reads.*) 'I clung to him to prevent myself falling through the door that had opened up beneath me and through which I had seen that summer's day so clearly. And the door righted itself and I knew it was now my choice to step through and remember whatever I wished. I am so deeply and eternally grateful to this man.'

Freud   Transference is common to all successful analyses.

Jessica   They all fall in love?

Freud   Without exception.

Dali   Wow.

Freud   And the gift that must be returned is an acceptance of that love, with no love returned, no demands made, no respect diminished.

Jessica   You never loved in return?

Freud   Of course not.

Jessica   She felt euphoric at the revelations tumbling from her past. And the symptoms began to disappear. She recognised the wiping gesture for what it was, and laughed when she caught herself doing it. Life opened up, she said, like a painted fan. What continued to disturb her were your questions about her intimate affairs. She had admitted her distaste for copulation, and acknowledged her husband's frustration. But still every week you pushed, probed and insisted that she spoke of these things.

Freud   This is indelicate. I've had enough.

Jessica   We've reached the crucial session.

Freud   You will leave my house, please.

Jessica   What have you to hide?

Freud   Don't be impertinent. Whatever confidences you are about to reveal from this poor woman's private reminiscences, and whatever conclusions you may have reached, I can assure you that no impropriety took place between us. And no such impropriety has ever taken place between myself and any patient.

Jessica   I'm not accusing you.

Freud   But you were about to.

Jessica   It's obviously something you feel very defensive about . . .

Freud   How dare you!

Jessica   But I have no intention of making any such accusations.

Freud   Then what is this about?

Jessica   One more visit. The seventh. She returns. Things are not good. The gagging has returned and she finds it impossible to keep any food down. Her fingers are useless, and her wiping tic incessant and exaggerated. She's distraught that in spite of all she's learned, she's iller than ever.

Freud   When she arrived. Not when she left.

Jessica   She was very angry with you, very angry, and you sensed this. Didn't you?

Freud   Of course.

Jessica   And you encouraged her to express her anger, didn't you?

Freud   Of course.

Jessica   And did she? Did she? *Did she?*

She hits him.

Dali   No.

Freud   It's all right. Yes she did.

Jessica   I'm almost there. Almost there now.

The hysterical symptoms take hold of her, more exaggerated and more frequent. Other physical tics manifest themselves. She returns to the couch in an increasingly distressed state.

Dali   Is what page, which, I don't know.

Jessica *moans loudly, an agonised exhalation that frightens* **Dali**.

Dali   Please.

Freud   It's all right.

Dali   To help me, please.

Freud   She's all right. She'll be all right.

He takes the chair.

Freud   Rebecca? Rebecca? What is wrong with your hand?

Jessica The excrement.

Freud Your breast?

Jessica And my fingers; covered in shit. I know! I know! But I can't, it's ... I'm still so angry!

Freud Angry.

Jessica Yes, angry.

Freud At the bird?

She breaks down. Gags.

What is wrong with your mouth?

Jessica The taste.

Freud Describe the taste.

Jessica The taste of salt. It's salt. Everything tastes of salt!! I'm filthy with this shit and all I can taste is salt.

Freud Associate. The taste of salt.

Jessica A candle burns upside down; its reflection in mahogany. The dinner party.

Freud A candle?

Jessica Put it out. No; the ... cutlery.

Freud Tell me about the candle.

Jessica It's in the middle of the dining table.

Freud No, the other candle.

Jessica What other? There is no other candle. Except the one I was allowed. I hate the dark; my mother allows me a candle. My father thinks it a waste. He will open my door and bark 'put it out'. The door opens ...

Pause. She's still for a moment.

Don't put the knife in your mouth. He opens the door. Put out the candle. The taste of salt and my ... my fingers.

She sobs quietly.

Freud   Why are you crying?

Jessica   I don't know.

Freud   I think you know.

Jessica   The candle is burning.

Freud   He opens the door.

Sobbing openly, growing in violence.

Jessica   He says 'put it out'. Put it . . . ! Put it . . . !

Freud   That's enough.

Jessica   The candle is not upside down! It's me, I'm upside down! My head is hanging over the side of the bed! Put it . . . !

Freud   That's enough now. Rebecca.

Jessica   Put it in your mouth!

Incapable of continuing, she stops.

Freud   Rebecca. No more now.

Jessica   She remembered. She remembered. The mess on her breast and her fingers and the taste of salt.

Dali   Don't cry. Please.

Jessica   I'm sorry. I'll be all right in a minute.

Dali   What was this?

Freud   She had remembered being raped. Orally. Before she was five years old.

Jessica   The taste of salt was the taste of her father's semen. The filth on her breast that she tried to clean off was his. When she woke in the morning her fingers were stuck together. She had to be carried from your study, and accompanied home. She slept for almost three days.

Freud   Over the next few sessions she discarded a great deal of anger and guilt. She regained her appetite and her physical symptoms disappeared.

Jessica She was ecstatic. (*Reads.*) 'For the first time in my adult life I am happy. A simple thing to have been so painfully elusive. I feel there is nothing now in my past that can throw a shadow over my future. This morning I shall prepare . . . a picnic basket.'

Freud However. The events that Rebecca had remembered . . .

Jessica Miriam! Her name was Miriam!

Dali And she and her husband?

Jessica Oh, eventually. Sexual relations were resumed. Which I suppose means *I* also have you to thank, Professor Freud.

Freud What for?

Jessica My life.

Freud She was your mother.

Jessica You cured her.

Freud You have her mouth.

Jessica You released her, enabled her. You were her saviour.

Dali Is good. You come not to criticise, but to pay homage.

Jessica What did you think, Professor?

Freud *lowers his head, thinking.*

Jessica When I found her journal I had to come.

Dali I like this. Your mother is cured and is a happy ending, yes?

Jessica Not really, no.

Dali No?

Jessica   Nine years later my mother died in the washroom of an insane asylum near Paris. She took a rubber tube they used for giving enemas and swallowed it; force-fed it to herself. The other end she attached to a faucet, turned the tap and drowned. In case you're still wondering, Professor, that is why I'm here.

Act Two

The same. Twilight.

Dali Is serious now, yes?

Jessica Yes.

Dali I go put my trousers on.

He retires to the closet.

Freud I had no knowledge of your mother's death.

Jessica That's hardly surprising. Rebecca S. has little in common with Miriam Stein. Your patient Rebecca is a successful case history; my mother Miriam a suicidal hysteric.

Freud The last time I saw her was one year after our final session. She returned to inform me of her health and happiness.

Jessica She was pregnant, with me.

Freud She had had, she said, a wonderful year.

Jessica 1897.

Freud What?

Jessica 1897.

An air-raid siren sounds.

What is that?

Freud A warning, is all.

Frightened, **Jessica** *covers her head with her arms.*

Freud To alert us, not harm us.

Dali *comes out of the closet, crosses and exits out the door.*

Dali Scuse.

Freud *draws the curtains.*

The intercom buzzes.

Freud   Yes?

Anna   Father? We are going to the shelter.

Freud   I'm not. I told you when you built it.

Anna   This might not be another drill.

Freud   I have been thrown out of my home, shunted over Europe, and shipped across the channel. No further.

Anna   It's just down the garden. Fifty yards.

Freud   I shall soon be spending a substantial amount of time in a hole in the ground. I don't intend to climb into one while I can still argue the point.

Anna   Very well. But keep the curtains closed.

Freud   Of course.

Anna   And if there are bombs, get under the desk.

Freud   Don't be absurd.

He switches it off. **Dali** *enters in a gas mask.*

Dali   Scuse.

And goes back into the closet.

Freud   If you would prefer to shelter . . .

Jessica   No. I prefer to talk.

Freud   What were you looking for last night?

Jessica   Unpublished notes. Relevant material. I wanted to find out if you knew what you did to her?

Freud   I?

Jessica   On that final visit.

Freud   She was strong, healthy, and functioning well.

Jessica   Obviously you *had* managed to turn her into a horse.

Freud   Her symptoms had subsided, her neuroses were negligible.

Jessica   And my father could penetrate her whenever he so desired. Thank you, Doctor; my wife is cured.

Freud   Not cured no, rendered capable. Remarkably so, considering.

Jessica   What?

Freud   That her analysis was incomplete.

Jessica   Was it? Was it?

She takes a book from the shelf. Opens it at a page she's previously marked.

The Aetiology of Hysteria. 1896. 'In every case, the cause of hysteria is a passive sexual experience before puberty, ie, a traumatic seduction.' This is what you wrote.

Freud   Yes it is.

Jessica   No equivocation, no trace of doubt. You wrote to your friend Fliess: 'Have I revealed the great clinical truth to you? Hysteria is the consequence of presexual shock.' That's what you believed.

Freud   Yes it is.

Jessica   And you published.

Freud   Yes I did.

Jessica   You were absolutely certain.

Freud   Yes I was.

She pulls a crumpled letter from a wellington boot.

Jessica   One year later. 'My Dear Fliess. Let me tell you straight away the great secret which has been slowly dawning on me in recent months. I no longer believe in my neurotica.'

Freud   What is the point you wish to make?

Jessica   Just one year later. And you what, you . . .

Freud   A year?

Jessica   Change your mind in less than a . . .

Freud   The year of my life! 1897 may have been a wonderful year for your mother, but it was torture for me.

Jessica   Why?

Freud   My clinical cases. I suffered disappointment after disappointment; the analyses refused to come to a satisfactory conclusion; the results were imperfect therapeutically and scientifically. I came to the inevitable conclusion that I was wrong.

Jessica   And when my mother returned, smiling, to confide her happiness and my genesis to you . . . you took back your blessing.

Freud   At first I believed I had uncovered the inciting trauma. A year later I knew this was not the case.

Jessica   You told my mother that her memory of abuse was a fantasy born of desire.

Freud   It is more complex than that.

Jessica   It's not that complex, Professor. You said her father did not seduce her; that it was she who wished to seduce her father.

Freud   That is a gross over-simplification.

Jessica   And by the autumn all the childhood seductions unearthed by your patients . . . none of them had ever occurred.

Freud   In the unconscious there is no criterion of reality. Truth cannot be distinguished from emotional fiction.

Jessica   So you abandoned them.

Freud   I abandoned the theory. It was false and erroneous.

Jessica I don't have many vivid memories of my mother. She ate alone; couldn't bear to be seen eating. I never ate a single meal with my mother. I don't remember her treating me badly, but nor do I have the faintest recollection of her loving me. My father had her committed when I was five years old.

The journal.

Freud If we had the time I could help you understand . . .

Jessica There's no need. I understand perfectly. I've spent a long time working to understand this. When you proposed that abuse was the root cause of so much mental illness your movement was at its most vulnerable. You needed the support of the intelligentsia, of institutions, of publishers and instead you were laughed at and reviled. Doors were closed. Anti-Semitic tracts appeared. Everything you'd worked for was threatened.

Freud True.

Jessica Your patients were the daughters and wives of wealthy and privileged men. Whom you began to accuse of molesting their own children. And then suddenly, you decide you were wrong. How convenient.

Freud Convenient? To have shared a Revelation and then discover it was false? All I had to steer myself through that terrible year was my integrity.

Jessica Huh.

Freud I have weathered many storms of protest, but I have never bowed to outrage or to ignorance.

Jessica Had you not changed your mind, the outraged and ignorant would have crucified you!! My own grandfather, who my mother accused, was friend or acquaintance to every publisher in Austria!

Freud You are accusing me of the most heinous opportunism!

Jessica   Yes. Yes I am!

Freud   Do you realise how many women retrieved 'memories' of abuse while lying there?

Jessica   Many.

Freud   More than many. You will forgive my astonishment at being asked to believe that sexual perversion was prevalent amidst the genteel classes in epidemic proportions. I was proposing a virtual plague of perversion. Not merely socially unacceptable; fundamentally unthinkable!

Jessica   So you thought up something else.

Freud   The theory of infantile sexuality . . .

Jessica   . . . Is the cornerstone of your entire edifice! Change your mind about that and psychoanalysis would be rubble.

Freud   No one has been readier than I to risk our movement in the pursuit of truth.

Jessica   My mother . . .

Freud (*harsh*)   Your mother was a hysteric! Her memories of seduction were wishful fantasies based on her unconscious desire to possess her father, his penis and his child.

Jessica   But my mother . . .

Freud   These desires in turn based on her desire to possess her mother, to suckle indefinitely, and to give her a child.

Jessica   I've read all this . . .

Freud (*rapid*)   A premature rejection of her mother, an unresolved anger at having no penis, a fierce fixation on her father. At the crucial age of seven, if my memory serves me, her mother dies. She believes herself to be guilty of killing her mother to attain her father. Her development is arrested, her guilt repressed along with her desires. Years

later she develops the hysterical symptoms and the fantasies
begin to emerge alongside the memories.

Jessica   But it's all so . . .

Freud   Complex.

Jessica   All I know is that my mother's father . . .

Freud   You know nothing! You are ignorant,
presumptuous and obsessed. Your theories are simplistic.
Your motives malicious. I have given you quite enough of
my time. Thank you.

Jessica   Why so angry?

Freud   I AM ANGRY WITH NO ONE!

Dali (*off*)   Arrgh!

He bursts out of the cupboard, holding his forefinger before him like a
beacon. It's bleeding.

Dali   Maphu mothur ufgud! Haffmee!

He tears off his gas mask.

Is my blood.

Jessica   What have you done?

Dali   Please call an ambulance and alert the hospital.
Look, is my blood. Is coming out of my finger.

Jessica   Calm down, it's not that bad.

Dali   Is my blood.

Jessica   Have you first aid?

Freud   In the drawer. How did you cut yourself?

Dali   Is not! I sit in the closet, I notice on the wall the
piece of . . . how you say this? Nasal mucus. Fastened to
the wall with much exhibitionism. Very old; a previous
owner I am sure. Is pearly green with a sharp point that
makes a gesture which is a trumpet call for intervention. Is
disgusting, so I take my courage, wrap my finger in

handkerchief and savagely tear the mucus from the wall!
But is hard and steely point like a needle! Look; is here. It
penetrate between the nail and the flesh! All the way down.

Jessica   All right, calm down.

Dali   Is great painful.

Jessica   I'm sure it is.

Dali   Is to the bone.

Jessica   I'll pull it out.

Dali   Please. Be carefully.

Jessica *pulls out the mucus. Wraps it in handkerchief.*

Dali   Argh!

Jessica   Here; disinfect it with this.

Dali   Is throbbing.

Jessica   Be a brave soldier.

Freud *begins reading his letters to Fliess.*

Dali   Is go boom, boom, boom; the music of perfidious
infection. Argh!

Jessica   What?

Dali   Is still there! The pointy part is still deep down. I
see it through the nail. Get it out.

Jessica   Well, I can't.

Dali   Do this!

Jessica   It's far too deep.

Dali   No! Is, but . . . ! It still throb. Is will be infected. Is
death. Death weigh in my hand like ignominious kilo of
gesticulating worms.

Jessica   It's only a splinter.

Dali   Is unknown nasal mucus! This finger is swelled. This
hand is begin to rot. Please, get me to a hospital. I have it

surgically dismissed at the wrist. Buried. It decompose without me.

Jessica   It's not snot anyway.

Dali   It's not?

Jessica   No, it's not.

Dali   *Si si!* It's snot. Is what I said.

Jessica   It's a bit of glue.

Dali   It's not.

Jessica   No. A drop of wood glue.

Dali   Oh. *Si.*

Jessica   You'll survive.

Dali   Is possible. Thank you.

Freud *replacing letters in cabinet.*

Jessica   What are you doing?

Freud   I'm sorry?

Jessica   I haven't read them all yet.

Freud   And why should I allow you to examine my personal correspondence?

Jessica   Why should you not?

Freud   Because it is personal.

Jessica   You said things to Fleiss you would never say to others.

Freud   Our communications were at times a little unguarded.

Jessica   Give them to me.

Freud   No.

Jessica   Why not?

Freud   The discovery of your mother's sad history has

been very traumatic for you, but whatever quest you have set yourself is a hopeless one. I have nothing to hide.

Loud knocks from the front door.

Jessica   Then let me have the letters.

Freud   Indeed, to hide nothing has been my sole quest.

He leaves, taking the letters with him.

Jessica   What are you drawing?

Dali   Him.

She looks.

Jessica   You are a cruel man.

Dali   No.

Jessica   Then you have cruel eyes.

Yahuda's *voice off, then both enter.*

Yahuda   Freud. Apologies for this but I must beg hospitality. Every time I turn on my bicycle lamp I'm yelled at by cockney plebeians in flat caps and armbands. It's pitch black; I can't get home. Ah.

Freud   Nor can Mr Dali and his wife.

Dali *looks for his wife.*

Freud   Your wife.

Dali   Please?

Yahuda   We met earlier.

Dali   Oh, *si. Si.*

Yahuda   How's the training going? Both pretty fit?

Dali   Which is this?

Yahuda   I got on top of one or two myself when I was younger.

Dali   Please?

Yahuda   Couldn't keep it up though.

Dali   Oh, *si*.

Yahuda   The nice thing is, they don't have to be enormous to be satisfying, wouldn't you agree? If you're not used to it, small ones are sufficiently stimulating. How far up her do you hope to get?

Dali   This man is a doctor?

Freud   I mentioned that you and your wife . . .

Yahuda   A word of advice – always use the best quality rope and don't attempt anything vertical the first time.

Dali   Please?

Freud   That you and your wife much enjoyed mountaineering.

Dali   Oh?

Jessica   I think it's time Dr Yahuda was told the truth.

Freud   No.

Jessica   Mr Dali and I are not married.

Freud   But share a common-law agreement. It's a changing world, Yahuda.

Jessica   We met for the first time earlier this afternoon.

Freud   A rapidly changing world.

Yahuda   So why were you here in the first place?

Jessica   It is true that I am Russian.

Freud   Is it? Good.

Jessica   And I have been engaged by Professor Doctor Freud to translate some of his letters.

Freud   Yes, that's it. Precisely.

Jessica   And those are the only ones I haven't done.

Freud   Ah.

Jessica   May I continue?

Freud   No.

Jessica   Why not?

Yahuda   Why not?

Freud   Very well. If you must.

Jessica *takes the letters.* **Freud** *can't let go of them. She pulls, third time lucky.*

Jessica   Thank you, Professor.

She retires to read.

Yahuda   What's wrong with your hand?

Freud   Nothing. Hysterical grip reflex. When I was young I er . . .

Makes a repeated gesture with his wrist. Recognises it as an obscene gesture.

. . . dropped an ice cream.

Yahuda *finds the manila envelope containing the Moses article.*

Yahuda   Stamped and addressed, I see. Off to the publishers?

Freud   Yes.

Yahuda   You realise, of course, you have a Moses complex?

Freud   I beg your pardon?

Yahuda   I read an article. Some woman you once sent barmy. Said you identified with Moses.

Freud   Moses is nothing but the flesh of sublimation.

Dali   Superb.

He makes a note.

Yahuda   It is a bad time to discourage men from putting their faith in God.

Freud On the contrary.

Yahuda Have you read this evening's paper?

Freud No.

Yahuda Then do so.

Slaps it at him.

Seven thousand Jewish shops looted. Three hundred synagogues burned to the ground. Babies held up to watch Jews being beaten senseless with lead piping. They are calling it *Kristallnacht*.

Freud *takes the paper.*

Yahuda Apparently Goerring is displeased that so much replacement glass will have to be imported. He said they should have broken less glass and killed more Jews. Have you heard from your sisters?

Freud No.

Jessica Sisters?

Freud Four elderly ladies. We have not been successful in our attempts to bring them out.

Yahuda Don't blame yourself.

Freud It is entirely my fault.

Yahuda No.

Freud If I myself had left sooner, I would have been more able to make suitable arrangements.

Yahuda You've done what you can.

Freud I do not believe I shall see them again.

Yahuda They say it is to be the last war. Do you think so?

Freud My last.

Yahuda *swings the light-pull like a bar skittles game. It knocks over half a dozen figures.*

Yahuda   You lead us from the wilderness and then
abandon us. If you think you're Moses why for the love of
God throw doubt upon him now?

Jessica   Why indeed?

Freud   Have you finished with those?

Jessica   It couldn't mean you wish to be doubted, could
it?

Freud   I wish to be left in peace!

Jessica   You doubt nothing?

Freud   Nothing!

Yahuda   What are you reading?

Freud   Nothing.

Jessica   You should read them also.

Freud   Yahuda. A cigar?

Yahuda   You stink of cigars.

Freud   No more lectures. I have already smoked myself to
death. I now do it purely for pleasure.

Freud *lights a cigar.*

Jessica   This one's interesting.

Yahuda   Is it?

Freud   No, it isn't. Come on, Yahuda. I need some fresh
air.

Yahuda   What about the Luftwaffe?

Freud   You think from two thousand feet, they could spot
the butt of an old cigar?

Yahuda   With my luck they'll recognise you instantly.

Yahuda *and* **Freud** *exit.*

Jessica   It's not a dream then, us being here?

Dali Whose?

Jessica His. If he's not here we can't be a dream.

Dali Strictly speaking is quite possible. All peoples in a dream being representative of the dreamer.

Jessica That's what I told him, that I was a facet. He denied it quite vehemently.

Dali What are you looking for?

Jessica I don't know, but I think he does.

Dali Lift your arm. You owe this.

She does. He draws. She reads.

Later, you and I; we have dinner of seafood. Crush the complacent shell of crab and lobster and eat the flesh while still surprised. Then break into National Gallery and visit the London Exhibition of Degenerate Art courtesy of Adolf Hitler, then tomorrow at dawn, by the light of the sun rising over Primrose Hill I shall render your armpit through my eyes and into history.

Jessica I'm washing my hair.

Dali Heaven, to Dali, is the depilated armpit of a woman.

Jessica Forget it. That's the hair I'm washing. Do you expect to make love to all your models?

Dali Never. Sometimes they make love to one another, but Dali only watches.

Jessica Is that honourable or sad?

Dali Please, do not try to understand Dali. This is only his job, and believe me, is too difficult.

Jessica You don't like being touched, do you? I noticed earlier, it makes you anxious. It makes you squirm.

Dali Please.

Jessica Do you make love to your wife?

Dali We did this, but no more.

Jessica Why not?

Dali The last time we made love, Dali, at the climax of his passion, cried out the name of another.

Jessica Your mistress?

Dali No, my own. Gala she say is over, and goes fuck fishermen.

Jessica Does that bother you?

Dali Gala I adore. She is everything. But no, I cannot let her to touch me. Always, I hate to be touched.

Jessica So have I.

Dali Is true?

Jessica Unlike you I find it very painful.

Dali Touching?

Jessica Not touching. I pray I shall not have to live my entire life like this.

He stands, she stiffens, he sits again. She stands and sits beside him. Their hands rise, fall, courting. Finally they hold hands for about four seconds, then let go.

Dali How was it for you?

Jessica Wonderful, thank you.

She moves away, wiping her hand.

Dali You feel the bones too? Is enough sex for Dali. How these ugly millions do this thing to get these gruesome children, all this sucking and prodding and body fluids in and out of one another I will never understand. Inside a beautiful woman is always the putrefying corpse of Dali's passion.

Freud *returns.*

Freud Scrape them off on the rockery! I'll fetch you a

shoe brush. Are you finished?

Jessica   No. Where's your friend?

Freud   He wished to be left alone. He is a good and powerful man. It is hard to see him powerless.

Jessica   It is hard to believe in good and powerful men, it is so often a contradiction in terms.

Freud   Give me the letters.

Jessica   No.

She leaps up and goes into the closet. Pops out again.

You regret nothing?

Freud   Nothing! In my life. Nothing! Except perhaps one inadvisable evening at *Rookery Nook.*

Jessica   Don't worry, I shan't be in here for ever.

Closes and locks the door behind her.

Freud   Then come out for pity's sake! Say what you have to say and leave me alone! Is this me?

Dali   No. Is a drawing by Dali.

Freud   But is this what I look like?

Dali   To Dali, *si.*

Freud   I look dead.

Dali   Is no offence. Dali sees beneath.

Freud   Soon, then.

Dali   But before you go. Please. One thing you do for him.

Freud   What?

Dali   To judge the work of Dali. The world is a whore, there is no one can tell me. Only you.

Freud   Your work?

Dali   Please. You see, if this is no good in your eyes ...
I have wasted the time of my life. When you look at my
paintings, what do you see? Well, you see what I see,
obviously, that is the point. But have I caught what we are
chasing, you and I? Can you *see* the unconscious?

Freud   Oh, Mr Dali. When I look at a classical picture, a
landscape, or a simple still life, I see a world of unconscious
activity. A fountain of hidden dreams.

Dali   *Si?*

Freud   But when I look at your work I'm afraid all I see
is what is conscious. Your ideas, your conceit, your
meticulous technique. The conscious rendition of conscious
thoughts.

Dali   Then this ... He ... I see.

Freud   You murder dreams. You understand?

Dali   Of course. (*Pause.*)

Freud   I hope I've not offended you.

Dali   No, no no. Is just the Death of the Surrealist
Movement, is all.

Freud   Surely not.

Dali   Is no matter, but is kaput. You tell me nothing I do
not know already. I shall give up the paint.

Freud   Oh please, not on account of me.

Dali   No, no no ...

Freud   You must continue.

Dali   No. No no no. No. All right, I shall continue. You
and me, we know is shit, but the world is a whore. She
will buy the shit. I shall buy a small island.

Freud   Could you spend your life pursuing something you
no longer believed in?

Dali   Oh yes, no problem.

Jessica *emerges from the closet.*

Freud *is now genuinely frightened of her.*

Jessica   I'm ready. I have it now. 1897. Who can tell me what is odd about this sentence? 'Those guilty of these infantile seductions are nursemaids, governesses and domestic servants. Teachers are also involved, as are siblings.' Well?

Dali   Give us a clue.

Jessica   If you like.

She finds another letter.

'The old man died on the night of October 23rd, and we buried him yesterday.' This was your father. 'He bore himself bravely, like the remarkable man that he was. By one of the obscure routes behind my consciousness his death has affected me deeply. By the time he died his life had been long over, but at death the whole past stirs within one.'

Freud   Give them to me.

Jessica   No. Nursemaids, governesses, servants, siblings . . . no mention of fathers, Professor?

Freud   I've had enough of your inquisitory meanderings.

Jessica   I need look no further! I know why you changed your mind. Another letter to Fliess, justifying your decision. Pleading your seduction theory could not stand up because 'In every case of hysteria the father, *not even excluding my own*, had to be blamed as a pervert'. Not even excluding my own!

Freud   My father was a warm-hearted man possessed of deep wisdom.

Jessica   And?

Freud   I loved and respected him.

Jessica   And.

Freud   This is preposterous.

Jessica   An earlier letter. 'I have now to admit that I have identified signs of psychoneuroses in Marie.' Who was Marie? Marie was your sister.

Freud   The error into which I fell was a bottomless pit which could have swallowed us all.

Jessica   Perhaps it should have done. You suspected your father.

Freud   That is quite enough.

Jessica   Your family leave for the summer, you stay alone. You embark on your own self-analysis.

She flicks pages.

Freud   Those letters are private.

Jessica   Analyse this sentence, Professor Freud. 'Not long ago I dreamt that I was feeling over-affectionate towards Matilde (my eldest daughter, aged nine) but her name was Hella and I saw the word Hella in heavy type before me.' I looked up the name. Hella means Holy. You desired that which was holy to you.

Dali   No. No more. This is a great man. It takes one to know one, which is proof.

Jessica   Your mind was in turmoil! The year your father died you found him condemned out of your own mouth. And then you realised your own potential for complicity in such things. Your own daughter.

Freud   There was no desire. The dream fulfilled my wish to pin down a father as the originator of neurosis.

Jessica   Then you admit you suspected . . .

Freud   My *wish* to do so!

Jessica   And yet the year of his death . . .

Freud   I suspected nothing.

Jessica   The year of your own analysis ...

Freud   Do not presume ...

Jessica   You choose to denounce your own theories!

Freud   I had no choice!

Jessica   Other than denounce your own father! Other than denounce yourself!

Dali   No! You, miss-prissy-kiss-my-armpit-tight-arsed-girlie say this slanderous things no more!

Jessica   It only remains for me to make my findings known.

Freud   To whom?

Jessica   I believe Dr Yahuda may lend a sympathetic ear.

She exits into the garden.

Freud   Come back here!

Jessica (*off*)   Dr Yahuda!

Dali   She is cast aspersions on integrity of all great men!

Freud   Stop her.

Dali   She is need have her head examined!

Freud   Bring me those letters.

Dali   Is a pleasure! Dali, he Look for the Nookie!

Dali *pursues.* **Yahuda** *enters through the DS door.*

Yahuda   I've mislaid my gas mask. Did I leave it in here?

Freud   I've not seen it.

Yahuda   Maybe on the porch.

Freud   No. I think I saw it in the hall.

Yahuda   I've looked in the hall.

Freud   I'll look with you.

190 Hysteria

The sound of breaking glass.

Yahuda What's that?

Freud Nothing. I'm not sure. Probably just a . . . bomb.

Yahuda A bomb!?

Freud Very likely.

Yahuda Highly unlikely.

Freud Unexploded. So far. I suggest we take immediate refuge.

Yahuda In the shelter?

Freud No! Under the stairs.

Yahuda Under the what?

Freud *hustles* **Yahuda** *out of the door.* **Jessica** *enters through the window. Scrunching through broken glass off.*

Dali *(off)* You think it discourage Dali you wield at him the greenhouse? No! Scabrous little non-fornicating fantasists like you Dali will squeeze between his fingernails!

Jessica *notices the buff envelope on the desk. An idea comes to her. She removes the* Moses *and* Monotheism *text from the envelope and puts the* Fliess *letters in its place, resealing the envelope. The other text she puts in the maroon file.*

Dali *(off)* You must learn to respect for betters and olders and men who struggle in the mind like a silly girl could not begin to do!

As **Jessica** *finishes,* **Dali** *bursts in holding a length of hemp rope.*

Dali Is swing, from tree. You want to give me papers and shut up and be good girl, or I do this worst thing to you.

Jessica *picks up a phallic stone figure.*

Jessica Try it.

Dali What a woman. Is heavy, no?

Jessica Yes.

Dali So. I am fearless, *si?*

Dali *takes a step forward,* **Jessica** *swings the figure, he cowers.*

Dali Donta hita the head! Is full of precious stuff!

Enter **Freud**.

Freud Move the Ewbank and tuck yourself well in.

Yahuda (*off*) This is absurd.

Freud I'll find your mask.

Closes the door behind him.

Dali Dali is got her but she grow violent, so best cure her quickly, *si?*

Jessica There's nothing wrong with me.

Dali Put this down or be warned.

Jessica Go to hell.

Dali OK. OK. You push Dali to employ his superior intellect!

He picks up a similar but much larger figure.

Freud That is four thousand years old!

Jessica What about this one?

She throws hers at **Dali**.

Freud Catch that!

Dali *catches it but drops his own on his foot.*

Dali Argh!

Jessica *runs out of the french windows.*

Jessica Dr Yahuda!

Dali All right, now is personal.

Dali *pursues* **Jessica**, *taking a really big figure.* **Freud** *picks up* *the maroon file and goes to the filing cabinet.*

Freud *changes his mind, crosses to the stove, opens the lid, and drops the file in the fire. The fire roars.*

Yahuda *enters.*

Yahuda   What do you want?

Freud   Nothing.

Yahuda   Not you; her.

Freud   Who?

Yahuda   I heard shouts.

Freud   For the warden. There is a large unexploded bomb in the greenhouse.

Jessica *(off)*   I need your help, Yah . . . *(Hand clamped over her mouth.)* . . . huda!

Yahuda   There, you see?

Freud   No, no. Our local warden is Mr Yahoohaa.

Jessica *(off)*   Yahuda!

Yahuda   I distinctly heard my name.

Freud   Nonsense. It's all in my head. Your head.

Yahuda   Was that a Freudian slip?

Freud   Certainly not.

He trips over the rug.

Excuse me. I must . . . the bomb.

He picks up a soda syphon and exits into the garden. **Yahuda** *spots the buff envelope and picks it up. Unable to restrain himself, he takes it to the stove and hesitates.*

Jessica *(off)*   Dr Yahuda!

This spurs **Yahuda** *to action. He lifts the lid.*

Jessica *enters, her head bleeding, and tied round the waist by a* *rope. On the end of the rope, attempting to restrain her,* **Freud** *and* **Dali**.

Jessica   Oh, thank Go ... no! Don't do that!

Yahuda   I was er ... warming my hands!

Jessica   What's that envelope doing in them?

Yahuda   Good grief; thank God you spotted that.

Freud   How dare you!

He takes the envelope from **Yahuda**.

Freud   Have you no regard for a man's life work?

Yahuda   Life's work? Senile piffle.

Jessica   There's something you must know. The story of infantile sexuality is based upon ... (a false premise!)

Freud *puts a gas mask on her.*

Freud   This woman has turned violently psychotic.

Jessica *yells her findings unintelligibly.*

Freud   In extreme cases I'm afraid only extreme methods will suffice.

Jessica *tries her best.*

Freud   You see; senseless ramblings.

Dali   Please to calm down like the good little girl should be seen and not heard.

Jessica *gives up.*

Freud   But you, Yahuda; you should be ashamed of yourself. A man's words are his legacy. They should not be censored or selectively distorted. They should stand in their entirety as a monument to his human fallibility and to his ...

Checks the contents.

... Aahg! No, you're right, let's burn the damn stuff.

Jessica   No!

Yahuda   Bravo!

She grabs it. **Dali** *tries to get it off her.*

Dali   Leave this things alone now; is none of little girl's business.

Freud   Give it to me!

Jessica   Yahuda ... read this.

She gives the envelope to **Yahuda**.

Yahuda   What?

Jessica   Read it. Read it!

Yahuda   I've already read it.

Freud *takes the envelope.*

Freud   It has been a very stimulating afternoon, but I must ask you all to leave now.

Freud *goes for the door. He pulls the handle, but the door has become rubber-like. It bends without opening.*

Freud   Good God.

Dali   How you do this?

Freud   What's going on?

Dali   Do it again.

Jessica   Don't let him destroy the letters.

Yahuda   What?

Jessica   The envelope; don't let him burn it.

Freud *uses the intercom.*

Freud   Anna!

Dali *tries the door.*

Dali   Is fantastic.

Freud   Anna!

From the intercom a **Child**'*s scream.*

Child   No, Papa! No!

And a **Father**'*s solemn reprimand.*

Father   Sigmund.

Freud   No.

Turns off the intercom and retreats in fright.

Yahuda   What was that?

Freud   Nothing. You heard it?

Jessica   I will not be silenced.

Freud   You will leave this house.

Jessica   I shall go to the papers.

Freud   I shall call the police.

Jessica   I shall publish the letters.

Freud *picks up the phone. It turns into a lobster.*

Freud   Hello? Would you please connect me with . . .
aaaargh!

Yahuda   What the hell is going on here?

Dali   Don't look at me.

Freud, *frightened now, goes for the door, thinks better of it, heads
for the french windows.*

Freud   Everything's fine. But reluctantly I must bring the
evening to a close.

*He opens the curtains. A train is hurtling across the garden towards
him. Steam, bright lights glaring straight ahead, and a piercing
whistle.*

Arrgh!

Yahuda   What the devil?

Freud *closes the curtains.*

Yahuda   What was that?

The clock strikes. **Freud***, terrified, compares his watch. The clock melts.*

Yahuda   What's happening?

Dali   Is the Camembert of time and space, no?

A deep, dangerous, thunderous music begins, low at first, building. The edges of the room begin to soften.

Jessica   Dr Yahuda, you have to hear me, before it's too late.

Freud   No!

Yahuda   Are you all right?

Freud   Please, Yahuda ...

Yahuda   You look unwell.

Freud   Go home.

Yahuda   I'm your physician, Freud, not another figment of your addled imagination.

Freud   But if you were it would please me most to imagine you sitting by the fire with a good book ... *at home.*

Yahuda *disappears through a trap door, or in a puff of pantomime smoke.*

Jessica *gets a hand free and tears off the mask.*

Jessica   Dr Yahuda!

Freud   Gone! Ha, ha!

Jessica   Then I shall go too. And find someone willing to listen.

Freud   No. No. I'm getting the hang of this now. You are nothing more than a neurotic manifestation . . .

Jessica   Of what?

Freud   Of a buried subconscious . . . of a . . .

Jessica   What?

Freud   You don't exist. I can't hear you.

Jessica   Of a what?

Freud   The vaguest sense . . .

Jessica   Of what?

Freud   Of g . . . Get out of my head! House! Head!

The room continues to melt.

Dali   Back in the closet and there to stay.

Jessica   Let me go!

She kicks **Dali** *in the crotch and dashes out of the DS door. He dives for and catches the rope.*

Dali   Is no panic. He is got her!

Jessica*'s momentum pulls him out of the room.*

Freud   And stay out.

But **Dali** *reappears almost instantly, pulling the rope.*

Dali   Is OK. She not got anywhere.

Freud   Let her go.

Dali   I bring her back.

Freud   No!

Dali   Is no problem.

Freud   Just . . . let the rope go.

Dali   You and me we sort this woman out once and for all, *si?*

Freud   No, please . . .

Dali Come back here, you hysterical bitch!

Freud Please, don't . . .

Dali *gives an almighty tug.* **Jessica** *is no longer tied to the rope. Into the room spills a nude* **Woman***. Glittering music.*

Freud No.

Dali Who is this?

Freud No, please . . .

The **Woman** *moves towards* **Freud***; he is both attracted and repelled.*

Dali Is fantastic! But is who?

Freud Matilde?

Woman Papa.

Freud No. Matilde?

The **Woman** *embraces* **Freud***.*

Woman Papa.

Freud Oh, my Matilde.

The embrace turns sexual.

No.

Dali Is the most desirable, no?

Freud No! Don't touch me!

He disengages.

I never . . . ! I never even imagined . . . !

Woman Papa!

Freud Leave me alone!

He runs to the window. She pursues him. Train whistles, and curtains billow. **Freud** *tries to hide in the closet. Opens the door and through it topples a cadaverous, festering, half-man, half-corpse. Screeching music.*

Freud Ahhh!

Dali   Aaaargh!

Corpse   Sigmund!

Freud   God help me.

The **Corpse** *pursues* **Freud**. **Dali**, *in terror, climbs onto the filing cabinet.*

Woman   Papa!

Sounds of shunting trains compete with music; a drowning cacophony. Grotesque **Images** *appear, reminiscent of* **Dali***'s work, but relevant to* **Freud***'s doubts, fears and guilts. More* **Bodies** *appear on the rope, the* **Bodies** *reminiscent of concentration camp victims, as are the antique figures being scattered by the* **Woman** *and the* **Corpse**. *Distant chants from the Third Reich. Four* **Old Ladies** *make their way to a gas chamber.*

Old Ladies   Sigmund. Siggy. Sigmund.

Heads hung, they undress . . .

Freud *is horrified as the contents of his unconscious are spilled across the stage.*

Dali *is hit by a swan. Suddenly there appears a huge, crippled, faceless* **Patriarch**. *He enters and towers over* **Freud**. *Music descends to a rumble.*

Jessica *enters, searching blindly.*

Freud   Papa?

Jessica   Mama?

Woman   Papa?

Jessica   Mama?

Corpse   Sigmund!

The **Patriarch** *lifts his crutch and swings it, striking the cowering* **Freud** *a massive blow on the jaw.* **Freud** *screams in agony and collapses.*

Jessica   Mama? Mama? Mama?

Jessica *is grasped and awkwardly embraced by the* **Patriarch**.
Her eyes are screwed shut so as not to see his face.

Patriarch   Open your eyes.

Jessica *shakes her head.*

Patriarch   Open your eyes. Then I shall open them for
you.

The razor appears in his hand and he cuts open one of her eyes.

Music crashes. Lights crash to a tight downlight on **Freud**. *Stillness.*
Silence.

Freud   Deeper than cancer. The past. And of all the
years, the year I looked into myself, is the year that has
been killing me. In the months of May and April, one by
one, I hunted down my fears, and snared them.
Throughout the summer, mounted, pinned and labelled
each of them. In October, my anger, for the most part, I
embalmed. And in December I dissected love. Love has
ever since been grey and lifeless flesh to me. But there has
been little pain. The past, for the most part, has passed. I
chose to think, not feel.

Dali *leans into his light, smiles.*

Dali   Better now?

Freud   Am I dying?

Dali   *Si.*

Freud   And all this?

Dali   Don't blame me for this; is nothing to do with. I tell
you already; surrealism is dead. Besides; is impossible to
understand.

Dali *gestures. The* **Patriarch**, *the* **Woman**, *the* **Corpse** *and*
the **Old Ladies** *all disappear. The set begins to return to normal.*

Freud   What about you?

Dali   Dali? Is true. He visit you. This was two months
ago. And he look at the death in your face of Freud and

he understand how many things were at last to end in
Europe with the end of your life. But apart from this he
visit and . . . nothing happens much.

Freud   Yahuda?

Dali   Many Jews.

Freud   Her?

Dali   She is nothing. Please. (*He sits* **Freud** *in his chair.*) So
. . . Dali visits. Freud remembers . . . sleeps. Goodnight.

Exit **Dali**.

*The air-raid all-clear siren sounds. The set completes its return to
normal, as do the lights.* **Jessica** *stands looking at the sleeping*
Freud.

Jessica   Professor?

His eyes open.

Were you sleeping?

Freud   I don't believe so.

Jessica   I'm sorry I got angry.

Freud   To get angry is most necessary.

Jessica   Better out than in?

Freud   Certainly.

Jessica   But what about those that get hurt?

Freud   If the anger is appropriately expressed . . .

Jessica   What about the children?

Freud   No one gets hurt.

Jessica   Ha!

Freud   It is painful to understand one's complicity in
these things.

Jessica   Do you still insist my mother was never molested
by my grandfather?

Freud   No, she was not.

Jessica   Well, that's a remarkable thing.

Freud   Why?

Jessica   Because I was. And please don't suggest that I imagined this. He was no beloved, half-desired father to me. He was a wiry old man who smelt of beer and cheese and would limp to my bed and masturbate on me. Only once was it an unexpected thing. And once, he whispered that if I told my father, he would do worse to me with this.

She shows the razor.

My mother knew what he would do, if she were not there to listen for the door, the creaking stair. That's why she protested at being sent away. And so fierce and vehement her protest, sent away she surely was.

Freud *bows his head.*

Jessica   What was it you remembered in your self-analysis, Professor? About your father?

Freud   What is more relevant is what I could not remember.

Jessica   Have you no feelings?

Freud   I chose to think. And if now I am not so much a man as a museum, and my compassion just another dulled exhibit, so be it. All I have done, what I've become . . . was necessary. To set the people free.

Jessica   Dead already.

Freud   Oh, a few bats hang like heartbeats in the tower. Fear. The odd rat still scampers through the basement. Guilt. Other than that the building is silent.

Jessica   Liar.

Freud   I hear nothing.

Jessica   You heard me.

Freud Nothing.

Jessica Listen harder.

Freud *breaks down. Weeps.*

Jessica What? What is it?

Freud The exhibits are screaming.

She comforts him briefly.

Jessica Goodbye.

Freud I don't know your name.

Jessica Jessica.

Freud God is looking.

Jessica Goodbye.

Freud Jessica. The young may speak what the old cannot bear to utter.

Jessica Because I can articulate these things does not mean I am able to bear them.

She leaves. **Yahuda** *enters and examines the chessboard.* **Freud** *speaks with difficulty.*

Freud Yahuda?

Yahuda Freud?

Freud You will remember you promised to help me when the time came. Well, it's torture now.

Yahuda *nods.*

Yahuda Have you spoken to Anna?

Freud She will understand.

Yahuda *nods. From his bag he takes a hypodermic, prepares it, and injects* **Freud** *with two centigrams of morphine.*

Freud Thank you, my friend. On the desk. There are some carbons . . .

Yahuda Which, these?

Freud To Fliess.

Yahuda I have them.

Freud The one on the top.

Yahuda Yes?

Freud Take a pen. A pen; use ink. Find 'The fathers'.

Yahuda Yes?

Freud Delete for me the five words that follow. 'Not even excluding my own.'

Yahuda Done.

Freud Illegible?

Yahuda Gone.

Freud Thank you.

He closes his eyes. Grimaces.

Yahuda I shall repeat the dose in twelve hours' time. Two centigrams, a little more, whatever's called for. You may hallucinate. Don't be afraid.

The grimace tightens, then the drug takes hold.

Freud Oh ... heaven.

And **Freud***'s face relaxes as he falls into a sleep which will become his last.*

Yahuda *dismisses a tear, takes a last move at the chessboard and leaves quietly.*

The sound of rain beyond the window, and a subtle change of light.

Freud *wakes. Looks at his watch.*

Freud If you are waiting for me to break the silence you will be deeply disappointed. The silence is yours alone, and is far more eloquent than you might imagine.

He turns in his chair and looks towards the couch. Frowns when he sees there is no one on it.

Jessica *appears through the rain and stops outside the french windows. Her hair hangs dripping to her shoulders.*

She taps on the glass. **Freud** *looks at her. Closes his eyes, too tired to go through all this again, but knowing he may have to.*

Jessica *continues to tap as the lights fade.*

Blasted

Sarah Kane

Sarah Kane was born in 1971. Her first play, *Blasted*, was produced at the Royal Court Theatre Upstairs in 1995. Her second play, *Phaedra's Love*, was produced at the Gate Theatre, London, in 1996. In April 1998, *Cleansed* was produced at the Royal Court Theatre Downstairs, and in September 1998, *Crave* was produced by Paines Plough and Bright Ltd at the Traverse Theatre, Edinburgh. Her last play, *4.48 Psychosis*, premiered at the Royal Court Theatre Upstairs in June 2000. Her short film, *Skin*, produced by British Screen/Channel Four, premiered in June 1997. Sarah Kane died in 1999.

For Vincent O'Connell, with thanks.

Blasted was first performed at the Royal Court Theatre Upstairs, London, on 12 January 1995. The cast was as follows:

Ian	Pip Donaghy
Cate	Kate Ashfield
Soldier	Dermot Kerrigan

Directed by James Macdonald
Designed by Franziska Wilcken
Lighting by Jon Linstrum
Sound by Paul Arditti

Characters

Ian
Cate
Soldier

Author's note

Punctuation is used to indicate delivery, not to conform to the rules of grammar.

A stroke (/) marks the point of interruption in overlapping dialogue.

Words in square brackets [ ] are not spoken, but have been included in the text to clarify meaning.

Stage directions in brackets ( ) function as lines.

Editor's note

This edition of *Blasted*, first reprinted in 2000, incorporates minor revisions made to the original text by Sarah Kane shortly before her death. It should therefore be regarded as the definitive version in all respects.

Scene One

A very expensive hotel room in Leeds – the kind that is so expensive it could be anywhere in the world.

There is a large double bed.
A mini-bar and champagne on ice.
A telephone.
A large bouquet of flowers.
Two doors – one is the entrance from the corridor, the other leads off to the bathroom.

Two people enter – **Ian** *and* **Cate**.

Ian *is 45, Welsh born but lived in Leeds much of his life and picked up the accent.*

Cate *is 21, a lower-middle-class Southerner with a south London accent and a stutter when under stress.*

They enter.

Cate *stops at the door, amazed at the classiness of the room.*
Ian *comes in, throws a small pile of newspapers on the bed, goes straight to the mini-bar and pours himself a large gin.*
He looks briefly out of the window at the street, then turns back to the room.

Ian   I've shat in better places than this.

   (*He gulps down the gin.*)

   I stink.
   You want a bath?

Cate   (*Shakes her head.*)

Ian *goes into the bathroom and we hear him run the water. He comes back in with only a towel around his waist and a revolver in his hand. He checks it is loaded and puts it under his pillow.*

Ian   Tip that wog when he brings up the sandwiches.

He leaves fifty pence and goes into the bathroom.
Cate *comes further into the room.*
She puts her bag down and bounces on the bed.
She goes around the room, looking in every drawer, touching everything.
She smells the flowers and smiles.

Cate   Lovely.

Ian *comes back in, hair wet, towel around his waist, drying himself off.*
He stops and looks at **Cate** *who is sucking her thumb.*
He goes back in the bathroom where he dresses.
We hear him coughing terribly in the bathroom.
He spits in the sink and re-enters.

Cate   You all right?

Ian   It's nothing.

He pours himself another gin, this time with ice and tonic, and sips it at a more normal pace.
He collects his gun and puts it in his under-arm holster.
He smiles at **Cate**.

Ian   I'm glad you've come. Didn't think you would.

   (*He offers her champagne.*)

Cate   (*Shakes her head.*)

   I was worried.

Ian   This? (*He indicates his chest.*) Don't matter.

Cate   I didn't mean that. You sounded unhappy.

Ian   (*Pops the champagne. He pours them both a glass.*)

Cate   What we celebrating?

Ian   (*Doesn't answer. He goes to the window and looks out.*)

   Hate this city. Stinks. Wogs and Pakis taking over.

Cate   You shouldn't call them that.

Ian Why not?

Cate It's not very nice.

Ian You a nigger-lover?

Cate Ian, don't.

Ian You like our coloured brethren?

Cate Don't mind them.

Ian Grow up.

Cate There's Indians at the day centre where my brother goes. They're really polite.

Ian So they should be.

Cate He's friends with some of them.

Ian Retard, isn't he?

Cate No, he's got learning difficulties.

Ian Aye. Spaz.

Cate No he's not.

Ian Glad my son's not a Joey.

Cate Don't c- call him that.

Ian Your mother I feel sorry for. Two of you like it.

Cate Like wh- what?

Ian (*Looks at her, deciding whether or not to continue. He decides against it.*)

   You know I love you.

Cate (*Smiles a big smile, friendly and non-sexual.*)

Ian Don't want you ever to leave.

Cate I'm here for the night.

Ian   (*Drinks.*)

Sweating again. Stink. You ever thought of getting married?

Cate   Who'd marry me?

Ian   I would.

Cate   I couldn't.

Ian   You don't love me. I don't blame you, I wouldn't.

Cate   I couldn't leave Mum.

Ian   Have to one day.

Cate   Why?

Ian   (*Opens his mouth to answer but can't think of one.*)

There is a knock at the door.
Ian *starts, and* **Cate** *goes to answer it.*

Ian   Don't.

Cate   Why not?

Ian   I said.

He takes his gun from the holster and goes to the door.
He listens.
Nothing.

Cate   (*Giggles.*)

Ian   Shh.

He listens.
Still nothing.

Ian   Probably the wog with the sarnies. Open it.

Cate *opens the door.*
There's no one there, just a tray of sandwiches on the floor.
She brings them in and examines them.

Cate   Ham. Don't believe it.

Ian   (*Takes a sandwich and eats it.*)

Champagne?

Cate   (*Shakes her head.*)

Ian   Got something against ham?

Cate   Dead meat. Blood. Can't eat an animal.

Ian   No one would know.

Cate   No, I can't, I actually can't, I'd puke all over the place.

Ian   It's only a pig.

Cate   I'm hungry.

Ian   Have one of these.

Cate   I CAN'T.

Ian   I'll take you out for an Indian.
Jesus, what's this? Cheese.

Cate *beams.*
She separates the cheese sandwiches from the ham ones, and eats.
Ian *watches her.*

Ian   Don't like your clothes.

Cate   (*Looks down at her clothes.*)

Ian   You look like a lesbos.

Cate   What's that?

Ian   Don't look very sexy, that's all.

Cate   Oh.

(*She continues to eat.*)

Don't like your clothes either.

Ian   (*Looks down at his clothes.*
Then gets up, takes them all off and stands in front of her, naked.)

Put your mouth on me.

Cate   (*Stares. Then bursts out laughing.*)

Ian   No?
Fine.
Because I stink?

Cate   (*Laughs even more.*)

> **Ian** *attempts to dress, but fumbles with embarrassment.*
> *He gathers his clothes and goes into the bathroom where he dresses.*
> **Cate** *eats, and giggles over the sandwiches.*
> **Ian** *returns, fully dressed.*
> *He picks up his gun, unloads and reloads it.*

Ian   You got a job yet?

Cate   No.

Ian   Still screwing the taxpayer.

Cate   Mum gives me money.

Ian   When are you going to stand on your own feet?

Cate   I've applied for a job at an advertising agency.

Ian   (*Laughs genuinely.*)

No chance.

Cate   Why not?

Ian   (*Stops laughing and looks at her.*)

Cate. You're stupid. You're never going to get a job.

Cate   I am. I am not.

Ian   See.

Cate   St- Stop it. You're doing it deliberately.

Ian   Doing what?

Cate   C- Confusing me.

Ian   No, I'm talking, you're just too thick to understand.

Cate   I am not, I am not.

>   **Cate** *begins to tremble.* **Ian** *is laughing.*
>   **Cate** *faints.*
>   **Ian** *stops laughing and stares at her motionless body.*

Ian   Cate?

>   (*He turns her over and lifts up her eyelids.*
>   *He doesn't know what to do.*
>   *He gets a glass of gin and dabs some on her face.*)

Cate   (*Sits bolt upright, eyes open but still unconscious.*)

Ian   Fucking Jesus.

Cate   (*Bursts out laughing, unnaturally, hysterically, uncontrollably.*)

Ian   Stop fucking about.

Cate   (*Collapses again and lies still.*)

>   **Ian** *stands by helplessly.*
>   *After a few moments,* **Cate** *comes round as if waking up in the*
>   *morning.*

Ian   What the Christ was that?

Cate   Have to tell her.

Ian   Cate?

Cate   She's in danger.

>   (*She closes her eyes and slowly comes back to normal.*
>   *She looks at* **Ian** *and smiles.*)

Ian   What now?

Cate   Did I faint?

Ian   That was real?

Cate   Happens all the time.

Ian   What, fits?

Cate   Since Dad came back.

Ian   Does it hurt?

Cate   I'll grow out of it the doctor says.

Ian   How do you feel?

Cate   (*Smiles.*)

Ian   Thought you were dead.

Cate   [I] Suppose that's what it's like.

Ian   Don't do it again, fucking scared me.

Cate   Don't know much about it, I just go. Feels like I'm away for minutes or months sometimes, then I come back just where I was.

Ian   It's terrible.

Cate   I didn't go far.

Ian   What if you didn't come round?

Cate   Wouldn't know. I'd stay there.

Ian   Can't stand it.

(*He goes to the mini-bar and pours himself another large gin and lights a cigarette.*)

Cate   What?

Ian   Death. Not being.

Cate   You fall asleep and then you wake up.

Ian   How do you know?

Cate   Why don't you give up smoking?

Ian   (*Laughs.*)

Cate   You should. They'll make you ill.

Ian   Too late for that.

Cate   Whenever I think of you it's with a cigarette and a gin.

Ian   Good.

Cate   They make your clothes smell.

Ian   Don't forget my breath.

Cate   Imagine what your lungs must look like.

Ian   Don't need to imagine. I've seen.

Cate   When?

Ian   Last year. When I came round, surgeon brought in this lump of rotting pork, stank. My lung.

Cate   He took it out?

Ian   Other one's the same now.

Cate   But you'll die.

Ian   Aye.

Cate   Please stop smoking.

Ian   Won't make any difference.

Cate   Can't they do something?

Ian   No. It's not like your brother, look after him he'll be all right.

Cate   They die young.

Ian   I'm fucked.

Cate   Can't you get a transplant?

Ian   Don't be stupid. They give them to people with a life. Kids.

Cate   People die in accidents all the time, they must have some spare.

Ian   Why? What for? Keep me alive to die of cirrhosis in three months' time.

Cate   You're making it worse, speeding it up.

Ian   Enjoy myself while I'm here.

> (*He inhales deeply on his cigarette and swallows the last of the gin neat.*)

[I'll] Call that coon, get some more sent up.

Cate   (*Shakes.*)

Ian   Wonder if the conker understands English.

*He notices **Cate**'s distress and cuddles her.*
He kisses her.
She pulls away and wipes her mouth.

Cate   Don't put your tongue in, I don't like it.

Ian   Sorry.

*The telephone rings loudly. **Ian** starts, then answers it.*

Ian   Hello?

Cate   Who is it?

Ian   (*Covers the mouthpiece.*) Shh.

> (*Into the mouthpiece.*) Got it here.

> (*He takes a notebook from the pile of newspapers and dictates down the phone.*)

A serial killer slaughtered British tourist Samantha Scrace, S – C – R – A – C – E, in a sick murder ritual comma, police revealed yesterday point new par. The bubbly nineteen-year-old from Leeds was among seven victims found buried in identical triangular tombs in an isolated New Zealand forest point new par. Each had been stabbed more than twenty times and placed face down comma, hands bound behind their backs point new par. Caps up, ashes at the site showed the maniac had stayed to cook a meal, caps down point new par. Samantha comma, a beautiful redhead with dreams of becoming a model comma, was on the trip

of a lifetime after finishing her A levels last year point.
Samantha's heartbroken mum said yesterday colon
quoting, we pray the police will come up with something
dash, anything comma, soon point still quoting. The
sooner this lunatic is brought to justice the better point
end quote new par. The Foreign Office warned tourists
Down Under to take extra care point. A spokesman said
colon quoting, common sense is the best rule point end
quote, copy ends.

(*He listens. Then he laughs.*)

Exactly.

(*He listens.*)

That one again, I went to see her. Scouse tart, spread
her legs. No. Forget it. Tears and lies, not worth the
space.

(*He presses a button on the phone to connect him to room service.*)

Tosser.

Cate How do they know you're here?

Ian Told them.

Cate Why?

Ian In case they needed me.

Cate Silly. We came here to be away from them.

Ian Thought you'd like this. Nice hotel.

(*Into the mouthpiece.*)

Bring a bottle of gin up, son.

(*He puts the phone down.*)

Cate We always used to go to yours.

Ian That was years ago. You've grown up.

Cate   (*Smiles.*)

Ian   I'm not well any more.

Cate   (*Stops smiling.*)

> **Ian** *kisses her.*
> *She responds.*
> *He puts his hand under her top and moves it towards her breast.*
> *With the other hand he undoes his trousers and starts masturbating.*
> *He begins to undo her top.*
> *She pushes him away.*

Cate   Ian, d- don't.

Ian   What?

Cate   I don't w- want to do this.

Ian   Yes you do.

Cate   I don't.

Ian   Why not? You're nervous, that's all.

> (*He starts to kiss her again.*)

Cate   I t- t- t- t- t- t- t- told you. I really like you but I
c- c- c- c- can't do this.

Ian   (*Kissing her.*) Shhh.

> (*He starts to undo her trousers.*)

> **Cate** *panics.*
> *She starts to tremble and make inarticulate crying sounds.*
> **Ian** *stops, frightened of bringing another 'fit' on.*

Ian   All right, Cate, it's all right. We don't have to do
anything.

> *He strokes her face until she has calmed down.*
> *She sucks her thumb.*
> *Then.*

Ian   That wasn't very fair.

Cate What?

Ian Leaving me hanging, making a prick of myself.

Cate I f- f- felt –

Ian Don't pity me, Cate. You don't have to fuck me 'cause I'm dying, but don't push your cunt in my face then take it away 'cause I stick my tongue out.

Cate I- I- Ian.

Ian What's the m- m- matter?

Cate I k- k- kissed you, that's all. I l- l- like you.

Ian Don't give me a hard-on if you're not going to finish me off. It hurts.

Cate I'm sorry.

Ian Can't switch it on and off like that. If I don't come my cock aches.

Cate I didn't mean it.

Ian Shit. (*He appears to be in considerable pain.*)

Cate I'm sorry. I am. I won't do it again.

> **Ian**, *apparently still in pain, takes her hand and grasps it around his penis, keeping his own hand over the top.*
> *Like this, he masturbates until he comes with some genuine pain.*
> *He releases* **Cate**'*s hand and she withdraws it.*

Cate Is it better?

Ian (*Nods.*)

Cate I'm sorry.

Ian Don't worry. Can we make love tonight?

Cate No.

Ian Why not?

Cate I'm not your girlfriend any more.

Ian   Will you be my girlfriend again?

Cate   I can't.

Ian   Why not?

Cate   I told Shaun I'd be his.

Ian   Have you slept with him?

Cate   No.

Ian   Slept with me before. You're more mine than his.

Cate   I'm not.

Ian   What was that about then, wanking me off?

Cate   I d- d- d- d-

Ian   Sorry. Pressure, pressure. I love you, that's all.

Cate   You were horrible to me.

Ian   I wasn't.

Cate   Stopped phoning me, never said why.

Ian   It was difficult, Cate.

Cate   Because I haven't got a job?

Ian   No, pet, not that.

Cate   Because of my brother?

Ian   No, no, Cate. Leave it now.

Cate   That's not fair.

Ian   I said leave it.

(*He reaches for his gun.*)

There is a knock at the door.
Ian *starts, then goes to answer it.*

Ian   I'm not going to hurt you, just leave it. And keep quiet. It'll only be Sooty after something.

Cate   Andrew.

Ian   What do you want to know a conker's name for?

Cate   I thought he was nice.

Ian   After a bit of black meat, eh? Won't do it with me but you'll go with a whodat.

Cate   You're horrible.

Ian   Cate, love, I'm trying to look after you. Stop you getting hurt.

Cate   You hurt me.

Ian   No, I love you.

Cate   Stopped loving me.

Ian   I've told you to leave that.
Now.

He kisses her passionately, then goes to the door.
When his back is turned, **Cate** *wipes her mouth.*
Ian *opens the door. There is a bottle of gin outside on a tray.*
Ian *brings it in and stands, unable to decide between gin and champagne.*

Cate   Have champagne, better for you.

Ian   Don't want it better for me.

   (*He pours himself a gin.*)

Cate   You'll die quicker.

Ian   Thanks. Don't it scare you?

Cate   What?

Ian   Death.

Cate   Whose?

Ian   Yours.

Cate   Only for Mum. She'd be unhappy if I died. And my brother.

Ian   You're young.
When I was your age –
Now.

Cate   Will you have to go to hospital?

Ian   Nothing they can do.

Cate   Does Stella know?

Ian   What would I want to tell her for?

Cate   You were married.

Ian   So?

Cate   She'd want to know.

Ian   So she can throw a party at the coven.

Cate   She wouldn't do that. What about Matthew?

Ian   What about Matthew?

Cate   Have you told him?

Ian   I'll send him an invite for the funeral.

Cate   He'll be upset.

Ian   He hates me.

Cate   He doesn't.

Ian   He fucking does.

Cate   Are you upset?

Ian   Yes. His mother's a lesbos. Am I not preferable to that?

Cate   Perhaps she's a nice person.

Ian   She don't carry a gun.

Cate   I expect that's it.

Ian   I loved Stella till she became a witch and fucked off with a dyke, and I love you, though you've got the potential.

Cate   For what?

Ian   Sucking gash.

Cate   (*Utters an inarticulate sound.*)

Ian   You ever had a fuck with a woman?

Cate   No.

Ian   You want to?

Cate   Don't think so. Have you? With a man.

Ian   You think I'm a cocksucker? You've seen me. (*He vaguely indicates his groin.*) How can you think that?

Cate   I don't. I asked. You asked me.

Ian   You dress like a lesbos. I don't dress like a cocksucker.

Cate   What do they dress like?

Ian   Hitler was wrong about the Jews who have they hurt the queers he should have gone for scum them and the wogs and fucking football fans send a bomber over Elland Road finish them off.

(*He pours champagne and toasts the idea.*)

Cate   I like football.

Ian   Why?

Cate   It's good.

Ian   And when was the last time you went to a football match?

Cate   Saturday. United beat Liverpool 2–0.

Ian   Didn't you get stabbed?

Cate   Why should I?

Ian   That's what football's about. It's not fancy footwork and scoring goals. It's tribalism.

Cate   I like it.

Ian   You would. About your level.

Cate   I go to Elland Road sometimes. Would you bomb me?

Ian   What do you want to ask a question like that for?

Cate   Would you though?

Ian   Don't be thick.

Cate   But would you?

Ian   Haven't got a bomber.

Cate   Shoot me, then. Could you do that?

Ian   Cate.

Cate   Do you think it's hard to shoot someone?

Ian   Easy as shitting blood.

Cate   Could you shoot me?

Ian   Could you shoot me stop asking that could you shoot me you could shoot me.

Cate   I don't think so.

Ian   If I hurt you.

Cate   Don't think you would.

Ian   But if.

Cate   No, you're soft.

Ian   With people I love.

(*He stares at her, considering making a pass.*)

Cate   (*Smiles at him, friendly.*)

Ian   What's this job, then?

Cate Personal Assistant.

Ian Who to?

Cate Don't know.

Ian Who did you write the letter to?

Cate Sir or madam.

Ian You have to know who you're writing to.

Cate It didn't say.

Ian How much?

Cate What?

Ian Money. How much do you get paid.

Cate Mum said it was a lot. I don't mind about that as long as I can go out sometimes.

Ian Don't despise money. You got it easy.

Cate I haven't got any money.

Ian No and you haven't got kids to bring up neither.

Cate Not yet.

Ian Don't even think about it. Who would have children. You have kids, they grow up, they hate you and you die.

Cate I don't hate Mum.

Ian You still need her.

Cate You think I'm stupid. I'm not stupid.

Ian I worry.

Cate Can look after myself.

Ian Like me.

Cate No.

Ian You hate me, don't you.

Cate   You shouldn't have that gun.

Ian   May need it.

Cate   What for?

Ian   (*Drinks.*)

Cate   Can't imagine it.

Ian   What?

Cate   You. Shooting someone. You wouldn't kill anything.

Ian   (*Drinks.*)

Cate   Have you ever shot anyone?

Ian   Your mind.

Cate   Have you though?

Ian   Leave it now, Cate.

She takes the warning.
Ian *kisses her and lights a cigarette.*

Ian   When I'm with you I can't think about anything else.
You take me to another place.

Cate   It's like that when I have a fit.

Ian   Just you.

Cate   The world don't exist, not like this.
Looks the same but –
Time slows down.
A dream I get stuck in, can't do nothing about it.
One time –

Ian   Make love to me.

Cate   Blocks out everything else.
Once –

Ian   [I'll] Make love to you.

Cate   It's like that when I touch myself.

Ian *is embarrassed.*

Cate   Just before I'm wondering what it'll be like, and just after I'm thinking about the next one, but just as it happens it's lovely, I don't think of nothing else.

Ian   Like the first cigarette of the day.

Cate   That's bad for you though.

Ian   Stop talking now, you don't know anything about it.

Cate   Don't need to.

Ian   Don't know nothing. That's why I love you, want to make love to you.

Cate   But you can't.

Ian   Why not?

Cate   I don't want to.

Ian   Why did you come here?

Cate   You sounded unhappy.

Ian   Make me happy.

Cate   I can't.

Ian   Please.

Cate   No.

Ian   Why not?

Cate   Can't.

Ian   Can.

Cate   How?

Ian   You know.

Cate   Don't.

Ian   Please.

Cate   No.

Ian I love you.

Cate I don't love you.

Ian (*Turns away. He sees the bouquet of flowers and picks it up.*)

These are for you.

Blackout.

The sound of spring rain.

Scene Two

The same.

Very early the following morning.
Bright and sunny – it's going to be a very hot day.
The bouquet of flowers is now ripped apart and scattered around the room.

Cate *is still asleep.*
Ian *is awake, glancing through the newspapers.*

Ian *goes to the mini-bar. It is empty.*
He finds the bottle of gin under the bed and pours half of what is left into a glass.
He stands looking out of the window at the street.
He takes the first sip and is overcome with pain.
He waits for it to pass, but it doesn't. It gets worse.
Ian *clutches his side – it becomes extreme.*
He begins to cough and experiences intense pain in his chest, each cough tearing at his lung.

Cate *wakes and watches* **Ian**.

Ian *drops to his knees, puts the glass down carefully, and gives in to the pain.*
It looks very much as if he is dying.
His heart, lung, liver and kidneys are all under attack and he is making involuntary crying sounds.

Just at the moment when it seems he cannot survive this, it begins to ease.
Very slowly, the pain decreases until it has all gone.

Ian *is a crumpled heap on the floor.*

He looks up and sees **Cate** *watching him.*

Cate   Cunt.

Ian   (*Gets up slowly, picks up the glass and drinks.*
He lights his first cigarette of the day.)

I'm having a shower.

Cate   It's only six o'clock.

Ian   Want one?

Cate   Not with you.

Ian   Suit yourself. Cigarette?

Cate   (*Makes a noise of disgust.*)

They are silent.

Ian *stands, smoking and drinking neat gin.*
When he's sufficiently numbed, he comes and goes between the bedroom and bathroom, undressing and collecting discarded towels.
He stops, towel around his waist, gun in hand, and looks at **Cate**.
She is staring at him with hate.

Ian   Don't worry, I'll be dead soon.

(*He tosses the gun onto the bed.*)

Have a pop.

Cate *doesn't move.*
Ian *waits, then chuckles and goes into the bathroom.*
We hear the shower running.

Cate *stares at the gun.*
She gets up very slowly and dresses.
She packs her bag.
She picks up **Ian**'s *leather jacket and smells it.*

She rips the arms off at the seams.
She picks up his gun and examines it.
We hear **Ian** *coughing up in the bathroom.*
Cate *puts the gun down and he comes in.*
He dresses.
He looks at the gun.

Ian   No?

(*He chuckles, unloads and reloads the gun and tucks it in his holster.*)

We're one, yes?

Cate   (*Sneers.*)

Ian   We're one.
Coming down for breakfast? It's paid for.

Cate   Choke on it.

Ian   Sarky little tart this morning, aren't we?

He picks up his jacket and puts one arm through a hole.
He stares at the damage, then looks at **Cate**.
A beat, then she goes for him, slapping him around the head hard and fast.
He wrestles her onto the bed, her still kicking, punching and biting.
She takes the gun from his holster and points it at his groin.
He backs off rapidly.

Ian   Easy, easy, that's a loaded gun.

Cate   I d- d- d- d- d- d- d- d- d-

Ian   Catie, come on.

Cate   d- d- d- d- d- d- d- d- d- d-

Ian   You don't want an accident. Think about your mum.
And your brother. What would they think?

Cate   I d- d- d- d- d- d- d- d- d- d- d- d- d-

Cate *trembles and starts gasping for air.*
She faints.

Ian *goes to her, takes the gun and puts it back in the holster.*
Then lies her on the bed on her back.
He puts the gun to her head, lies between her legs, and simulates sex.
As he comes, **Cate** *sits bolt upright with a shout.*
Ian *moves away, unsure what to do, pointing the gun at her from behind.*
She laughs hysterically, as before, but doesn't stop.
She laughs and laughs and laughs until she isn't laughing any more, she's crying her heart out.
She collapses again and lies still.

Ian Cate? Catie?

Ian *puts the gun away.*
He kisses her and she comes round.
She stares at him.

Ian You back?

Cate Liar.

Ian *doesn't know if this means yes or no, so he just waits.*
Cate *closes her eyes for a few seconds, then opens them.*

Ian Cate?

Cate Want to go home now.

Ian It's not even seven. There won't be a train.

Cate I'll wait at the station.

Ian It's raining.

Cate It's not.

Ian Want you to stay here. Till after breakfast at least.

Cate No.

Ian Cate. After breakfast.

Cate No.

Ian (*Locks the door and pockets the key.*)

   I love you.

Cate   I don't want to stay.

Ian   Please.

Cate   Don't want to.

Ian   You make me feel safe.

Cate   Nothing to be scared of.

Ian   I'll order breakfast.

Cate   Not hungry.

Ian   (*Lights a cigarette.*)

Cate   How can you smoke on an empty stomach?

Ian   It's not empty. There's gin in it.

Cate   Why can't I go home?

Ian   (*Thinks.*)

   It's too dangerous.

   Outside, a car backfires – there is an enormous bang.
   Ian *throws himself flat on the floor.*

Cate   (*Laughs.*)

   It's only a car.

Ian   You. You're fucking thick.

Cate   I'm not. You're scared of things when there's nothing
   to be scared of. What's thick about not being scared of
   cars?

Ian   I'm not scared of cars. I'm scared of dying.

Cate   A car won't kill you. Not from out there.
   Not unless you ran out in front of it.

   (*She kisses him.*)

   What's scaring you?

Ian   Thought it was a gun.

Cate   (*Kisses his neck.*)

Who'd have a gun?

Ian   Me.

Cate   (*Undoes his shirt.*)

You're in here.

Ian   Someone like me.

Cate   (*Kisses his chest.*)

Why would they shoot at you?

Ian   Revenge.

Cate   (*Runs her hands down his back.*)

Ian   For things I've done.

Cate   (*Massages his neck.*)

Tell me.

Ian   Tapped my phone.

Cate   (*Kisses the back of his neck.*)

Ian   Talk to people and I know I'm being listened to. I'm sorry I stopped calling you but –

Cate   (*Strokes his stomach and kisses between his shoulder blades.*)

Ian   Got angry when you said you loved me, talking soft on the phone, people listening to that.

Cate   (*Kisses his back.*)

Tell me.

Ian   In before you know it.

Cate   (*Licks his back.*)

Ian   Signed the Official Secrets Act, shouldn't be telling you this.

Cate   (*Claws and scratches his back.*)

Ian   Don't want to get you into trouble.

Cate   (*Bites his back.*)

Ian   Think they're trying to kill me. Served my purpose.

Cate   (*Pushes him onto his back.*)

Ian   Done the jobs they asked. Because I love this land.

Cate   (*Sucks his nipples.*)

Ian   Stood at stations, listened to conversations and given the nod.

Cate   (*Undoes his trousers.*)

Ian   Driving jobs. Picking people up, disposing of bodies, the lot.

Cate   (*Begins to perform oral sex on* **Ian**.)

Ian   Said you were dangerous.

So I stopped.

Didn't want you in any danger.

But

Had to call you again

Missed

This

Now

I do

The real job

I

Am

A

Killer

On the word 'killer' he comes.
As soon as **Cate** *hears the word she bites his penis as hard as she can.*
Ian*'s cry of pleasure turns into a scream of pain.*
He tries to pull away but **Cate** *holds on with her teeth.*
He hits her and she lets go.
Ian *lies in pain, unable to speak.*
Cate *spits frantically, trying to get every trace of him out of her mouth.*
She goes to the bathroom and we hear her cleaning her teeth.
Ian *examines himself. He is still in one piece.*
Cate *returns.*

Cate   You should resign.

Ian   Don't work like that.

Cate   Will they come here?

Ian   I don't know.

Cate   (*Begins to panic.*)

Ian   Don't start that again.

Cate   I c- c- c- c- c-

Ian   Cate, I'll shoot you myself you don't stop.
I told you because I love you, not to scare you.

Cate   You don't.

Ian   Don't argue I do. And you love me.

Cate   No more.

Ian   Loved me last night.

Cate   I didn't want to do it.

Ian   Thought you liked that.

Cate   No.

Ian   Made enough noise.

Cate   It was hurting.

Ian   Went down on Stella all the time, didn't hurt her.

Cate   You bit me. It's still bleeding.

Ian   Is that what this is all about?

Cate   You're cruel.

Ian   Don't be stupid.

Cate   Stop calling me that.

Ian   You sleep with someone holding hands and kissing you
wank me off then say we can't fuck get into bed but
don't want me to touch you what's wrong with you Joey?

Cate   I'm not. You're cruel. I wouldn't shoot someone.

Ian   Pointed it at me.

Cate   Wouldn't shoot.

Ian   It's my job. I love this country. I won't see it destroyed
by slag.

Cate   It's wrong to kill.

Ian   Planting bombs and killing little kiddies, that's wrong.
That's what they do. Kids like your brother.

Cate   It's wrong.

Ian   Yes, it is.

Cate   No. You. Doing that.

Ian   When are you going to grow up?

Cate   I don't believe in killing.

Ian   You'll learn.

Cate   No I won't.

Ian   Can't always be taking it backing down letting them
think they've got a right turn the other cheek SHIT

some things are worth more than that have to be
protected from shite.

Cate   I used to love you.

Ian   What's changed?

Cate   You.

Ian   No. Now you see me. That's all.

Cate   You're a nightmare.

She shakes.
Ian *watches a while, then hugs her.*
She is still shaking so he hugs tightly to stop her.

Cate   That hurts.

Ian   Sorry.

He hugs her less tightly.
He has a coughing fit.
He spits into his handkerchief and waits for the pain to subside.
Then he lights a cigarette.

Ian   How you feeling?

Cate   I ache.

Ian   (*Nods.*)

Cate   Everywhere.
         I stink of you.

Ian   You want a bath?

Cate *begins to cough and retch.*
She puts her fingers down her throat and produces a hair.
She holds it up and looks at **Ian** *in disgust. She spits.*
Ian *goes into the bathroom and turns on one of the bath taps.*
Cate *stares out of the window.*
Ian *returns.*

Cate   Looks like there's a war on.

Ian   (*Doesn't look.*)

Turning into Wogland.
You coming to Leeds again?

Cate   Twenty-sixth.

Ian   Will you come and see me?

Cate   I'm going to the football.

She goes to the bathroom.
Ian *picks up the phone.*

Ian   Two English breakfasts, son.

He finishes the remainder of the gin.
Cate *returns.*

Cate   I can't piss. It's just blood.

Ian   Drink lots of water.

Cate   Or shit. It hurts.

Ian   It'll heal.

There is a knock at the door. They both jump.

Cate   DON'T ANSWER IT DON'T ANSWER IT
DON'T ANSWER IT

She dives on the bed and puts her head under the pillow.

Ian   Cate, shut up.

He pulls the pillow off and puts the gun to her head.

Cate   Do it. Go on, shoot me. Can't be no worse than what
you've done already. Shoot me if you want, then turn
it on yourself and do the world a favour.

Ian   (*Stares at her.*)

Cate   I'm not scared of you, Ian. Go on.

Ian   (*Gets off her.*)

Cate   (*Laughs.*)

Ian   Answer the door and suck the cunt's cock.

    Cate *tries to open the door. It is locked.*
    Ian *throws the key at her.*
    She opens the door.
    The breakfasts are outside on a tray. She brings them in.
    Ian *locks the door.*
    Cate *stares at the food.*

Cate   Sausages. Bacon.

Ian   Sorry. Forgot. Swap your meat for my tomatoes and mushrooms. And toast.

Cate   (*Begins to retch.*)

       The smell.

    Ian *takes a sausage off the plate and stuffs it in his mouth and keeps a rasher of bacon in his hand.*
    He puts the tray of food under the bed with a towel over it.

Ian   Will you stay another day?

Cate   I'm having a bath and going home.

    She picks up her bag and goes into the bathroom, closing the door.
    We hear the other bath tap being turned on.
    There are two loud knocks at the outer door.
    Ian *draws his gun, goes to the door and listens.*
    The door is tried from outside. It is locked.
    There are two more loud knocks.

Ian   Who's there?

    Silence.
    Then two more loud knocks.

Ian   Who's there?

    Silence.
    Then two more knocks.
    Ian *looks at the door.*
    Then he knocks twice.
    Silence.

Then two more knocks from outside.

Ian *thinks.*
Then he knocks three times.

Silence.
Three knocks from outside.

Ian *knocks once.*
One knock from outside.

Ian *knocks twice.*
Two knocks.

Ian *puts his gun back in the holster and unlocks the door.*

Ian   (*Under his breath.*) Speak the Queen's English fucking
    nigger.

He opens the door.
Outside is a **Soldier** *with a sniper's rifle.*
Ian *tries to push the door shut and draw his revolver.*
The **Soldier** *pushes the door open and takes* **Ian**'s *gun*
easily.
The two stand, both surprised, staring at each other.
Eventually.

Soldier   What's that?

Ian *looks down and realises he is still holding a rasher of bacon.*

Ian   Pig.

The **Soldier** *holds out his hand.*
Ian *gives him the bacon and he eats it quickly, rind and all.*
The **Soldier** *wipes his mouth.*

Soldier   Got any more?

Ian   No.

Soldier   Got any more?

Ian   I –
    No.

Soldier   Got any more?

Ian   (*Points to the tray under the bed.*)

The **Soldier** *bends down carefully, never taking his eyes or rifle off* **Ian***, and takes the tray from under the bed.*
He straightens up and glances down at the food.

Soldier   Two.

Ian   I was hungry.

Soldier   I bet.

The **Soldier** *sits on the edge of the bed and very quickly devours both breakfasts.*
He sighs with relief and burps.
He nods towards the bathroom.

Soldier   She in there?

Ian   Who?

Soldier   I can smell the sex.

(*He begins to search the room.*)

You a journalist?

Ian   I –

Soldier   Passport.

Ian   What for?

Soldier   (*Looks at him.*)

Ian   In the jacket.

The **Soldier** *is searching a chest of drawers.*
He finds a pair of **Cate***'s knickers and holds them up.*

Soldier   Hers?

Ian   (*Doesn't answer.*)

Soldier   Or yours.

(*He closes his eyes and rubs them gently over his face, smelling with pleasure.*)

What's she like?

Ian   (*Doesn't answer.*)

Soldier   Is she soft?
Is she – ?

Ian   (*Doesn't answer.*)

*The **Soldier** puts **Cate**'s knickers in his pocket and goes to the
bathroom.
He knocks on the door. No answer.
He tries the door. It is locked.
He forces it and goes in.
Ian waits, in a panic.
We hear the bath taps being turned off.
Ian looks out of the window.*

Ian   Jesus Lord.

*The **Soldier** returns.*

Soldier   Gone. Taking a risk. Lot of bastard soldiers out
there.

***Ian** looks in the bathroom. **Cate** isn't there.
The **Soldier** looks in **Ian**'s jacket pockets and takes his keys, wallet
and passport.*

Soldier   (*Looks at **Ian**'s press card.*)

Ian Jones.
Journalist.

Ian   Oi.

Soldier   Oi.

They stare at each other.

Ian   If you've come to shoot me –

Soldier   (*Reaches out to touch **Ian**'s face but stops short of
physical contact.*)

Ian You taking the piss?

Soldier Me?

> (*He smiles.*)

> Our town now.

> (*He stands on the bed and urinates over the pillows.*)

Ian *is disgusted.*

There is a blinding light, then a huge explosion.

Blackout.

The sound of summer rain.

Scene Three

The hotel has been blasted by a mortar bomb.

There is a large hole in one of the walls, and everything is covered in dust which is still falling.

The **Soldier** *is unconscious, rifle still in hand.*
He has dropped **Ian***'s gun which lies between them.*

Ian *lies very still, eyes open.*

Ian Mum?

> *Silence.*
> *The* **Soldier** *wakes and turns his eyes and rifle on* **Ian** *with the minimum possible movement.*
> *He instinctively runs his free hand over his limbs and body to check that he is still in one piece. He is.*

Soldier The drink.

> **Ian** *looks around. There is a bottle of gin lying next to him with the lid off.*
> *He holds it up to the light.*

Ian Empty.

Soldier   (*Takes the bottle and drinks the last mouthful.*)

Ian   (*Chuckles.*)

Worse than me.

The **Soldier** *holds the bottle up and shakes it over his mouth, catching any remaining drops.*

Ian *finds his cigarettes in his shirt pocket and lights up.*

Soldier   Give us a cig.

Ian   Why?

Soldier   'Cause I've got a gun and you haven't.

Ian considers the logic.
Then takes a single cigarette out of the packet and tosses it at the **Soldier***.*
The **Soldier** *picks up the cigarette and puts it in his mouth.*
He looks at **Ian***, waiting for a light.*
Ian *holds out his cigarette.*
The **Soldier** *leans forward, touching the tip of his cigarette against the lit one, eyes always on* **Ian***.*
He smokes.

Soldier   Never met an Englishman with a gun before, most of them don't know what a gun is. You a soldier?

Ian   Of sorts.

Soldier   Which side, if you can remember.

Ian   Don't know what the sides are here.
Don't know where . . .

(*He trails off confused, and looks at the* **Soldier***.*)

Think I might be drunk.

Soldier   No. It's real.

(*He picks up the revolver and examines it.*)

Come to fight for us?

Ian   No, I –

Soldier   No, course not. English.

Ian   I'm Welsh.

Soldier   Sound English, fucking accent.

Ian   I live there.

Soldier   Foreigner?

Ian   English and Welsh is the same. British. I'm not an import.

Soldier   What's fucking Welsh, never heard of it.

Ian   Come over from God knows where have their kids and call them English they're not English born in England don't make you English.

Soldier   Welsh as in Wales?

Ian   It's attitude.

(*He turns away.*)

Look at the state of my fucking jacket. The bitch.

Soldier   Your girlfriend did that, angry was she?

Ian   She's not my girlfriend.

Soldier   What, then?

Ian   Mind your fucking own.

Soldier   Haven't been here long have you.

Ian   So?

Soldier   Learn some manners, Ian.

Ian   Don't call me that.

Soldier   What shall I call you?

Ian   Nothing.

Silence.

The **Soldier** *looks at* **Ian** *for a very long time, saying nothing.*
Ian *is uncomfortable.*
Eventually.

Ian What?

Soldier Nothing.

Silence.
Ian *is uneasy again.*

Ian My name's Ian.

Soldier I
　　　　Am
　　　　Dying to make love
　　　　Ian

Ian (*Looks at him.*)

Soldier You got a girlfriend?

Ian (*Doesn't answer.*)

Soldier I have.
　　　　Col.
　　　　Fucking beautiful.

Ian Cate –

Soldier Close my eyes and think about her.
　　　　She's –
　　　　She's –
　　　　She's –
　　　　She's –
　　　　She's –
　　　　She's –
　　　　She's –
　　　　When was the last time you – ?

Ian (*Looks at him.*)

Soldier When? I know it was recent, smell it, remember.

Ian Last night. I think.

Soldier   Good?

Ian   Don't know. I was pissed. Probably not.

Soldier   Three of us –

Ian   Don't tell me.

Soldier   Went to a house just outside town. All gone. Apart
from a small boy hiding in the corner. One of the
others took him outside. Lay him on the ground
and shot him through the legs. Heard crying in the
basement. Went down. Three men and four
women. Called the others. They held the men while
I fucked the women. Youngest was twelve. Didn't
cry, just lay there. Turned her over and –
Then she cried. Made her lick me clean. Closed my
eyes and thought of –
Shot her father in the mouth. Brothers shouted.
Hung them from the ceiling by their testicles.

Ian   Charming.

Soldier   Never done that?

Ian   No.

Soldier   Sure?

Ian   I wouldn't forget.

Soldier   You would.

Ian   Couldn't sleep with myself.

Soldier   What about your wife?

Ian   I'm divorced.

Soldier   Didn't you ever –

Ian   No.

Soldier   What about that girl locked herself in the bathroom.

Ian   (*Doesn't answer.*)

Soldier Ah.

Ian You did four in one go, I've only ever done one.

Soldier You killed her?

Ian (*Makes a move for his gun.*)

Soldier Don't, I'll have to shoot you. Then I'd be lonely.

Ian Course I haven't.

Soldier Why not, don't seem to like her very much.

Ian I do.
She's . . . a woman.

Soldier So?

Ian I've never –
It's not –

Soldier What?

Ian (*Doesn't answer.*)

Soldier Thought you were a soldier.

Ian Not like that.

Soldier Not like that, they're all like that.

Ian My job –

Soldier Even me. Have to be.
My girl –
Not going back to her. When I go back.
She's dead, see. Fucking bastard soldier, he –

He stops.
Silence.

Ian I'm sorry.

Soldier Why?

Ian It's terrible.

Soldier What is?

Ian Losing someone, a woman, like that.

Soldier You know, do you?

Ian I –

Soldier Like what?

Ian Like –
You said –
A soldier –

Soldier You're a soldier.

Ian I haven't –

Soldier What if you were ordered to?

Ian Can't imagine it.

Soldier Imagine it.

Ian (*Imagines it.*)

Soldier In the line of duty.
For your country.
Wales.

Ian (*Imagines harder.*)

Soldier Foreign slag.

Ian (*Imagines harder. Looks sick.*)

Soldier Would you?

Ian (*Nods.*)

Soldier How.

Ian Quickly. Back of the head. Bam.

Soldier That's all.

Ian It's enough.

Soldier You think?

Ian Yes.

Soldier   You never killed anyone.

Ian   Fucking have.

Soldier   No.

Ian   Don't you fucking –

Soldier   Couldn't talk like this. You'd know.

Ian   Know what?

Soldier   Exactly. You don't know.

Ian   Know fucking what?

Soldier   Stay in the dark.

Ian   What? Fucking what? What don't I know?

Soldier   You think –

>   (*He stops and smiles.*)

>   I broke a woman's neck. Stabbed up between her legs, on the fifth stab snapped her spine.

Ian   (*Looks sick.*)

Soldier   You couldn't do that.

Ian   No.

Soldier   You never killed.

Ian   Not like that.

Soldier   Not
Like
That

Ian   I'm not a torturer.

Soldier   You're close to them, gun to head. Tie them up, tell them what you're going to do to them, make them wait for it, then ... what?

Ian   Shoot them.

Soldier   You haven't got a clue.

Ian   What then?

Soldier   You never fucked a man before you killed him?

Ian   No.

Soldier   Or after?

Ian   Course not.

Soldier   Why not?

Ian   What for, I'm not queer.

Soldier   Col, they buggered her. Cut her throat. Hacked her ears and nose off, nailed them to the front door.

Ian   Enough.

Soldier   Ever seen anything like that?

Ian   Stop.

Soldier   Not in photos?

Ian   Never.

Soldier   Some journalist, that's your job.

Ian   What?

Soldier   Proving it happened. I'm here, got no choice. But you. You should be telling people.

Ian   No one's interested.

Soldier   You can do something, for me –

Ian   No.

Soldier   Course you can.

Ian   I can't do anything.

Soldier   Try.

Ian   I write . . . stories. That's all. Stories. This isn't a story anyone wants to hear.

Soldier   Why not?

Ian   (*Takes one of the newspapers from the bed and reads.*)

'Kinky car dealer Richard Morris drove two teenage prostitutes into the country, tied them naked to fences and whipped them with a belt before having sex. Morris, from Sheffield, was jailed for three years for unlawful sexual intercourse with one of the girls, aged thirteen.'

(*He tosses the paper away.*)

Stories.

Soldier   Doing to them what they done to us, what good is that? At home I'm clean. Like it never happened.
Tell them you saw me.
Tell them . . . you saw me.

Ian   It's not my job.

Soldier   Whose is it?

Ian   I'm a home journalist, for Yorkshire. I don't cover foreign affairs.

Soldier   Foreign affairs, what you doing here?

Ian   I do other stuff. Shootings and rapes and kids getting fiddled by queer priests and schoolteachers. Not soldiers screwing each other for a patch of land. It has to be . . . personal. Your girlfriend, she's a story. Soft and clean. Not you. Filthy, like the wogs. No joy in a story about blacks who gives a shit? Why bring you to light?

Soldier   You don't know fuck all about me.
I went to school.
I made love with Col.

Bastards killed her, now I'm here.
Now I'm here.

(*He pushes the rifle in* **Ian**'s *face.*)

Turn over, Ian.

Ian   Why?

Soldier   Going to fuck you.

Ian   No.

Soldier   Kill you then.

Ian   Fine.

Soldier   See. Rather be shot than fucked and shot.

Ian   Yes.

Soldier   And now you agree with anything I say.

He kisses **Ian** *very tenderly on the lips.*
They stare at each other.

Soldier   You smell like her. Same cigarettes.

The **Soldier** *turns* **Ian** *over with one hand.*
He holds the revolver to **Ian**'s *head with the other.*
He pulls down **Ian**'s *trousers, undoes his own and rapes him – eyes closed and smelling* **Ian**'s *hair.*
The **Soldier** *is crying his heart out.*

Ian's *face registers pain but he is silent.*

When the **Soldier** *has finished he pulls up his trousers and pushes the revolver up* **Ian**'s *anus.*

Soldier   Bastard pulled the trigger on Col.
What's it like?

Ian   (*Tries to answer. He can't.*)

Soldier   (*Withdraws the gun and sits next to* **Ian**.)

You never fucked by a man before?

Ian   (*Doesn't answer.*)

Soldier   Didn't think so. It's nothing. Saw thousands of people packing into trucks like pigs trying to leave town. Women threw their babies on board hoping someone would look after them. Crushing each other to death. Insides of people's heads came out of their eyes. Saw a child most of his face blown off, young girl I fucked hand up inside her trying to claw my liquid out, starving man eating his dead wife's leg. Gun was born here and won't die. Can't get tragic about your arse. Don't think your Welsh arse is different to any other arse I fucked. Sure you haven't got any more food, I'm fucking starving.

Ian   Are you going to kill me?

Soldier   Always covering your own arse.

The **Soldier** *grips* **Ian**'s *head in his hands.*

He puts his mouth over one of **Ian**'s *eyes, sucks it out, bites it off and eats it.*

He does the same to the other eye.

Soldier   He ate her eyes.
Poor bastard.
Poor love.
Poor fucking bastard.

Blackout.

The sound of autumn rain.

Scene Four

The same.

The **Soldier** *lies close to* **Ian**, *the revolver in his hand. He has blown his own brain out.*

Cate *enters through the bathroom door, soaking wet and carrying a baby.*
She steps over the **Soldier** *with a glance.*
Then she sees **Ian**.

Cate You're a nightmare.

Ian Cate?

Cate It won't stop.

Ian Catie? You here?

Cate Everyone in town is crying.

Ian Touch me.

Cate Soldiers have taken over.

Ian They've won?

Cate Most people gave up.

Ian You seen Matthew?

Cate No.

Ian Will you tell him for me?

Cate He isn't here.

Ian Tell him –
Tell him –

Cate No.

Ian Don't know what to tell him.
I'm cold.
Tell him –
You here?

Cate A woman gave me her baby.

Ian You come for me, Catie? Punish me or rescue me makes no difference I love you Cate tell him for me do it for me touch me Cate.

Cate Don't know what to do with it.

Ian I'm cold.

Cate Keeps crying.

Ian Tell him –

Cate I CAN'T.

Ian Will you stay with me, Cate?

Cate No.

Ian Why not?

Cate I have to go back soon.

Ian Shaun know what we did?

Cate No.

Ian Better tell him.

Cate No.

Ian He'll know. Even if you don't.

Cate How?

Ian Smell it. Soiled goods. Don't want it, not when you can have someone clean.

Cate What's happened to your eyes?

Ian I need you to stay, Cate. Won't be for long.

Cate Do you know about babies?

Ian No.

Cate What about Matthew?

Ian He's twenty-four.

Cate When he was born.

Ian They shit and cry. Hopeless.

Cate Bleeding.

Ian Will you touch me?

Cate   No.

Ian   So I know you're here.

Cate   You can hear me.

Ian   Won't hurt you, I promise.

Cate   (*Goes to him slowly and touches the top of his head.*)

Ian   Help me.

Cate   (*Strokes his hair.*)

Ian   Be dead soon anyway, Cate.
And it hurts.
Help me to –
Help me –
Finish
It

Cate   (*Withdraws her hand.*)

Ian   Catie?

Cate   Got to get something for Baby to eat.

Ian   Won't find anything.

Cate   May as well look.

Ian   Fucking bastards ate it all.

Cate   It'll die.

Ian   Needs its mother's milk.

Cate   Ian.

Ian   Stay.
Nowhere to go, where are you going to go?
Bloody dangerous on your own, look at me.
Safer here with me.

Cate *considers.*
Then sits down with the baby some distance from **Ian**.
He relaxes when he hears her sit.

Cate *rocks the baby.*

Ian   Not as bad as all that, am I?

Cate   (*Looks at him.*)

Ian   Will you help me, Catie?

Cate   How.

Ian   Find my gun?

> **Cate** *thinks.*
> *Then gets up and searches around, baby in arms.*
> *She sees the revolver in the* **Soldier**'s *hand and stares at it for some time.*

Ian   Found it?

Cate   No.

> *She takes the revolver from the* **Soldier** *and fiddles with it.*
> *It springs open and she stares in at the bullets.*
> *She removes them and closes the gun.*

Ian   That it?

Cate   Yes.

Ian   Can I have it?

Cate   I don't think so.

Ian   Catie.

Cate   What?

Ian   Come on.

Cate   Don't tell me what to do.

Ian   I'm not, love. Can you keep that baby quiet.

Cate   It's not doing anything. It's hungry.

Ian   We're all bloody hungry, don't shoot myself I'll starve to death.

Cate   It's wrong to kill yourself.

Ian   No it's not.

Cate   God wouldn't like it.

Ian   There isn't one.

Cate   How do you know?

Ian   No God. No Father Christmas. No fairies. No Narnia. No fucking nothing.

Cate   Got to be something.

Ian   Why?

Cate   Doesn't make sense otherwise.

Ian   Don't be fucking stupid, doesn't make sense anyway. No reason for there to be a God just because it would be better if there was.

Cate   Thought you didn't want to die.

Ian   I can't see.

Cate   My brother's got blind friends. You can't give up.

Ian   Why not?

Cate   It's weak.

Ian   I know you want to punish me, trying to make me live.

Cate   I don't.

Ian   Course you fucking do, I would. There's people I'd love to suffer but they don't, they die and that's it.

Cate   What if you're wrong?

Ian   I'm not.

Cate   But if.

Ian   I've seen dead people. They're dead. They're not somewhere else, they're dead.

Cate   What about people who've seen ghosts?

Ian   What about them? Imagining it. Or making it up or wishing the person was still alive.

Cate   People who've died and come back say they've seen tunnels and lights –

Ian   Can't die and come back. That's not dying, it's fainting. When you die, it's the end.

Cate   I believe in God.

Ian   Everything's got a scientific explanation.

Cate   No.

Ian   Give me my gun.

Cate   What are you going to do?

Ian   I won't hurt you.

Cate   I know.

Ian   End it.
Got to, Cate, I'm ill.
Just speeding it up a bit.

Cate   (*Thinks hard.*)

Ian   Please.

Cate   (*Gives him the gun.*)

Ian   (*Takes the gun and puts it in his mouth.
He takes it out again.*)

Don't stand behind me.

*He puts the gun back in his mouth.
He pulls the trigger. The gun clicks, empty.
He shoots again. And again and again and again.
He takes the gun out of his mouth.*

Ian   Fuck.

Cate   Fate, see. You're not meant to do it. God –

Ian   The cunt.

(*He throws the gun away in despair.*)

Cate   (*Rocks the baby and looks down at it.*)

Oh no.

Ian   What.

Cate   It's dead.

Ian   Lucky bastard.

Cate   (*Bursts out laughing, unnaturally, hysterically, uncontrollably. She laughs and laughs and laughs and laughs and laughs.*)

Blackout.

The sound of heavy winter rain.

Scene Five

The same.

Cate *is burying the baby under the floor.*

She looks around and finds two pieces of wood.
She rips the lining out of **Ian**'s *jacket and binds the wood together in a cross which she sticks into the floor.*
She collects a few of the scattered flowers and places them under the cross.

Cate   I don't know her name.

Ian   Don't matter. No one's going to visit.

Cate   I was supposed to look after her.

Ian   Can bury me next to her soon. Dance on my grave.

Cate   Don't feel no pain or know nothing you shouldn't know –

Ian   Cate?

Cate   Shh.

Ian   What you doing?

Cate   Praying. Just in case.

Ian   Will you pray for me?

Cate   No.

Ian   When I'm dead, not now.

Cate   No point when you're dead.

Ian   You're praying for her.

Cate   She's baby.

Ian   So?

Cate   Innocent.

Ian   Can't you forgive me?

Cate   Don't see bad things or go bad places –

Ian   She's dead, Cate.

Cate   Or meet anyone who'll do bad things.

Ian   She won't, Cate, she's dead.

Cate   Amen.

(*She starts to leave.*)

Ian   Where you going?

Cate   I'm hungry.

Ian   Cate, it's dangerous. There's no food.

Cate   Can get some off a soldier.

Ian   How?

Cate   (*Doesn't answer.*)

Ian   Don't do that.

Cate   Why not?

Ian   That's not you.

Cate   I'm hungry.

Ian   I know so am I.
But.
I'd rather –
It's not –
Please, Cate.
I'm blind.

Cate   I'm hungry.

　　　(*She goes.*)

Ian   Cate? Catie?
If you get some food –
Fuck.

Darkness.
Light.

Ian *masturbating.*

Ian   cunt cunt cunt cunt cunt cunt cunt cunt cunt cunt cunt

Darkness.
Light.

Ian *strangling himself with his bare hands.*

Darkness.
Light.

Ian *shitting.*
And then trying to clean it up with newspaper.

Darkness.
Light.

Ian *laughing hysterically.*

Darkness.
Light.

Ian *having a nightmare.*

Darkness.
Light.

Ian *crying, huge bloody tears.*
He is hugging the **Soldier***'s body for comfort.*

Darkness.
Light.

Ian *lying very still, weak with hunger.*

Darkness.
Light.

Ian *tears the cross out of the ground, rips up the floor and lifts the baby's body out.*

He eats the baby.

He puts the remains back in the baby's blanket and puts the bundle back in the hole.
A beat, then he climbs in after it and lies down, head poking out of the floor.

He dies with relief.

It starts to rain on him, coming through the roof.

Eventually.

Ian   Shit.

Cate *enters carrying some bread, a large sausage and a bottle of gin. There is blood seeping from between her legs.*

Cate   You're sitting under a hole.

Ian   I know.

Cate   Get wet.

Ian   Aye.

Cate   Stupid bastard.

She pulls a sheet off the bed and wraps it around her.

She sits next to **Ian**'s *head.*

She eats her fill of the sausage and bread, then washes it down with gin.

Ian *listens.*

She feeds **Ian** *with the remaining food.*

She pours gin in **Ian**'s *mouth.*

She finishes feeding **Ian** *and sits apart from him, huddled for warmth.*

She drinks the gin.
She sucks her thumb.

Silence.

It rains.

Ian   Thank you.

Blackout.

Shopping and Fucking

Mark Ravenhill

Mark Ravenhill's first full-length play, *Shopping and Fucking*, was produced by Out of Joint and the Royal Court Theatre and opened at the Royal Court Theatre Upstairs in September 1996. It transferred to the West End in 1997, and opened in New York in 1998. It has subsequently been produced all over the world. Other works include *Faust is Dead* (Actors Touring Company), *Sleeping Around* (Paines Plough), *Handbag* (Actors Touring Company), for which he won an Evening Standard Award, and *Some Explicit Polaroids* (Out of Joint).

Shopping and Fucking, an Out of Joint/Royal Court Theatre production, was first presented at the Royal Court Theatre Upstairs on 26 September 1996. The cast was as follows:

Lulu	Kate Ashfield
Robbie	Andrew Clover
Mark	James Kennedy
Brian	Antony Ryding
Gary	Robin Soans

Directed by Max Stafford-Clark
Designed by Julian McGowan
Lighting by Johanna Town
Sound by Paul Arditti

Scene One

Flat – once rather stylish, now almost entirely stripped bare.

Lulu and **Robbie** *are trying to get* **Mark** *to eat from a carton of takeaway food.*

Lulu Come on. Try some.

Pause.

Come on. You must eat.

Pause.

Look, please. It's delicious. Isn't that right?

Robbie That's right.

Lulu We've all got to eat.
Here.
Come on, come on.
A bit for me.

Mark *vomits.*

Robbie Shit. Shit.

Lulu Why does that alw . . . ?
Darling – could you? Let's clean this mess up.
Why does this happen?

Mark Please.

Lulu This will . . . come on . . . it's all right.

Mark Look, please.

Lulu Thank you.
See? It's going. Going . . . going . . . gone.

Robbie All right? OK?

Lulu Yes, yes. He's all right now.

Mark Look . . . you two go to bed.

Lulu Leave you like this?

Mark   I want to be alone for a while.

Robbie   Is someone coming round?

Lulu   Do you owe money?

Mark   No. No one's coming round. Now – go to bed.

Lulu   So what are you going to do?

Mark   Just sit here. Sit and think. My head's a mess. I'm
fucked.

Robbie   You'll be all right.

Mark   I'm so tired.
Look at me. I can't control anything. My . . . guts. My
mind.

Robbie   We have good times don't we?

Mark   Of course we have. I'm not saying that.

Robbie   Good times. The three of us. Parties. Falling into
taxis, out of taxis. Bed.

Mark   That was years ago. That was the past.

Lulu   And you said: I love you both and I want to look
after you for ever.

Mark   Look I . . .

Lulu   Tell us the shopping story.

Mark   Please I want to . . .

Robbie   Yeah, come on. You still remember the shopping
story.

Pause.

Mark   Well all right.
I'm watching you shopping.

Lulu   No. Start at the beginning.

Mark   That's where it starts.

Robbie   No it doesn't. It starts with: 'summer'.

Mark Yes. OK.

It's summer. I'm in a supermarket. It's hot and I'm sweaty.
Damp. And I'm watching this couple shopping. I'm
watching you. And you're both smiling. You see me and
you know sort of straight away that I'm going to have you.
You know you don't have a choice. No control.

Now this guy comes up to me. He's a fat man. Fat and
hair and lycra and he says:

See the pair by the yoghurt?

Well, says fat guy, they're both mine. I own them. I own
them but I don't want them – because you know
something? – they're trash. Trash and I hate them. Wanna
buy them?

How much?

Piece of trash like them. Let's say . . . twenty. Yeah, yours
for twenty.

So, I do the deal. I hand it over. And I fetch you. I don't
have to say anything because you know. You've seen the
transaction.

And I take you both away and I take you to my house.
And you see the house and when you see the house you
know it. You understand? You know this place.

And I've been keeping a room for you and I take you into
this room. And there's food. And it's warm. And we live
out our days fat and content and happy.

Pause.

Listen. I didn't want to say this. But I have to.
I'm going.

Lulu Scag. Loves the scag.

Mark Not any more.

Robbie Loves the scag more than he loves us.

Mark Look. Look now. That isn't fair. I hate the scag.

Lulu Still buying the scag though, aren't you?

Mark No. I'm off the scag. Ten days without the scag.
And I'm going away.

Robbie From us?

Mark   Yes. Tonight.

Lulu   Where are you going?

Mark   I want to get myself sorted. I need help. Someone has to sort me out.

Robbie   Don't do that. You don't need to do that. We're helping you.

Lulu   We're sorting you out.

Mark   It's not enough. I need something more.

Robbie   You're going? And leaving us?

Mark   I'm going to get help.

Robbie   Haven't we tried? We've tried. What do you think we've been doing? All this time. With the . . . clearing up when you, you . . .

Lulu   Where?

Mark   Just a place.

Lulu   Tell us.

Mark   A centre. For treatment.

Lola   Are you coming back?

Mark   Of course I am.

Robbie   When?

Mark   Well that all depends on how well I respond. To the treatment. A few months.

Robbie   Where is it? We'll visit.

Mark   No.

Robbie   We'll come and see you.

Mark   I mustn't see you.

Robbie   I thought you loved me. You don't love me.

Mark   Don't say that. That's a silly thing to say.

Lulu Hey. Hey, look. If you're going, then go.

Robbie You don't love me.

Lulu Look what you've done. Look what you've done to him.
What are you waiting for? A taxi? Maybe you want me to call a taxi? Or maybe you haven't got the money? You going to ask me for the money? Or maybe just take the money? You've sold everything. You've stolen.

Mark Yes. It's not working. That's why I'm going.

Lulu Yes. I think you should. No. Because we're going to be fine. We're going to do very well. And I think maybe you shouldn't come back. We won't want you back.

Mark Let's wait and see.

Lulu You don't own us. We exist. We're people. We can get by. Go.
Fuck right off. Go. GO.

Mark Goodbye.

Exit **Mark.**

Robbie Stop him. Tell him to stay. Tell him I love him.

Lulu He's gone now. Come on. He's gone.
We'll be all right. We don't need him. We'll get by.

Scene Two

Interview room.

Brian *and* **Lulu** *sit facing each other.* **Brian** *is showing* **Lulu** *an illustrated plastic plate.*

Brian And there's this moment. This really terrfific moment. Quite possibly the best moment. Because really, you see, his father is dead. Yes? The Lion King was crushed – you feel the sorrow welling up in you – crushed by a wild herd of these big cows. One moment, lord of all he

surveys. And then ... a breeze, a wind, the stamping of a
hundred feet and he's gone. Only it wasn't an accident.
Somebody had a plan. You see?

Lulu   Yes. I see.

Brian   Any questions. Any uncertainties. You just ask.

Lulu   Of course.

Brian   Because I want you to follow.

Lulu   Absolutely.

Brian   So then we're ... there's ...

Lulu   Crushed by a herd of wild cows.

Brian   Crushed by a herd of wild cows. Yes.

Lulu   Only it wasn't an accident.

Brian   Good. Excellent. Exactly. It wasn't an accident. It
may have looked like an accident but. No. It was arranged
by the uncle. Because –

Lulu   Because he wanted to be King all along

Brian   Thought you said you hadn't seen it.

Lulu   I haven't.
Instinct. I have good instincts. That's one of my qualities.
I'm an instinctive person.

Brian   Is that right?

Brian *writes down 'instinctive' on a pad.*

Brian   Good. Instinctive. Could be useful.

Lulu   Although of course I can also use my rational side.
Where appropriate.

Brian   So you'd say you appreciate order?

Lulu   Order. Oh yes. Absolutely. Everything in its place.

Brian *writes down 'appreciates order'.*

Brian   Good. So now the father is dead. Murdered. It

was the uncle. And the son has grown up. And you know –
he looks like the dad. Just like him. And this sort of
monkey thing comes to him. And this monkey says: 'It's
time to speak to your dead dad.' So he goes to the stream
and he looks in and he sees –

Lulu / His own reflection.

Brian his own reflection. You've never seen this?

Lulu Never.

Brian But then . . . The water ripples, it hazes. Until he
sees a ghost. A ghost or a memory looking up at him.
His . . .

Pause.

Excuse me. It takes you right here. Your throat tightens.
Until . . . he sees . . . his . . . dad.
My little one. Gets to that bit and I look round and he's
got these big tears in his eyes. He feels it like I do.
Because now the dad speaks. And he says: 'The time has
come. It is time for you to take your place in the Cycle of
Being (words to that effect). You are my son and the one
true King.'
And he knows what it is he's got to do. He knows who it is
he has to kill.
And that's the moment. That's our favourite bit.

Lulu I can see that. Yes.

Brian Would you say you in any way resembled your
father?

Lulu No. Not really. Not much.

Brian Your mother?

Lulu Maybe. Sometimes. Yes.

Brian You do know who your parents are?

Lulu Of course. We still . . . you know. Christmas. We
spend Christmas together. On the whole.

Brian *writes down 'celebrates Christmas'.*

Brian   So many today are lost. Isn't that so?

Lulu   I think that's right. Yes.

Brian   And some come here. They look to me. You're looking to me, aren't you?
Well, aren't you?

Lulu   Yes. I'm looking to you.

Brian (*proffers plate*)   Here. Hold it. Just hold it up beside you. See if you look right. Smile. Look interested. Because this is special. You wouldn't want to part with this. Can you give me that look?

Lulu *attempts the look.*

Brian   That's good. Very good. Our viewers, they have to believe that what we hold up to them is special. For the right sum – life is easier, richer, more fulfilling. And you have to believe that too. Do you think you can do that?

Again **Lulu** *attempts the look.*

Brian   Good. That's very good. We don't get many in your league.

Lulu   Really?

Brian   No. That really is very . . . distinctive.

Lulu   Well. Thank you. Thanks.

Brian   And now: 'Just a few more left. So dial this number now.'

Lulu   Just a few more left. So dial this number now.

Brian   Excellent. Natural. Professional. Excellent.

Lulu   I have had training.

Brian   So you're . . . ?

Lulu   I'm, a trained actress.

Brian *writes down 'trained actress'.*

Brian   I don't recognise you.

Lulu   No? Well, probably not.

Brian   Do some for me now.

Lulu   You want me to . . . ?

Brian   I want to see you doing some acting.

Lulu   I didn't realise. I haven't prepared.

Brian   Come on. You're an actress. You must be able to do some acting.
An actress – if she can't do acting when she's asked then what is she?
She's nothing.

Lulu   All right.

She stands up.

I haven't actually done this one before. In front of anyone.

Brian   Never mind. You're doing it now.

Lulu   One day people will know what all this was for. All this suffering.

Brian   Take your jacket off.

Lulu   I'm sorry?

Brian   I'm asking you to take your jacket off. Can't act with your jacket on.

Lulu   Actually, I find it helps.

Brian   In what way?

Lulu   The character.

Brian   Yes. But it's not helping me. I'm here to assess your talents and you're standing there acting in a jacket.

Lulu   I'd like to keep it on.

Brian (*stands*)   All right. I'll call the girl. Or maybe you remember the way.

Lulu No.

Brian What do you mean – no?

Lulu I mean . . . please I'd like this job. I want to be considered for this job.

Brian Then we'll continue. Without the jacket. Yes?

Lulu *removes her jacket. Two chilled ready meals fall to the floor.*

Brian Look at all this.

They both go to pick up the meals. **Brian** *gets there first.*

Exotic.

Lulu We've got really into them. That's what we eat. For supper.

Brian Did you pay for these?

Lulu Yes.

Brian Stuffed into your jacket. Did you pay for them?

Lulu Yes.

Brian Look me in the eyes. Did. You. Pay?

Lulu No.

Brian Stolen goods.

Lulu We have to eat. We have to get by. I don't like this. I'm not a shoplifter. By nature. My instinct is for work. I need a job. Please.

Brian You're an actress by instinct but theft is a necessity. Unless you can persuade me that I need you. All right. Carry on. Act a bit more.
No shirt.

Lulu No . . . ?

Brian Carry on without the . . . (what's the . . . ?) . . . blouse. And the . . .

Lulu *removes her blouse.*

Lulu   One day people will know what all this was for. All this suffering. There'll be no more mysteries. But until then we have to carry on living. We must work. That's all we can do. I'm leaving by myself tomorrow ...

Brian *(stifling a sob)*   Oh God.

Lulu   I'm sorry. Shall I stop?

Brian   Carry on. Please.

Lulu   I'm leaving by myself tomorrow. I'll teach in a school and devote my whole life to people who need it. It's autumn now. It will soon be winter and there'll be snow everywhere. But I'll be working.
That's all.

Lulu *puts her skirt and jacket on.*

Brian *(wipes away a tear)*   Perfect. Brilliant. Did you make it up?

Lulu   No. I learnt it. From a book.

Brian   Brilliant. So you think you can sell?

Lulu   I know I can sell.

Brian   Because you're an actress?

Lulu   It helps.

Brian   You seem very confident.

Lulu   I am.

Brian   All right then. A trial. Something by way of a test. I'm going to give you something to sell and we're going to see how well you do. Clear so far?

Lulu   Totally.

Brian   Do you know this place?

Lulu   Yes.

Brian   Show them this on the way in tonight.

You understand that I am *entrusting* you?

Lulu   I understand.

Brian   I am entrusting you to pass this important test.

Lulu   I'm not going to let you down.

Brian *reaches for his briefcase and starts to open it.*

Scene Three

Flat.

Robbie *is sitting. He is wearing the uniform of a leading burger chain.* **Lulu** *stands over him.*

Robbie   And all I've said was: With cheese, sir?
And he just looks at me blankly. Just stares into my eyes.
And there's this . . . fear.
Try again. 'Would you like cheese on your burger, sir?'
This is too much for him. I see the bottom lip go. The
eyes are filling up.

Lulu   So you told him. And they sacked you?

Robbie   Someone had to. If you were there you'd . . .
I decide I'm going to have to tell him. And I say:
Look, here you have a choice. For once in your life you
have a choice so for fuck's sake make the most of it.

Lulu   And then they / sacked you?

Robbie   And then. Then. He gets his fork. Grabs this
fork. And he jumps over the counter. And he goes for me.

Lulu   With the fork?

Robbie   Goes for me with the fork. Gets me down and
stabs me.

Lulu   He stabbed you?

Beat.

Robbie   It's nothing.

Lulu You're wounded. You should have told me.

Robbie No. It's nothing.

Lulu Where's the wound then?

Robbie It snapped. Before it did any damage.

Lulu ?

Robbie The fork. It was a plastic fork. It snapped before it did any damage.

Pause.

Lulu So . . . no wound? So. Where's the money going to come from? Who's gonna pay for everything?

Robbie You'll come up with something.

Lulu Me?

Robbie Yeah. You'll sort it out.
Did you get it?

Lulu Did I get . . . ?

Robbie The job. The TV.

Lulu Well. Yes. They're taking me on . . .

Robbie Brilliant. / That's brilliant.

Lulu They're offering me a sort of temporary assignment.

Robbie Yeah? What sort of . . . ?

Lulu *produces three hundred E in a clear plastic bag.*

Robbie You're gonna sell them?

Lulu We're going to sell them. You can make yourself useful.
Should be three hundred. You can count them.

Exit **Lulu. Robbie** *starts counting the tablets.* **Mark** *enters and watches* **Robbie**, *who doesn't see him until* –

Mark Are you dealing?

Robbie   Fuck. You made me –
How long have you – ?

Mark   Just now. Are you dealing?

Robbie   That doesn't . . .

Pause.

So. They let you out.

Mark   Sort of.

Pause.

Robbie   Thought you said months. Did you miss me?

Mark   I missed you both.

Robbie   I missed you. So, I s'pose . . .
I sort of hoped you'd miss me.

Mark   Yeah. Right.

Robbie *moves to* **Mark**. *They kiss.*

Robbie *moves to kiss* **Mark** *again.*

Mark   No.

Robbie   No?

Mark   Sorry.

Robbie   No. That's OK.

Mark   No, sorry. I mean it. Because actually I'd decided
I wasn't going to do that. I didn't really want that to
happen, you know? Commit myself so quickly to . . .
intimacy.

Robbie   OK.

Mark   Just something I'm trying to work through.

Robbie   . . . Work through?

Mark   Yeah. Sort out. In my head.
We've been talking a lot about dependencies. Things you
get dependent on.

Robbie   Smack.

Mark   Smack, yes absolutely. But also people. You get dependent on people. Like . . . emotional dependencies. Which are just as addictive, OK?

Robbie   (*pause*)   So – that's it, is it?

Mark   No.

Robbie   That's me finished.

Mark   No.

Robbie   'Goodbye.'

Mark   I didn't say that. No. Not goodbye.

Robbie   Then . . . kiss me.

Mark   Look . . . (*Turns away.*)

Robbie   Fuck off.

Mark   Until I've worked this through.

Pause.

Robbie   Did you use?

Mark   No.

Robbie   Right. You used, they chucked you out.

Mark   Nothing. I'm clean.

Robbie   So . . . ?

Pause.

Mark   There are these rules, you see. They make you sign – you agree to this set of rules. One of which I broke. OK?

Robbie   Which one?

Mark   It was nothing.

Robbie   Come on.

Mark   I told them. It wasn't like that. I put my case / but –

Robbie   *Tell me.*

Pause.

Mark   No personal relations.

Robbie   Fuck.

Mark   You're not supposed to – form an attachment.

Robbie   Ah, I see.

Mark   Which I didn't.

Robbie   So that's why / you won't kiss me.

Mark   It wasn't an attachment.

Robbie (*pause*)   If you were just honest. / We said we'd be honest.

Mark   It wasn't like that. I told them 'You can't call this a personal relationship.'

Robbie   What was it then?

Mark   More of a . . . transaction. I paid him. I gave him money. And when you're paying, you can't call that a personal relationship, can you? / What would you call it?

Robbie   You can't kiss me. You fucked someone / but you can't kiss me.

Mark   That would mean something.

Robbie   Who was it?

Mark   Somebody.

Robbie   Tell me who.

Mark   He was called Wayne.

Robbie   Well get you.

Mark   I just – you know – in the shower. Shower and I . . . Saw his bottom. Saw the hole, you know. And I felt like – I wanted to . . . lick it.

Robbie (*pause*)   That's it?

Mark   We did a deal. I paid him. We confined ourselves to the lavatory. It didn't mean anything.

Robbie   Nothing for afters?

Mark   That's all.

Robbie   Just Lick and Go.

Mark   It wasn't a personal relation.

Robbie (*lets trousers drop*)   Well, if you can't kiss my mouth.

Mark   No. With you – there's ... baggage.

Robbie   Well, excuse me. I'll just have to grow out of it.

Robbie *pulls his trousers up. Pause.*

Mark   I'm sorry.

Robbie   Sorry? No. It's not ... sorry doesn't work. Sorry's not good enough.

Pause.

Mark   You're dealing?

Robbie   Doesn't matter.

Mark   Thought so.

Robbie   Listen, this stuff is happiness. Little moment of heaven. And if I'm spreading a little – no a great big fuck off load of happiness –

Pause. **Robbie** *picks up an E between thumb and forefinger.*

Mark   It's not real.

Robbie   Listen, if you, if this, this ... planet is real ...

He takes an E. Pause.

Waiting for you. Do you know what it's like – waiting? Looking forward to this day – for you to ... And you – Oh fuck it. Fuck it all.

Robbie *takes another E.*

Enter **Lulu** *with two microwaved ready meals on a tray.*

Lulu   I . . . They let you out. It's sooner . . .

Mark   Yeah. They let me out. Thought I'd come back. See if you're all right.

Pause.

Lulu   I've only got enough for two.

Mark   Never mind.

Lulu   It's just hard to share them. They're done individually.

Mark   Oh well.

Lulu   Well . . . hello.

Mark   Hello.

Lulu   We've got really into the little boxes with the whole thing in it. One each.

Robbie   Looks great, doesn't she?
Gonna be on TV, aren't you?

Mark   You've got a job?

Lulu   They're . . . considering it. It's just a / little . . .

Robbie   Just she says. Only. It's TV.

Mark   Great.

Robbie   You see, we're doing something? Aren't we?

Lulu   Yes.

Robbie   We're working. Providing.

Mark   So will I. Yes. I'll sort myself out and we'll be OK.

Lulu   They're really not made for sharing. It's difficult.

Mark   It's OK. I'll go out.

Robbie   Back to Wayne?

Mark   No. Out. Find some food. Shopping.

Robbie   Don't just – don't stand there and judge us.

Mark   Cheeseburger. Some chocolate maybe.

Robbie   I want you to be part of this.

Mark   I've hurt you. I see that. But – please just let me
... I've got to take this a step at a time, OK?

Exit **Mark**.

Robbie   Cunt. Cunt. / Cunt.

Lulu   I know, I know.

Robbie   Hate the cunt.

Lulu   That's it. Come on. / Come on.

Robbie   Hate him now.

Lulu   Yes. Yes. Yes.

Robbie   I want him to suffer.

Pause.

Lulu   Did you count them?

Robbie   Oh. Yes. Yesyesyes.

Lulu   And was it? Three hundred. Exactly.

Robbie   Yes. Three hundred. Exactly.

Scene Four

A bedsit.

Gary *is sitting on a tatty armchair.* **Mark** *is standing.*

Gary   Course, any day now it'll be virtual. That's what
they reckon.

Mark   I suppose that's right.

Gary   I'm planning on that. Looking to invest. The Net
and the Web and that. You ever done that?

Mark   No. Never.

Gary   Couple of years' time and we'll not even meet.
We'll be like holograph things. We could look like whatever
we wanted. And then we wouldn't want to meet 'cos we
might not look like our holographs. You know what I
mean?
I think a lot about that kind of stuff me.
See, I called you back. Don't do that for everyone.

Mark   Thank you.

Gary   Why d'ya pick me?

Mark   I liked your voice.

Gary   There must have been something special.

Mark   I just thought you had a nice voice.

Gary   How old did you think I was – on the lines?

Mark   I didn't think about it.

Gary   How old do you want me to be?

Mark   It doesn't matter.

Gary   Everybody's got an age they want you to be.

Mark   I'd like you to be yourself.

Gary   That's a new one.

Mark   I'd like to keep things straightforward.

Gary   You're in charge. Make yerself at home.
D'you want porn? I mean, it's mostly women and that but
it's something.
(*Indicating porn.*) She looks rough, doesn't she? Would you
shag her?

Mark   No. Let's leave the porn.

Gary   Or we could do some like . . . stuff, y'know.

He pulls out a packet of cocaine.

Share it with you.

Mark No. Thank you.

Gary It's thrown in. There's no / extra cost.

Mark I don't want any.

Gary It's quality. He don't give me rubbish.

Mark Put it away.

Gary I int gonna poison ya.

Mark Put the fucking stuff away.

Gary All right, all right. Don't get knocky.

Pause.

Mark I'm going to have to go.

Gary You only just got here.

Mark I can't be around people who use.

Gary All right. Look. I'm putting it away.

He puts the packet in his trouser pocket

See? All gone.
You stopping?

Mark I'm sorry. I'm really sorry but I suppose I was threatened by your actions. And my fear led me to an ... outburst. Which I now regret. It's just very important to me. And I'd like you to acknowledge that.

Gary You God Squad?

Mark I'm sorry?

Gary I had 'em before. We're at it and he kept going on about Lamb of Jesus. Hit me. I give as good as I took.

Mark No. I'm not God Squad.

Gary Just got a thing about druggies?

Mark I have a history of substance abuse.

Gary You're a druggie?

Mark I'm a recovering substance abuser.

Gary You're not a druggie?

Mark I used to be a druggie.

Gary Got you. So what you into?

Mark You mean . . .

Gary Sexwise.

Mark Sexwise, I'd say I'm into the usual things.

Gary So, you're looking for regular?

Mark Pretty regular. The important thing for me right now, for my needs, is that this doesn't actually mean anything, you know?
Which is why I wanted something that was a transaction. Because I thought if I pay then it won't mean anything. Do you think that's right – in your experience?

Gary Reckon.

Mark Because this is a very important day for me. I'm sorry, I'm making you listen.

Gary Everyone wants you to listen.

Mark Right. Well. Today you see is my first day of a new life. I've been away to get better, well to acknowledge my needs anyway, and now I'm starting again and I suppose I wanted to experiment with you in terms of an interaction that was sexual but not personal, or at least not needy, OK?

A distant sound of coins clattering.

Gary Downstairs. The arcade. Somebody's just had a win. You gotta know which ones to play otherwise all you

get is tokens. I've a lucky streak me. Good sound, int it?
Chinkchinkchinkchinkchink.

Mark   I suppose what I'd like, what I'd realy like is to
lick your arse.

Gary   That all?

Mark   Yes. That's all

Gary   Right. We can settle up now.

Mark   How much do you want?

Gary   Hundred.

Mark   A hundred pounds? No, I'm sorry.

Gary   All right. If it's just licking, fifty.

Mark   Look, I can give you twenty.

Gary   Twenty. What d'you expect for twenty?

Mark   It's all I've got.
I've got to keep ten for the taxi.

Gary   You're taking the piss, int ya?

Mark   Look, I'll walk. Thirty. It's all I've got.

Gary   I should kick you out, you know that? I shouldn't
be wasting my time with losers like you. Look at you.
Druggie with thirty quid. I'm in demand me. I don't have
to be doing this.
There's a bloke, right, rich bloke, big house. Wants me to
live with him.
So tell me: why should I let you lick my arse?

Mark   Why don't you think of him? You could lie there
and think of him.
Just a few minutes, OK? Thirty quid.
Just get my tongue up, wiggle it about and you can think
of him.
This isn't a personal thing. It's a transaction, OK?

Gary *pulls down his trousers and underpants.* **Mark** *starts to lick* **Gary**'s *arse.*

Gary   He's a big bloke. Cruel like but really really he's kind. Phones me on the lines and says: 'I really like the sound of you. I want to look after you.'

Clatter of coins.

Listen to that. They're all winning tonight.
So I'll probably move in. Yeah, probably do it tomorrow.

Mark *pulls away. There's blood around his mouth.*

Mark   There's blood.

Pause.

You're bleeding.

Gary   Didn't think that happened any more.
Thought I'd healed, OK? That's not supposed to happen.
I'm not infected, OK?
Punter gave me a bottle somewhere. Rinse it out.

Mark *goes to take the money.*

Gary   You can't take that.
Lick me arse you said. Licked me arse didn' ya?

Mark   I'll leave you ten.

Gary   Rinse your mouth out.
We agreed thirty.

Mark   Twenty. I need ten for the taxi.

Gary   Thirty – look, I need the money – please – I owe him downstairs – can't live on tokens – give me the thirty. You promised.

Mark   Have the thirty.

Mark *gives* **Gary** *the thirty pounds.*

Gary   Stay. Rinse it out. You'll feel better. It's champagne.

Gary *exits.* **Mark** *sits.*

Scene Five

Pub.

Robbie *hands* **Lulu** *a drink.*

Robbie   After ten minutes I thought I'd got the wrong name. Checked the name. And then I thought: maybe it's the right name but the wrong pub. Because there could be two pubs with the same name. But probably not on the same street. So I checked. And there wasn't. The same name on this street. But then I thought there could be other streets with the same street name. So I looked it up, borrowed the book from this bloke and looked it – listen. Did you know? There's blood.

Lulu   On me?

Robbie   On you. You've got blood on your face.

Lulu   I thought so. Get it off.

Robbie   Why's that then?

Lulu   Please I want it off.

Robbie   Is that your blood?

Lulu *(pawing at her face)*   Where is it?

Robbie *(indicates forehead)*   Just – yeah – that's it.

Lulu   Is it all gone? Everything?

Robbie   Yes. It's all gone.
Was that your blood?

Lulu   No. It must have splashed me.

Robbie   Who's blood is it?

Lulu   Why does it have to be like this?

Robbie   I knew something was up.

Lulu   I mean, what kind of planet is this when you can't even buy a bar of chocolate?

Robbie   I think that's why I worried so much.

Lulu   And afterwards of course you feel so guilty. Like you could have done something.

Robbie   They attacked you?

Lulu   Not me. The Seven-Eleven.
Walking past and I think: I'd like a bar of chocolate. So I go in but I can't decide which one. There's so much choice. Too much. Which I think they do deliberately. I'm only partly aware – and really why should I be any more aware? – that an argument is forming at the counter. A bloke. Dirty, pissy sort of –

Robbie   Wino?

Lulu   Probably. Wino sort of bloke is having a go at this girl, young –

Robbie   Student?

Lulu   Yes. Student girl behind the counter. Wino is raising his voice to student.
There's a couple of us in there. Me – chocolate. Somebody else – TV guides. (Because now of course they've made the choice on TV guides so fucking difficult as well.)
And wino's shouting: You've given me twenty. I asked for a packet of ten and you've given me twenty.
And I didn't see anything. Like the blade or anything. But I suppose he must have hit her artery. Because there was blood everywhere.

Robbie   Shit.

Lulu   And he's stabbing away and me and TV guide we both just walked out of there and carried on walking.
And I can't help thinking: why did we do that?

Robbie   Look. It's done now.

Lulu   I could have stayed.
Am I clean?

Robbie   All gone.

Lulu   I could have intervened. Shopped him.
It's all off?

Robbie   Yes.

Lulu   It's like it's not really happening there – the same
time, the same place as you. You're here. And it's there.
And you just watch.
I'm going back.

Robbie   What for?

Lulu   Who called an ambulance? She could be lying
there.

Robbie   No. There must have been someone.

Lulu   Or I could give a description.

Robbie   Did you see his face?

Lulu   No. No, I didn't.

Robbie   He's a wino. How they going to find a wino out
there?

Lulu   I don't know.

Robbie   Look, they'll have a video. There's always like a
security camera. They'll have his face.

Lulu   And I've still got. You see I took.

She produces the chocolate bar from her pocket.

I took the bar of chocolate. She's being attacked and I
picked this up and just for a moment I thought: I can take
this and there's nobody to stop me. Why did I do that?
What am I?

Pause.

Robbie   They must be used to it. Work nights in a shop
like that, what do they expect?
You go home.

Lulu   I can't.

Robbie   You've had a shock. You need to rest.

Lulu   We've got to do this.

Robbie   I know.

Lulu   We've got to do it tonight.

Robbie   You're in no fit state. You've gotta sleep.

Lulu   I don't want to sleep. I want to get on with this.

Robbie   I'll do it.

Lulu   We've got to do it together.

Robbie   Think I can't manage? I can cope.

Lulu   Of course you can.

Robbie   I want to do it.

Lulu   Out there on your own?

Robbie   I'm educated. I've read the books. I've got the bits of paper. It's only selling. I can sell. Go home. Go to bed.

Lulu   You're right. I am tired.

Robbie   Then sleep.

Lulu   They'll have me on the video. With the chocolate.

Robbie   They'll be after him. Not you.

Lulu   Suppose.
It's all here.

Lulu *gives* **Robbie** *a bum-bag.*

Robbie   Right then.

Lulu   Look there's just one rule, OK? That's what they reckon. If you're dealing. There's just rule number one. Which is: He who sells shall not use.

Robbie   Yeah. Makes sense, doesn't it?

Lulu   Right. So just don't . . .

Robbie   Course not. Rule number one. I'm a big boy.

Lulu (*hands* **Robbie** *flyer*)   Show them this on the door.

Robbie   Still love you.

Lulu   Haven't said that for a long time. Wish we could go back to before. Just you and me.
Do you think I look great?

Robbie   In the right light. And a fair wind.

Lulu   And a couple of E?

Robbie   . . . I better go.

Exit **Robbie**.

Lulu *looks at the chocolate bar for a beat. Then eats it very quickly.*

Scene Six

Bedsit.

Gary *hands* **Mark** *the bottle of champagne*

Gary   Horrible int it? Little kid with his arse bleeding.

Mark   Sorry. I need to go.

Gary   Arse like a sore.

Mark   It's not that.

Gary   Thought I'd healed.

Mark   Yes, yes. Sure.

Gary   This bloke, my mum's bloke . . .

Mark   No. Don't, please.

Gary   I tried to fight him off, but I think he gets off on that.

Mark   Please, if you . . .

Gary   Whatever, you lie back, you fight, he still . . .
I started to bleed.

Mark No.

Gary He comes into my room after *News at Ten* . . . every night after *News at Ten* and it's, son. Come here, son. I fucking hate that, 'cos I'm not his son.

Mark Sure, sure. I understand.

Gary But I thought . . . now . . . I . . . got . . . away.

Mark FUCKING SHUT UP OK? KEEP YOUR FUCKING MOUTH SHUT.

Gary Sound like him.

Mark Listen. I want you to understand because. I have this personality you see? Part of me that gets addicted. I have a tendency to define myself purely in terms of my relationship to others. I have no definition of myself you see. So I attach myself to others as a means of avoidance, of avoiding knowing the self. Which is actually potentially very destructive. For me – destructive for me. I don't know if you're following this but you see if I don't stop myself I repeat the patterns. Get attached to people to these emotions then I'm back to where I started. Which is why, though it may seem uncaring, I'm going to have to go. You're gonna be OK?
I'm sorry it's just –

Gary *cries.*

Mark Hey. Hey. Hey.

He makes a decision. He takes **Gary** *in his arms.*

Come on. No. Come on. Please. It's OK.
Everything will be OK.
You don't have to say anything.

Gary I want a dad. I want to be watched. All the time, someone watching me. Do you understand?

Mark I think so.

Gary Does everyone feel like that?

Mark Well . . . yes.

Gary What do you want?

Mark I don't know yet.

Gary You must want something. Everybody's got something.

Mark I used to know what I felt. I traded. I made money. Tic Tac. And when I made money I was happy, when I lost money I was unhappy. Then things got complicated. But for so many years everything I've felt has been . . . chemically induced. I mean, everything you feel you wonder . . . maybe it's just the . . .

Gary The smack.

Mark Yes. The smack, coffee, you know, or the fags.

Gary The microwaves.

Mark The cathode rays.

Gary The madcow. Moooooo.

Mark Right. I mean, are there any feelings left, you know?

The coins clatter.

I want to find out, want to know if there are any feelings left.

Gary (*offering two Pot Noodles*) Beef or Nice and Spicy?

Scene Seven

Accident and Emergency waiting room.

Robbie *sits bruised and bleeding.* **Lulu** *is holding a bottle of TCP.*

Lulu I asked the Sister. She said I could.

It'll sting a bit. But with blood. It might get infected. Like gangrene.

Lulu *applies the TCP to* **Robbie**'s *face.*

Lulu   Keep still. Don't want to end up with like – one eye mmm?
Looks good actually.

Robbie   Yeah.

Lulu   Yes, suits you. Makes you look – well . . . tough.

Robbie   Good.

Lulu   I could go for you. Some people a bruise, a wound, doesn't suit them.

Robbie   No.

Lulu   But you – it fits. It belongs.

Lulu *slips her hand into* **Robbie**'s *trousers and starts to play with his genitals.*

Lulu   Is that good?

Robbie   Yeah.

Lulu   That's it. Come on. That's it.
Tell me about them.

Robbie   Who?

Lulu   The men. Attackers.

Robbie   Them.

Lulu   The attackers. Muggers.

Robbie   Well –

Lulu   Sort of describe what they did. Like a story.

Robbie   No.

Lulu   I want to know.

Robbie   It's nothing.

Lulu I don't want to just imagine.

Robbie It wasn't like that.

Lulu Come on then.

Robbie Look.

Lulu What was it like?

Pause.

Robbie There was only one.

Lulu Didn't you say gang?

Robbie No.
Just this one bloke.

Lulu A knife?

Robbie No.

Lulu Oh.
So. He pinned you down?

Robbie No.

Lulu Got the money.

Robbie I didn't – there wasn't any money all right? I
never took any money.

Lulu You never / sold?

Robbie No.

Lulu So before you even got there this man. With his
knife.

Robbie / There wasn't a knife.

Lulu attacks and gets the E.

Robbie No. I got there. I was there with the E.

Lulu So?

Robbie So.

Pause.

Lulu   You've lost it. (*His erection.*)

Robbie   Yeah.

Lulu   Gone limp on me.

Robbie   Yeah.

Lulu   Why's that then?

Pause.

Robbie   I was there. I was all ready. I was ready to deal.

Lulu   Right.

Robbie   There's a few other dealers. Stood around the
dance floor. I take up my position. I'm ready.
And this bloke comes up to me. Really, really nice-looking.
And he says: 'You selling?' Yeah, I say. Fifteen quid a go.
And the way he looks at me I know he fancies me, you
know?
And he reaches in his pocket and – oh shit. So stupid.

Lulu   It was the knife yes?

Robbie   There wasn't a knife.

Lulu   Gun?

Robbie   He. Look. He reaches in his pocket and says:
'Shit I left my money in my other jeans. Oh shit, now how
am I gonna have a good time, now how am I gonna enjoy
myself?'

Lulu   Right. Yes.
Go on.

Robbie   And he looked so . . . I felt sorry for him, all
right?
But then he says: 'How about this? How about you give
me the E? Give me the E now then later, at the end, you
can come back to mine and we can get the money from
my jeans.'

Lulu   Right so he was luring you. Luring you back to his
/ place.

Robbie No.

Lulu Get you back to his so that he could pull the gun /
or whatever.

Robbie No.

Lulu And get the Es off you.

Robbie No, it didn't happen. That's not it.

Lulu No?

Robbie No.
So I said yes. It's a deal. And I gave him the E and he
takes it and I watch him and he's dancing and he's
sweating and smiling and he looks – well – beautiful and
just really really happy.

Lulu How many?

Robbie What?

Lulu You broke the first rule – yes? Yes?

Robbie Yes.

Lulu How many?

Robbie I was out there on my own.

Lulu How many?

Robbie Three. Maybe four.

Lulu Shit. I told you. Rule number one.

Robbie I know.
But then, a few minutes later. A bloke. Even better, yes,
even better looking than the last bloke. And he says: 'Look,
you gave my mate some E and I was wondering, I get paid
at the end of the week and if I give you my phone
number will you give me a couple of E.'

Lulu You didn't?

Robbie Yes.

Lulu Fuck.

Robbie And I felt good, I felt amazing, from just giving, you see?

Lulu No, no I don't.

Robbie But imagine. Imagine you're there, imagine how it feels.

Lulu No.

Robbie And then – it sort of rolled. It flew.

Lulu You prick. Three hundred.

Robbie Until there's these guys, they're asking and I'm giving and everyone's dancing and smiling.

Lulu Three hundred E. / Silly prick.

Robbie Listen, listen to me. This is what I felt.

Lulu I don't want to know. / You gave away three hundred.

Robbie It's important.

Lulu No. Stupid. Fucking. / Cunt.

Robbie Just listen for a moment, OK?
Listen, this is the important bit. If you'd felt . . . I felt.
I was looking down on this planet. Spaceman over this earth. And I see this kid in Rwanda, crying, but he doesn't know why. And this granny in Kiev, selling everything she's ever owned. And this president in Bogota or . . . South America, And I see the suffering. And the wars. And the grab, grab, grab.
And I think: Fuck Money. Fuck it. This selling. This buying. This system. Fuck the bitching world and let's be . . . beautiful. Beautiful. And happy. You see?
You see?
But now you see, but then I've only got two left and this bloke comes up and says: 'You the bloke giving out the E?' I give him the two but he says 'What two? Two. Two's not going to do shit for me. You gotta have more.' And he starts to hit, he starts to punch me.

Lulu   Fucking fucker arsehole. Fuck.
Pillowbiter. (*Hit.*) Shitstabber. (*Hit.*)
Boys grow up you know and stop playing with each other's
willies. Men and women make the future. There are people
out there who need me. Normal people who have kind tidy
sex and when they want it. And boys? Boys just fuck each
other.
The suffering is going to be handed out. And I shouldn't
be part of that. But it'll be both of us. And that's not
justice. Is it?
You look like shit now. Look like you might get (*Throws the
bottle of TCP into* **Robbie**'s *eyes.*) gangrene.

Exit **Lulu**.

Robbie   Nurse. Nurse.

Scene Eight

Bedsit.

Mark *and* **Gary**.

Gary   I knew it wasn't right. I went to the council.
And I said to her, look, it's simple: he's fucking me.
Once, twice, three times a week he comes into my
room. He's a big man. He holds me down and he fucks me.
How long? she says. About two years, I say. I say, he
moved in then six months later it starts. I told her and she
says 'Does he use a condom?'

Mark   Yeah?

Gary   Yeah. I mean 'Does he use a condom?'
When it's like that he's not gonna use a condom, is he?
Just spit. All he uses is a bit of spit.

Mark   On his – ?

Gary   Spit on his dick.

Mark   Of course.

Gary   And then she / says –

Mark   / And you –

Gary   The next thing / she says –

Mark   Does he / spit –

Gary   I told her that and / she says –

Mark   Does he spit up you?

Gary   Listen. I tell her he's fucking me – without a condom – and she says to me – you know what she says?

Mark   No. No, I don't.

Gary   I think I've got a leaflet. Would you like to give him a leaflet?

Mark   Fuck.

Gary   Yeah. Give him a leaflet.

Mark   Well –

Gary   No, I don't want a leaflet. I mean, what good is a fucking leaflet? He can't even read a fucking leaflet, you know.

Mark   Yes.

Gary   And there's this look – like . . . panic in her eyes and she says: What do you want me to do?

Mark   Right.

Gary   Tell me what you want me to do.

Mark   And you said – ?

Gary   Well, I don't know. Inject him with something, put him away, cut something off. Do something. And I'm – I've got this anger, right? This great big fucking anger – here in front of my eyes. I mean, I fucking hate her now, right?

Mark   So did you / attack?

Gary   I go: Fuck. Fuck.

Mark   Maybe a knife or something?

Gary   So. In this little box, little white box room . . .

Mark   You attacked / her?

Gary   I stand on the table and I shout:
It's not difficult this is it? It's easy this. He's my stepdad.
Listen, he's my stepdad and he's fucking me.
And I walk away and I get on the coach and I come down
here and I'm never going back. Gonna find something else.
Because there's this bloke. Looking out for me. He'll come
and collect me. Take me to this big house.

Mark   Look, this person that you're looking for . . .

Gary   Yeah?

Mark   Well it's not me.

Gary   Of course not.

Mark   No.

Gary   Fuck, you didn't think . . . ? No. It's not meant to be
you. You and me we're looking for different things, right?

Mark   Right.

Gary   Mates?

Mark   Mates.

Gary   So – mate – do you wanna stay?

Mark   I don't know.

Gary   Stay if you like. Room on the floor. Someone
waiting up for you?

Mark   Not exactly.

Gary   You stay long as you want.

Mark   Thank you.

Gary   Stay around and you can keep yourself busy. Give

us a hand. Getting the messages, cleaning up. Chucking out
the mental ones.
Tell you what, you hand around long enough we can . . .

He pulls out a holdall from behind the chair.
He unzips the bag. It is full of fifty-pence pieces. He catches up
handfuls and lets them cascade through his fingers.

See? I'm a winner me. Every time. And I don't let them
give me tokens.
I can pay for what I want.
Stick around, you and me could go shopping yeah?

Mark I don't know.

Gary It's only shopping.

Mark All right then. Yeah. Let's go shopping.

*They both listen to the coins as they run through **Gary**'s fingers.*

Scene Nine

Flat.

Brian, **Lulu** *and* **Robbie**. **Brian** *inserts a video.*

Brian Watch. I want you to see this.

They watch a video of a schoolboy playing a cello. They sit for some
*time in silence. **Brian** starts to weep.*

Sorry. Sorry.

Lulu Would you like a – something to wipe?

Brian Silly. Me a grown man.

Lulu Maybe a handkerchief?

Brian No. No.

He pulls himself together. They sit and watch again for some time,
but eventually he starts to weep again.

Oh God. I'm so – I'm really sorry.

Lulu   No, no.

Brian   It's just the beauty, you see? The beauty of it.

Lulu   Of course.

Brian   Like a memory, you know, memory of what we've lost.

Pause.

Lulu   Are you sure you don't want – ?

Brian   Well –

Lulu   It's no problem.

Brian   Well then.

Lulu (*to* **Robbie**)   Could you – ?

Robbie   No problem.

Robbie *exits. They continue to watch the video.* **Robbie** *enters again with a toilet roll, takes it over to* **Brian**.

Brian   What's this?

Robbie   It's for your – you know to wipe your –

Brian   I asked you what it is.

Robbie   Well.

Brian   So tell me what it is. What is in your hand?

Robbie   Well –

Lulu   Darling.

Brian   Yes?

Robbie   Toilet paper.

Brian   Toilet paper exactly. Toilet paper. Which belongs in the –

Robbie   Toilet.

Brian   Exactly.

314 Shopping and Fucking

Lulu Darling, I didn't mean . . . that.

Brian And we use it to – ?

Robbie Well, wipe your arse.

Brian Exactly. Wipe your arse. While I – what is this? (*Wipes eye.*)

Lulu I didn't mean toilet paper.

Robbie It's a – like a tear.

Brian It is a tear. Little drop of pure emotion. Which requires a – ?

Robbie Well, a hanky.

Brian Handkerchief.

Robbie Handkerchief.

Lulu Of course, I meant a handkerchief.

Brian This is disrupting you know that?

Lulu Sorry.

Brian This isn't – we're not in a supermarket or, or a disco. Music like this, you listen.

Lulu Yes.

Again they all settle down to watch the video. After a while, **Brian** *starts to cry, but even more so this time.*

Brian Oh God. Oh God. God.

Lulu He's very good.

Brian You feel it like – like something you knew. Something so beautiful that you've lost but you'd forgotten that you've lost it. Then you hear this.

Lulu Play like that when he's how . . . how old?

Brian Hear this and know what you've . . . l-l-l-ooost.

Brian *starts to sob heavily.*

Lulu   Look, I think I've got one.

Robbie   A handkerchief?

Lulu   Yes. A handkerchief. In the bedroom.

Robbie   Shall I fetch it?

Lulu   Well – yes. Yes, I think you should.

Exit **Robbie**.

Brian   Because once it was paradise, you see? And you could hear it – heaven singing in your ears. But we sinned, and God took it away, took away music until we forgot we even heard it but sometimes you get a sort of glimpse – music or a poem – and it reminds you of what it was like before all the sin.

Enter **Robbie**, *offers handkerchief to* **Brian**.

Brian   Is it clean?

Robbie   Yes.

Brian   Again – is it clean?

Robbie   Yes.

Brian   Again – is it clean?

Robbie   Yes.

Brian   Look me in the eyes. Straight in the eyes. Yes?

Robbie (*does so*)   Yes.

Brian   And again – is it clean?

Robbie   No.

Brian   Then why did you offer it to me?

Robbie   Well –

Brian   Dirty handkerchief. Offer a dirty handkerchief.

Lulu   Darling –

Brian   Handkerchief for your nose.

Brian *punches* **Robbie**. *He slumps to the floor.*

Robbie   I'm – sorry.

Lulu   Take it away.

Robbie   Yes. Sorry.

Robbie *crawls out as they settle down in front of the video.*

Brian   His teacher says – and it's a religious school, very religious school – his teacher says 'It's a gift from God.' And I think that's right. Think that must be right because it can't be from us. Doesn't come from me and his mother. I mean, where does it come from if it's not from God, eh? Kid like that, nice kid – his father's son – but nothing special, picks up a bit of wood and string and – well – grown men cry.

Lulu   You must be very proud.

Robbie *enters.* **Brian** *removes a pristine handkerchief from his top pocket and carefully wipes his eyes.*

Brian (*to* **Robbie**)   See. You don't wipe your eyes with something that's been up your nose, all right?

Robbie   Yes. Sorry.

They continue to watch the video.

Brian   Think of the life he's gonna have, eh? Think of that.

Pause.

Brian   Because he doesn't know it now of course. But when he's older, when he knows about sin, about all this, then he's gonna thank God he's got this, isn't he? This little bit of purity.

Lulu   It is amazing, isn't it?

Robbie   Yeah. Yeah. Really – amazing.

Lulu   That it just looks so effortless.

Brian   But there is effort.

Lulu Of course.

Brian Behind it all is effort.

Lulu Have to practise all the time, don't they?

Brian His effort – yes.

Loin For like – hours a day.

Brian His efforts – of course – but also my efforts.

Lulu Of course.

Brian Because, at the end of the day, at the final reckoning, behind beauty, behind God, behind paradise, peel them away and what is there? (*To* **Robbie**.) Son, I'm asking you.

Robbie Well –

Brian Come on, son.

Robbie Well –

Brian Answer the question.

Robbie Well – a father.

Brian Sorry?

Robbie You've can't have them without a sort of a dad.

Brian No. No. Think again. Try again.

Robbie Well I –

Brian Think.

Robbie No.

Brian No, no. That's not good enough – no. Behind beauty, behind God, behind paradise –

Lulu Darling . . . ?

Robbie Money.

Brian Yes. Good. Excellent. Money.
Takes a few knocks, doesn't it, son?

Yeah.
But we get it knocked into us don't we, eh? Learn the
rules. Money. There's boarding fees and the uniforms, the
gear, the music, skiing.
Which is why I run such a tight ship you see? Which is
why I have to keep the cash flow flowing you see? Which
is why I can't let people FUCK. ME. AROUND. You
understand?

Lulu   Of course

Brian   Which is why, right now, I feel sad and sort of
angry. Yes?

Lulu   Yes.

Brian   I don't like mistakes. I don't like my mistakes. And
now you tell me I've made a mistake. And so I hate
myself.
Inside. My soul.
We have a problem. Three thousand pounds of a problem.
But what is the solution?

*They sit for a moment and contemplate this. Finally, **Brian** gets up,
ejects the video, puts it back into its case.*

This could be a stalemate. Unless one of us concedes. But
would you concede? Could you concede anything?

Lulu   No.

Brian   So what you're saying is – you're asking me to
concede?

Lulu   Yes.

Brian   You think I should concede?

Long pause.

Seven days. To make the money.

Lulu   Thank you.

Brian   You understand? Son?

Robbie   Yes. Seven Days. Yes.

Pause. **Brian** *produces a second video.*

Brian I'd like you to have a look at this. Camera's a bit shaky. Some people will tell you it's about 'production values'. But really . . . 'production values'? They're nothing without a good subject.

This one was recorded a couple of months ago. 11.53am. On a Wednesday.

He inserts the video, presses play: a Black and Decker being switched on.

You can't see the face, of course, but the hand belongs to one of my group.

Now a shot of a man with insulation tape over his mouth.

The man with the tape over his mouth is someone who failed his test.

The drill is moving towards the man's face.

There is so much fear, so much wanting. But we're all searching.
Searching aren't we?

Exit **Brian**.

Lulu *and* **Robbie** *watch as the video continues.*

Scene Ten

Flat. **Robbie** *is on the phone.*

Robbie Come on. Take it.
This is . . . it's a golden opportunity. We could change the course of history.

A mobile phone starts to ring. **Lulu** *enters.*

That's what I say. Standing in the Garden and it's: All of humanity, the course of history. / Look, I'm offering it to you. Because we are the first, we are the only ones. And I want you to take it.

Lulu (*on mobile*)   / Hello. Hello, Terry.
No. You call as often as you like.
Oh good. Yes, that's a good idea. A cord that reaches the bed.
Now, if you give me the number again. Yes.
And the expiry date. (*A second mobile rings.*) Yes.
Now I'm taking you into another.
Yes. I'm taking you into the bedroom.

Exit **Lulu**.

Robbie   Here in my hand. Skin. Core. Red. Red skin.
And there's juice.
And you see the juice and you want to bite.
Bite. Yes. Your tongue. The apple. Good. The forbidden fruit.

(*Answers second mobile.*) Yes? For the . . . ? If you can . . . ?
She's just. Yes. Coming. On her way. Yes.

(*To phone.*) And it's like you've never seen before, you've never looked at my body.

(*To second mobile.*) If you can wait, if you can hang on.
Because we're really very . . . sure, sure. A couple of minutes.

(*To phone.*) My, my cock. It's hard. And what's there between your . . . yes . . . because oh look you've got one too . . . that you've never noticed . . . yes. Your own big cock.

(*To second mobile.*) Still there? Still holding? So, you're done.
Another time. Of course.

(*To phone.*) And you want me and I want you and it's man on man and I'm Adam and you're Adam.

The second mobile starts to ring again.

And you want to take it right up the . . . yes . . . oh yes . . . / up against the Tree of Knowledge.

Enter **Lulu**, *still on first mobile.*

Lulu   / Smack. Smack. Smack.
Good. Good. Yes. Yes.

She puts down the first mobile and answers the second mobile.

Hello?
The name?
And the number.
Ah. Gallop. Yes.
Gallop apace you fiery-footed steeds towards Phoebus'
lodging! Such a waggoner as Phaeton would whip . . .
Yes . . .
Spread thy . . .
Good, that's right
Come, civil night. Come, gentle night. Come, loving black-
browed night. Come, Romeo.
Yes, nearly oh yes.
Oh I have bought the mansion of a love but have not
possessed it, and though I am sold not yet enjoyed.
Dirty fucking cunting fucker.
Yes. Yes. Good. Good. Bye then. Bye.

Robbie (*on phone*)   This is, I tell you this is Paradise. This
is Heaven on the Earth. And the spheres are sphering and
the firm . . .
Good good.
And now we're in the . . . ? Tower of . . . I see . . . the
Tower of Babel. All the tongues in the world. Splashinsky.
Mossambarish. Bam bam bam. Pashka pashka pashka.
All right then. You're done? Good good. That's good. You
take care now. Yeah.

(*To* **Lulu**.)   Nine hundred pounds and seventy-eight pence.

Lulu   Why are there so many sad people in this world?

Robbie   We're making money.

Lulu   Yeah. Making money.

Robbie   We're gonna be all right.

Scene Eleven

Changing room at Harvey Nichols. **Mark** *is trying on an expensive designer suit.*

Gary (*off*)   How's it going?

Mark   Yeah. Good.

Gary   Do you want the other size?

Mark   No. This is great.

Gary   All right then.

Mark   Have a look if you like.

Enter **Gary**. *He is transformed: top to toe designer gear and carrying bundles of expensive shopping bags.*

Gary   Oh yes.

Mark   Like it?

Gary   Oh yeah. It's you. Suits you. Do you want it?

Mark   I don't know.

Gary   If you like it, you have it.

Mark   I mean, it's not like I'm even gonna wear it.

Gary   You don't know that. You're starting over.

Mark   I do like it.

Gary   Could be anything. New life, new gear. It makes sense. Go on.

Mark   You sure you can / afford . . . ?

Gary   Hey. None of that.

Mark   All right then. Yes.

Gary   Good and now we'll . . .

He holds out a handful of credit cards as if they were playing cards.

Pick a card, any card.

Mark *picks a card. Reads the name on it.*

Mark   P. Harmsden.

Gary   You remember? Last night. Poppers. Kept on hitting himself.

Mark   Ah. P. Harmsden.

Gary   Right then. Get it off and then we're eating out. My treat.

Mark   Why don't you ... wait outside?

Gary   I'm not bothered.

Mark   Have a look round. I'll only be a few minutes.

Gary   Too late now. I've seen it.

Mark   Seen the ...?

Gary   Seen the hard-on.

Mark   Ah yes. The hard-on.

Gary   Must be aching by now. Up all day.
Is it the shopping does that?
You gotta thing about shopping?
Or is it 'cos of me?

Mark   Yes. That's right. It's because of you.

Gary   Right.
What's going on in your head?
I mean, I can see what's going on in your pants but what's in there?
Tell me.

Mark   Nothing. Look. It's just a physical thing, you know?

Gary   So why don't you say what you want?
Do you want to kiss me?

Mark   Yes.

Gary   Go on then.

Mark Listen, if we do . . . anything, it's got to mean nothing, you understand?

Gary Course.

Mark If I feel like it's starting to mean something then I'll stop.

Gary You can kiss me like a gentle kiss. Me mum, she's got a nice kiss.

Mark *kisses* **Gary**.

Gary How was that?

Mark Yes. That was all right.

Gary How old do you think I am?

Mark I don't know.

Gary When you met me – what did you think?

Mark I don't . . . sort of sixteen, seventeen.

Gary Right. Bit more?

Mark Bit more.

He kisses **Gary** *again. This time it becomes more sexual. Eventually,* **Mark** *pulls away.*

No. I don't want this.

Gary I knew it. You've fallen for me.

Mark Fuck. I really thought I'd broken this, you know?

Gary Do you love me? Is that what it is? Love?

Mark I don't know. How would you define that word? There's a physical thing, yes. A sort of wanting which isn't love is it? No, That's, well, desire. But then, yes, there's an attachment I suppose. There's also that. Which means I want to be with you, Now, here, when you're with me I feel like a person and if you're not with me I feel less like a person.

Gary So is that love then?
Say what you mean.

Mark Yes.
I love you.

Gary See.

Mark But what I'd like to do – now that I've said that which was probably very foolish – what I'd like to do is move forward from this point and try to develop a relationship that is mutual, in which there's a respect, a recognition of the other's needs.

Gary I didn't feel anything.

Mark No?

Gary When you kissed me. Nothing.

Mark I see.

Gary Which means . . . gives me the power, doesn't it? So I'll tell you. You're not what I'm after. I don't want it like that.

Mark But over a period of time . . .

Gary No.

Mark You see, if you've never actually been loved –

Gary I'm not after love. I want to be owned. I want someone to look after me. And I want him to fuck me. Really fuck me. Not like that, not like him. And, yeah, it'll hurt. But a good hurt.

Mark But if you had a choice.

Gary Then I wouldn't choose you. I want to be taken away. Someone who understands me.

Mark There's no one out there.

Gary Think just because you don't feel that way no one else does? There's lots of people who understand. And someone's gonna do it.
I'm going now.

Mark   Stay please. Please I . . .

Mark *kisses* **Gary**, *who pushes him away.*

Gary   That't not true about me mum. I don't let her kiss me. She's a slag.
You go home now. You go back where you belong.

Mark   I want to stay with you.
Give me a day, OK? Another day.

Gary   Don't waste your time with me.

Mark   You can . . . look yes. Come home with me.

Gary   What for? I'm nothing.

Mark   Show you where I live, who I live with.

Gary   You're pathetic you.

Mark   Just one more day. Give it a day.

Gary   You gonna take me home and fuck me?
All right then. One day. Take me home.

Mark   Suck my cock.

Gary   You taking me home?

Mark   Suck my cock now. Take you home later.

Gary   There's a security camera.

Mark   Doesn't matter.

Gary   All this for me? Fourteen.
You got it wrong. I'm fourteen.

Scene Twelve

Robbie *and* **Lulu** *looking at the phone.*

Robbie   Come on. Ring. Ring.
This shouldn't be happening.
Why is this happening?
I mean, we're close really. Nearly two thousand. Over two

thousand – that's good, isn't it? We're very, very close.
We've been working. We're making money. We're good at
it, aren't we? Isn't that right? You'd say that's right,
wouldn't you?

Lulu That's right.

Robbie So, it can't stop now. They've got to keep on
coming.
Ring you bastard ring.
Shit. I can't stand this.

Lulu It's just quiet. A quiet time. That happens.

Robbie Hasn't happened before.

Lulu Sit down. Relax.

Robbie I can't.

Lulu It'll start again.

Robbie There isn't time. We can't afford this.

Lulu Just a moment's peace. Make the most of it.

Robbie I want to live. I want to survive, don't you?

Lulu I don't know.

Robbie You want to die?

Lulu No. I want to be free. I don't want to live like this.

Robbie That's right. Another day yeah?

Lulu Yes.

Robbie One more day and we'll be free.

Lulu Yes.

Robbie If it keeps on ringing.

Ping of a microwave.

Lulu Food's ready.

Robbie Yeah.

Lulu   Eat something?

Robbie   Yes.

Exit **Lulu**.

Robbie   Come on. Come on. Please.

He picks up the phone and speaks into it.

Why aren't you ringing you . . . ?

He realises that the line is dead.
Checks the lead – finds it's been pulled out of the wall.
Checks the mobiles. They've been switched off.

Sits.

Enter **Lulu** *with microwave meals, offers one to* **Robbie**.

Robbie   No thanks.

Lulu   Eat something.

Robbie   No thanks.

Lulu   Come on.

Robbie   I'm not hungry.

Lulu   All right then.

Pause.

Have a bit.

Robbie   Don't want any.

Lulu   Might as well have a meal while it's quiet.

Robbie   You reckon?

Lulu   It'll all start again in a minute.

Robbie   They'll all be ringing?

Lulu   Of course.

Robbie   Don't think so. Do you?

Lulu   Course they will.

Robbie No. I reckon they're not gonna ring. I reckon that tomorrow we're gonna die.

Lulu Course not.

Robbie Because I reckon that one of us wants to die.

Lulu No.

Robbie No?

Lulu No.

Robbie Then tell me why one of us disconnected the phones.

Lulu For a few moments. I just wanted / a few moments peace.

Robbie And I want to live. That's what I want to do.

Lulu I just wanted to eat a meal without . . . all that.

Robbie There'll be time later.

Lulu I can't stand it. In my head.

Robbie And what about me?
We've got to do this together.

Robbie *moves to reconnect the phone.*

Lulu No. Please. Not yet.

Robbie We have to carry on.

Lulu After we've eaten this. Ten, five minutes.

Robbie Come on.

Lulu There was this phone call. I had this call. Twenty minutes, half an hour ago. Youngish. Quite well spoken really. And I did the . . . you know . . . where are you sitting? In the living-room. Right. And you're . . . ? Yes, yes, playing with his dick. Good. Fine. So far, auto-pilot. And then he says, I'm watching this video. Well, that's good. And then he starts to . . . he describes . . . because he got this video from his mate who copied it from his mate

who copied it from dahdahdah. And I mean, he's wanking
to this video of a woman, a student girl who's in the
Seven-Eleven, working behind the counter. And there's a
wino and ... yeah.

Robbie　Fuck.

Lulu　Yeah. He was wanking to the video.
So if we can just. A few more minutes.

Robbie　No. We're gonna carry on.

Lulu　Eat something first.

Robbie　There's no time.

Lulu　Eat. Eat. Eat first. Few minutes.

Robbie　I'm not eating.

Lulu　What's wrong with the / ... Look, if I'm eating ...
If I can ...

Robbie　I don't want the food, / it doesn't taste of
anything ...

Lulu　And why? / What is so wrong that you can't eat it?

Robbie　I'm not eating. / There isn't time.

Lulu　Come on, you've got the world here. You've got all
the tastes in the world. You've got an empire under
cellophane. Look, China. India. Indonesia. In the past
you'd have to invade, you'd have to occupy just to get one
of these things and now, when they're sitting here in front
of you, you're telling me you can't taste anything.

Lulu *holds* **Robbie** *back to prevent him reconnecting the phone.*

Robbie　Well, yes. Yes I am. / There's no taste. This
stuff tastes of nothing.

Lulu　Eat it. Eat it. Eat it.

Robbie　This stuff?

Lulu　Now. Eat it now.

Robbie   No. This? This is shit. This? I wouldn't feed a
fucking paraplegic with cancer this shit.

Lulu   Eat it. Eat it. Eat it. Eat it.

Lulu *pushes* **Robbie***'s face into the food.*

Enter **Mark** *and* **Gary***.*

Mark   Hello.

Robbie   Where have you been?
You went out to get chocolate. A week ago.
Chocolate or a cheeseburger from the shop.
So why have you brought him back?

Mark   Show him where I live.

Robbie   Been shopping? How did you pay for all that?

Mark   He paid.

Gary   Yeah. Paid for everything.

Mark   Who I lived with.

Robbie   And here we are. I'm Barney, this is Betty.
Pebbles is playing outside somewhere. And you must be
Wayne.

Gary   Wayne? I'm not Wayne. Who's Wayne?

Lulu   We're just eating. Sitting down for a meal. It's
actually very difficult to share them actually because they're
specifically designed as individual portions but I can get an
extra plate. Plate. Knife. Whatever.

Mark   No no no. I don't think we're that hungry.

Robbie   We? We? Listen to that: we.

Mark   Well, I don't think we are.

Gary   Didn't come round to eat, did we?

Mark   No, no, we didn't, no.

Robbie   You on special offer?

Gary   You what?

Robbie   Cheaper than a Twix?

Gary   He don't need to pay me.

Robbie   Really? He will do. He's got this thing. Has to make it a transaction.

Gary   Not with me.

Lulu   It all got a bit messy.

Robbie   Paid Wayne, didn't you?

Mark   Gary, this is Lulu.

Lulu   Things got out of hand.

Gary   Some people you just give it away, don't you?

Lulu   Let's sit down, shall we? Let's all just sit.

They sit.

Well, look at this mess. If you don't watch yourself, you just revert, don't you? To the playground or canteen and suddenly it's all food fights and mess.
So let's be adults. Not much but I think I can still . . . a portion. Anyone?
Darling?

Mark   No.

Robbie   So – you're special?

Gary   He thinks so.

Robbie   He said that? He told you that?

Mark   Come on now. Leave him alone.

Gary   Yes. He said that.

Robbie   Tell me.

Mark (*to* **Robbie**)   Leave him alone.

Robbie   I want to know.

Lulu Pudding is going to be quite a surprise I can tell you. / I'm really looking forward to pudding.

Robbie Tell me what he said to you.

Gary He said: I love you.

Mark It wasn't those words.

Gary Yeah, yeah. I love you. I'd be lost without you.

Mark I never said those words.

Robbie (*to* **Gary**) You're lying. Fucking lying.

Robbie *leaps on* **Gary** *and starts to strangle him.*

Gary No. It's true. Please. 'S true. He loves me.

Mark Leave him alone. Get off. Off.

Mark *attacks* **Robbie**, *who is attacking* **Gary**.
Lulu *tries to protect the ready meals, but most are crushed in the melee.*

Lulu Stop it. Stop. Now.

Mark *succeeds in pulling* **Robbie** *off* **Gary**. *The fight subsides.*

Gary Loony. You're a fucking headcase, you are.

Lulu Come on leave it now leave it.

Gary Fucking going for me.

Lulu Ssssh . . . quiet . . . quiet.

Long pause.

Robbie 'I love you.'

Lulu Forget it.

Robbie That's what he said you said.

Mark I never said – because – look – I don't.

Exit **Mark**.

Lulu Mess. Look at this. Why is everything such a mess?

Lulu *scrapes up as much as she can on to the tray and exits.*
Robbie *and* **Gary** *regard each other in silence.*

Gary He *does* loves me. He did say that.

Robbie Did he do this thing – ask you to lick his balls while he came?

Gary Yeah. Have you . . . ?

Robbie Too many times. I'm his boyfriend.

Gary He doesn't do nothing for me, all right?

Robbie No? Not your type?

Gary He's too soft.

Pause.

Do you love him?

Robbie Yes.

Pause.

Gary It's all gentle with him. That's not what I'm after. Got to find this bloke. I know he's out there. Just got to find him.

Robbie Someone who's not gentle?

Gary Yeah, someone strong. Firm, you know.

Robbie Yes.

Gary You think he's cruel but really he's looking out for you. I'm going to be somewhere. I'll be dancing. Shopping. Whatever. And he'll fetch me. Take me away.

Robbie If he exists.

Gary You what?

Robbie If he really exists.

Gary You saying I'm lying?

Robbie I didn't say that.

I think . . . I think we all need stories, we make up stories so that we can get by.

And I think a long time ago there were big stories. Stories so big you could live your whole life in them. The Powerful Hands of the Gods and Fate. The Journey to Enlightenments. The March of Socialism. But they all died or the world grew up or grew senile or forgot them, so now we're all making up our own stories. Little stories. It comes out in different ways. But we've each got one.

Gary Yes.

Robbie It's lonely. I understand. But you're not alone. I could help. I'm offering to help. Where you gonna start? Maybe I know what you're looking for.

Gary A helping hand? What do you wanna do that for?

Robbie For a fee.

Gary Yeah?

Robbie Yeah. Pay me and you'll get what you want. I've got instincts. I know about this other bloke.

Gary If I get what I want.

Robbie Cash. It's got to be cash.

Gary Course

Robbie You've got the money?

Gary Yeah. I've got the money.
So. What you gonna do? To help me.

Robbie We're gonna play a game.

Scene Thirteen

The flat.

Mark, **Gary**, **Lulu** *and* **Robbie**.

Mark Why are we playing this?

Robbie   Because he wants to.

Mark   It's a stupid game.

Robbie   Your friend. Isn't that right?

Gary   Right.

Mark   Why do you want to play this?

Gary   In my head, I see this picture, all right?

Lulu   Yes.

Gary   Well, like a picture but like a story, you know?

Robbie   Yes?

Gary   A sort of story of pictures.

Lulu   A film.

Gary   Yeah, story like a film.

Robbie   With you?

Gary   Yes.

Lulu   You're in the film?

Gary   Yes.

Robbie   You're the hero – ?

Gary   Well –

Lulu   You're the protag – you are the central character of
the film?

Gary   Sort of. Yeah.

Robbie   Right.

Gary   So there's this story, film and I – there's these
stairs.

Pause.

Robbie   What?

Gary   No. Look, I don't want to . . .

Lulu   You don't want to –

Gary   I thought I could but I can't, all right?
It's just saying it. Sorry.

Robbie   So – just wasting out time?

Gary   I'm sorry.

Robbie   We should have got the money first.

Lulu   You're not going through with this?

Gary   I don't know.

Robbie   He should have paid up front.

Mark   Paying for ... ?

Robbie   Paying to play the game.

Lulu   So do you want to do this?

Pause.

Robbie   Pointless. Wasting our time. I mean, how old are
you? What are you? Some kid wasting our time.

Gary   I'm not a kid.

Robbie   You don't know what you want.

Gary   I know what I want.

Lulu   So ... ?

Gary   It's just ... the words. It's describing it.

Mark   All right. Come back to him.

Robbie   Now, as I'm the judge –

Mark   Do me. Ask me – truth or dare?

Robbie   That's not fair. That's not in the rules, is it?

Mark   But if he's not ready.

Robbie   Right. A forfeit. Something I'd like you to ...
something by way of punishment.

Mark   Just leave it, OK?

Gary   Shit, I don't want to.

Robbie (*to* **Lulu**)   What do you think would be a suitable punishment?

Mark (*to* **Gary**)   It's all right. It's all right.

Gary   Shit.

Gary's *tears are close to hysteria.*

Mark   I'll do it. We can come back to you.
Now – ask me a question.

Robbie   No.

Mark   Come on – ask me a question.

Lulu   All right.

Robbie   It's cheating.

Lulu   I know. My question is . . . My question is: who is the most famous person you've ever fucked?

Mark   The most famous person?

Lulu   The most famous person.

Mark   Well OK then OK.

Robbie   If you're gonna . . . it's got to be the truth.

Mark   Yeah, yeah.

Robbie   Or it doesn't count.

Mark   I know.

Lulu   Come on. The most famous person.

Robbie   No because last time –

Lulu   Come on.

Robbie   No because before.

Lulu   Let him say it.

Robbie   You made it up last time.

Mark   I know, I know.

Robbie   So what I'm saying is –

Mark   I know what you're saying.

Robbie   I'm saying it's got to be true.

Mark   Right.

Beat.

Robbie   Right.

Beat.

Lulu   Well then –

Mark   Well then. I'm in Tramps, OK? Tramps or Annabel's, OK?

Robbie   Which – ?

Mark   I can't remember.

Robbie   Look, you've got to –

Lulu   Go on.

Mark   Tramps or Annabel's or somewhere, OK?

Robbie   If you don't know where.

Mark   It doesn't matter where, OK?

Robbie   If it's true then –

Mark   The place, the name doesn't matter.

Lulu   No. It doesn't matter.

Robbie   I think you should know –

Mark   What the fuck does it matter where?

Lulu   All right.

Mark   When what you said was who.

Lulu   Come on. Who? Who? Who?

Mark   Tramps or Annabel's or someplace. Someplace because the place is not of importance, OK? Because the place doesn't matter. So I'm at this somewhere place –

Robbie   When?

Mark   Jesus.

Lulu   It doesn't matter.

Robbie   I want to know when.

Lulu   Come on, you're there and –

Robbie   I want to know when?

Mark   Sometime. In the past.

Robbie   The last week past? The last year past? Your childhood past?

Lulu   The past past.

Mark   Well I don't –

Robbie   Come on –

Lulu   Why?

Robbbie   Veracity. For the /

Mark   / all right then all right /

Robbie   / veracity of it.

Mark   '84. '85. About then. OK?

Robbie   OK.

Mark   So I'm in this place – which is maybe Tramps maybe not – and it's possibly 1985 –

Robbie   That's all I wanted to know.

Mark   I'm having a good time.

Robbie   Meaning?

Mark   Meaning a good time. Meaning a time that is good.

Robbie   Meaning you've taken –

Mark   Meaning I'm having a time that is good.

Robbie   Because you've taken –

Mark   Not necessarily.

Robbie   But you had?

Mark   I don't know.

Robbie   Come on. '84. '85. You must have been on something.

Mark   Well yes.

Robbie   Yes.

Mark   Probably yes.

Robbie   Because really when can you say you're not –

Mark   What? Go on, what?

Robbie   When can you say you're not on something?

Mark   Now.

Robbie   Yeah?

Lulu   Come on. Come on.

Robbie   You're sure? Sure that you're not –

Mark   Yes.

Lulu   Let's – the story.

Mark   I'm fucking clean, all right?

Lulu   Come on. '84. '85. Tramps. Annabel's.

Robbie   Yeah. Right.

Mark   I mean, what the fuck do I have to – ? I'm clean, OK?

Lulu   Please. I want to know who.

Mark   All right. Just don't – all right. Tramps. '84. I'm having a good time.

Robbie   You're tripping?

Mark   No. And I need a piss, yes?

Lulu   In the toilet?

Mark   Yes, a piss in the toilet.

Lulu   This is a toilet story.

Mark   So, I'm making my way to the toilet, right? And there's this woman, OK? This woman is like watching me.

Lulu   Who? Who? Who?

Mark   Of course, I should have known then. I should have known who she was.

Lulu   Who?

Mark   But I mean I am so –

Robbie   You're tripping.

Mark   No.

Robbie   You should have known who she was but you're tripping.

Mark   Look, I was not tripping.

Robbie   You didn't recognise this famous person because you were completely out of it.

Mark   OK, OK, I was completely out of it.

Lulu   And you're on your way to the toilet.

Mark   Out of it. All I know is that this woman's eyes are like: give me your veiny bang stick, OK?

Lulu   Way with words.

Mark   So I'm pissing. Urinals. I'm pissing in the urinals and in the mirror I can see the door, OK? Well, OK. Pissing and the door opens. Door opens and it's her.

Lulu   So you're what – in the ladies?

Robbie   Urinals in the ladies?

Mark   Nope.

Robbie   So this is the –

Mark   Urinals in the gents.

Robbie   So she's –

Mark   She's there in the gents, OK? Standing in the gents watching me piss, OK? And now, we're in like bright – we're in fluorescent light I see.

Lulu   Who? Who? Who?

Mark   Not yet.

Robbie   Why not?

Mark   Because I'm out of it, OK. As you say, I'm on something. I should know who, but I don't recognise her, OK?

Lulu   So then bright light and you see . . . ?

Mark   See what she's wearing. A uniform. She is wearing a police uniform.

Lulu   Fuck. Who? Who? Who?

Robbie   A man's uniform or – ?

Mark   WPC. The Docs, the stockings, the jacket. The works. The hat. And she looks me in the eyes –

Gary   A woman?

Robbie   You're pissing?

Mark   Looks me in the eyes by way of the mirror, OK?

Robbie   OK, OK.

Gary   You did it with a woman?

Mark   She looks, she, she, she cruises me and then goes into one of the cubicles but looking at me all the time, you know? Goes into one of the cubicles and leaves the door ajar. I want to race right in there, you know? Get down to it but, like you do, I count to ten. Count to ten and then like coolly walk past. And as I walk past I take a cool glance to my left, cool look into the cubicle, cubicle with the door ajar and – wow.

Lulu   Wow?

Mark   Wow? The skirt is up around the waist. The skirt is up and the knickers are off or maybe she never had knickers – who knows? – but the skirt is up and she is like displaying this beautiful, come and get it snatch to die for, OK?

Gary   Said you didn't go for women.

Robbie   Facing / you?

Lulu   Who is it?

Mark   So I'm in there. I'm in and I kneel. I pay worship. My tongue is worshipping that pussy like it's God. And that's when she speaks. Speaks and I know who she is.

Lulu   Who?

Mark   She says 'Oh yah. Chocks away.'

Lulu   No.

Robbie   What?

Gary   Is this a woman?

Lulu   No – it can't be.

Robbie   I told you.

Lulu   That is fucking unbelievable.

Robbie   Yes, yes it is.

Lulu   What? Fergie?

Mark   Yup. Fergie

Lulu   Fucking hell.

Mark   I recognise the voice. Get a look at the face. It's her.

Robbie Come on –

Mark Fergie is like 'chocks away'. Fergie is right down to it. Fergie is ready to swallow anything, you know? I mean, any chocks there might have been have been chocked away.
So a couple of minutes later, I'm there and Fergie is fellating. It's gobbledeygobble up against the cistern.

Robbie Nobody believes this. How can you believe this?

Mark Gobbledeygobble and the door, door to the cubicle starts to open.

Robbie This is ridiculous.

Mark I haven't locked the door, you see.

Robbie We said the truth. It had to be the truth.

Mark Rule number one. Always lock the door.

Robbie No one believes this.

Mark Door opens and there's another woman. Yes. There's a second woman. Another policewoman like squeezes her way in.

Robbie Shut up.

Mark With blonde hair.

Robbie SHUT UP. SHUT THE FUCK UP.

Pause.

Mark What? What I thought you wanted to know . . .

Robbie The truth.

Mark Which is what . . .

Robbie No.
(*To* **Lulu**.) Do you believe him?
(*To* **Gary**.) Do you?

Pause.

Rule number one. Never believe a junkie.
Because a junkie is a cunt. And when a junkie looks you in
the eye and says 'I love you' that's when you know he's
gonna fill you full of shit.

Pause.

Gary Why didn't you tell me you'd done it with a
woman?

Robbie (*to* **Gary**) Back to you.

Gary All right.

Robbie It's your turn now.

Mark You don't have to –

Gary I want to.

Lulu We'll help you.

Gary Yeah?

Lulu Help you to find the words.

Robbie All right then. All right. Your story. Your film,
yeah?

Gary Yeah.

Robbie I think I know what it is. I see. I understand.

Gary Yeah.

Robbie Yes. These pictures in your head.
So if I help – yes? If I can help you to describe the
pictures then –

Gary Yes.

Robbie All right. All right. There's you yes and you're.
I see you . . . there's music yes?

Gary Music. Yes.

Robbie Loud music. Dum dum dum. Like / techno.

Gary Techno music. Yes.

Robbie   Techno music and you're moving like – you're dancing yes?

Gary   Dancing.

Robbie   Dancing on a dance floor. Dance floor in a club.

Gary   Yes. Yes. A club.

Robbie   And you're dancing with this bloke.

Gary   No. Not like that. He's just there.

Robbie   Dancing by yourself. But now . . .

Gary   Watching.

Robbie   Bloke who's watching you.

Gary   I'm dancing.

Lulu   He's watching.

Gary   Yeah. Watching me.

Lulu   And you smile.

Gary   No. No smile.

Robbie   But you know, you think: you don't have a choice.

Lulu   No control.

Gary   No control.

Robbie   Because he's . . .

Lulu   Because he's . . .

Gary   Because he's gonna / take me away.

Robbie   Have you. I'm going to have you.

Lulu   He's going to have you.

Mark   Come on, leave –

Robbie   No.

Mark   This is – it's getting heavy.

Gary   No.

Robbie   We're getting to the truth.

Gary   I want to do it.

Lulu   Now there's another – a fat bloke.

Gary   Yes? A fat bloke?

Lulu   Fat bloke who owns you.

Gary   I didn't know about him.

Lulu   Owns you but doesn't want you.
And the fat bloke says:
See that one dancing?

Robbie   Yeah. Yeah. I see him.

Lulu   Well, he's mine. I own him.

Mark   Fuck's sake.

Lulu   I own him but I don't want him.

Gary   Dunt want me.

Lulu   You know something.
He's trash and I hate him.

Robbie   Hate him.

Gary   Right. Hates me.

Robbie   And the fat bloke says –

Lulu   Well, you wanna buy him?

Gary   Yes.

Robbie   And / I say.

Gary   You say.

Robbie   How much?

Lulu   Piece of trash like that. Well, let's say twenty. He's yours for twenty.

Robbie   So you see the money.

Gary   I see money. See you pay him.

Robbie   You've seen the ...

Gary   Transaction. I've seen the transaction.

Robbie   Transaction.

Gary   Yes and you've come to fetch me. You don't say anything. Just take me away.

Robbie   Good. Take you away.

Gary   Big car. Through the security gates and we're in the house.
And now dark. I can't see because ... I'm wearing a, there's like a ...

Lulu   A blindfold?

Gary   Blindfold. Yes ... like a blindfold.

Lulu *produces a blindfold.*

Mark *pushes* **Lulu** *away and put his arms around* **Gary**.

Mark   All right. Stop now. See? You can choose this instead. You must like that.
Just to be loved.

Gary   What are you doing?

Mark   Just holding you.

Gary   You've not even fucked me.

He pushes **Mark** *away.*

You're taking the piss, aren't you?

Mark   I'm just trying to show you. Because, I don't think that you have ever actually been loved and if the world has offered us no practical ...

Gary   What are you?

Mark   I can take care of you.

Gary   You're nobody. You're not what I want.

Mark   If you can just get out of this trap.

Gary   I don't want you. Understand?
You're nothing.

Mark   Wait. I just need to get this.

Mark *takes coke from* **Gary***'s pocket and retreats.*

Lulu   Do you understand what we're going to do to you?

Gary   Yes.

Lulu   You understand and do you want us to do this?

Gary   Yes.

Lulu *puts the blindfold on* **Gary***.*

Robbie   Blindfold you and –

Gary   Take me up the stairs.

Robbie   In my house?

Gary   In your house.

Lulu *and* **Robbie** *spin* **Gary** *around.*

Robbie   And you feel . . . you know this house. Know
you've been here before.

Gary   Yeah. When have I been here before?

Lulu   And now. Now a bare room.
So – you're the new slave?

Robbie   Yes. Yes, old woman. This is the new slave.

Lulu   Beware. Beware. Do you know what the last slave
died of ?

Gary   No. There's no woman.

Robbie   Now.

Lulu   Sssssh. He's coming. The master is coming.
Ssssssshhh.

Gary   I know this house. I know who he is.

Robbie   Knob. Knob on the door turning.

Silence. **Gary** *stands very still.* **Robbie** *slowly approaches him from behind. Long pause –* **Robbie** *inches away from* **Gary**.

Gary   Go on.

Robbie   Yes?

Gary   Do it.

Robbie   It's what you want.

Gary   Yes.

Robbie *starts to undo* **Gary**'s *trousers.*

Robbie   Yes?

Gary   Yes.

Robbie *pulls down* **Gary**'s *trousers.*

He spits on his hand. Slowly he works the spit up **Gary**'s *arse.*

Now?

Gary   Do it now.

Robbie   Now.

Robbie *unzips his fly. Works spit onto his penis. He penetrates* **Gary**. *He starts to fuck him.*

Silence. **Robbie** *continues to fuck* **Gary**.

Lulu   Is that good? Do you like that?

More silent fucking.

Robbie (*to* **Mark**)   Do you want him?

Mark   I . . .

Robbie   Do you know what he is? Trash. Trash and I hate him. Want him, you can have him.

Mark   Yes.

Robbie *pulls away.* **Mark** *goes through the same routine –
spitting and penetrating* **Gary**. *He fucks him viciously.*

Mark Fuck you. Fuck you.

Lulu Does it hurt? Is it hurting you?

Gary Are you him? Are you my dad?

Mark No.

Gary Yes. You're my dad.

Mark I told you – no.

He hits **Gary**.
Then, he pulls away from **Gary**.

Gary See. See. I know who you are. So finish it.

Mark No.

He hits **Gary** *repeatedly.*

I'm. Not. Your. Dad.

Lulu Leave him. Leave him now. Finished. It's over.

Gary No. Don't stop now.

Robbie No?

Robbie *gets into position to continue fucking* **Gary**.

Gary Because – look – this bit. It doesn't end like this.
He's always got something. He gets me in the room,
blindfolds me. But he doesn't fuck me. Well not him, not
his dick. It's the knife. He fucks me – yeah – but with a
knife. So . . .

Pause.

Lulu No.

Mark Gotta have something.

Gary In the kitchen. Or, or a screwdriver. Or something.

Lulu No.

Gary Got to be fucking something. That's how it ends.

Robbie *pulls off* **Gary**'s *blindfold.*

Robbie No. I can't do that.

Gary You're not gonna finish like this?

Robbie I'm not gonna do that.

Lulu You'll bleed.

Gary Yeah.

Lulu You could die.

Gary No. I'll be OK. Promise.

Robbie It'll kill you.

Gary It's what I want.

Lulu Go home now.

Gary Just do it. Just fucking do it.
You're losers – you're fucking losers you know that?

Robbie Yeah.

Gary Listen, right. When someone's paying, someone
wants something and they're paying, then you do it.
Nothing right. Nothing wrong. It's a deal. So then you
do it.
I thought you were for real.
Pretending, isn't it? Just a story.

Robbie Yes. It's just a story.

Mark (*to* **Robbie** *and* **Lulu**) Please leave us now.

Lulu We needed his money.

Mark I know. If you leave us alone. I'll take care of this.
Yes?

Lulu Come on, come on.

Exit **Robbie** *and* **Lulu**.

Gary Are you gonna do it? I want you to do it. Come

on. You can do it.
Because he's not out there.
I've got this unhappiness. This big sadness swelling like it's
gonna burst.
I'm sick and I'm never going to be well.

Mark I know.

Gary I want it over. And there's only one ending.

Mark I understand.

Gary He's got no face in the story. But I want to put a
face to him. Your face.

Mark Yes.

Gary Do it. Do it and I'll say 'I love you'.

Mark All right. You're dancing and I take you away.

Scene Fourteen

The flat.

Brian *has the holdall of money.*

Brian You know, life is hard. On this planet. Intractable.
I can tell you this because I feel it. Yes, like you I have felt
this. We work, we struggle. And we find ourselves asking:
what is this for? Is there meaning? I know you've . . . I can
see this question in your eyes. You ask yourself these
questions. Right now – yes?

Robbie Yes.

Brian And you – what is there to guide me on my
lonely journey?
Yes?

Lulu Yes.

Brian We need something. A guide. A talisman. A set of
rules. A compass to steer us through this everlasting night.
Our youth is spent searching for this guide until we . . .

some give up. Some say there is nothing. There is chaos.
We are born into chaos. But this is . . . no. This is too
painful. This is too awful to contemplate. This we deny.
Am I right?

Robbie   Yes.

Brian   Yes. I have a rung a bell. Good, good. Bells are
rung.
Chaos or . . . order. meaning. Something that gives us
meaning.

Pause.

My dad once said to me. My dad said it to me and now
I'm going to say it to you. One day my dad says to me:
Son, what are the first few words in the Bible?

Robbie   In the beginning.

Brian   No.

Robbie   Yes. In the beginning.

Brian   I'm telling you no.

Robbie   That's what it says. In the beginning.

Brian   No, son. I'm telling you no. And you listen to me
when I'm telling you no, all right?

Robbie   All right.

Brian   Tell me, son, says my dad, what are the first few
words in the Bible? I don't know, Dad, I say, what are the
first few words in the Bible? And he looks as me, he looks
me in the eye and he says: Son, the first few words in the
Bible are . . . get the money first. Get. The Money. First.

Pause.

It's not perfect, I don't deny it. We haven't reached
perfection. But it's the closest we've come to meaning.
Civilisation is money. Money is civilisation. And civilisation
– how did we get here? By war, by struggle, kill or be
killed. And money – it's the same thing, you understand?

The getting is cruel, is hard, but the having is civilisation. Then we are civilised. Say it. Say it with me. Money is . . .

Pause.

SAY IT. Money is . . .

Lulu *and* **Robbie**   Civilisation.

Brian   Yes. Yes. I'm teaching. You're learning. Money is civilisation. And civilisation is . . . SAY IT. Don't get frightened now. And civilisation is . . .

Lulu *and* **Robbie**   Money.

Brian *offers them the holdall.*

Brian   Here. Take it.

Lulu   You . . . ?

Brian   I want you to take it.

Lulu   It's all there.

Brian   Yes.

Lulu   Look – if you want to count it. Three thousand.

Brian   Take it from me when I tell you to take it.

Lulu *takes the bag.*

Brian   Good. Good. You see? Do you understand? I am returning the money. You see?

Lulu   I . . . yes.

Brian   And now – you have a question. Ask me the question. Please. Ask the question?

Lulu   Why?

Brian   If you formulate the question . . .

Lulu   Why didn't you take the money? Why did you give us back the money?

Brian   And now I can answer you. I answer: Because you have learnt. The lesson has been learnt you see. You

understand this (*Indicates the money.*) and you are civilised.
And so – I return it. I give it to you.

Lulu Thank you.

Brian *gets up, moves to video player. He ejects the video of his son.
Takes another video from his pocket. Places it in the machine. Pushes
play.*

Lulu (*TV*) One day we'll know what all this was for, all
this suffering, there'll be no more mysteries, but until then
we have to carry on living . . . we must work, / that's all
we can do. I'm leaving by myself tomorrow, I'll teach in a
school, and devote my whole life to people who need it. It's
autumn now, it'll soon be winter, and there'll be snow
everywhere but I'll be working . . . yes, working.

Brian We must work.
What we've got to do is make the money. For them. My
boy. Generations to come. We won't see it of course – that
purity. But they will. Just as long as we keep on making
the money.
Not in chemicals. Not pure. Supplies aren't the best. So a
kid dies. And then it's headlines and press conferences. And
you watch the dad, you watch a grown man cry and you
think: time to move out of chemicals.

He pauses the tape.

That's the future, isn't it? Shopping, Television.
And now you've proved yourselves, I'd like you to join us.
All of you. Think about it.

He moves to the exit.

Our second favourite bit was the end. Because by then he's
got married. And he's got a kid of his own. Right at the
end he stands alone. He's on a rock and he looks up at the
night, he looks up at the stars and he says: 'Father.
Everything is all right, Father. I remembered. The Cycle of
Being.' Or words to that effect.
You ought to see it. You'd like it.

Exit **Brian**. **Mark** *comes forward.*

Mark   It's three thousand AD. Or something. It's the
future. The Earth has died. Died or we killed it. The
ozone, the bombs, a meteorite. It just doesn't matter. But
humanity has survived. A few of us ... jumped ship. And
on we go.
So it's three thousand and blahdeblah and I'm standing in
the market, some sort of bazaar. A little satellite circling
Uranus. Market day. And I'm looking at this mutant. Some
of them, the radiation it's made them so ugly, twisted. But
this one. Wow. It's made him ... he's tanned and blond
and there's pecs and his dick ... I mean, his dick is three-
foot long.
This fat sort of ape-thing comes up to me and says ...
See the mute with the three-foot dick?
Yeah. I see him.
Well, he's mine and I own him. I own him but I hate him.
If I don't sell him today I'm gonna kill him.
So ... a deal is struck, a transaction, I take my mutant
home and I get him home and I say:
I'm freeing you. I'm setting you free. You can go now. And
he starts to cry. I think it's gratitude. I mean, he should be
grateful but it's ...
He says – well, he telepathises into my mind – he doesn't
speak our language – he tells me:
Please. I'll die. I don't know how to ... I can't feed myself.
I've been a slave all my life. I've never had a thought of
my own. I'll be dead in a week.
And I say: That's a risk I'm prepared to take.

Robbie   Thirty-six inches and no shag?

Mark   That's right.

Lulu   I like that ending.

Robbie   It's not bad.

Mark   It's the best I can do.

Robbie   Hungry now? I want you to try some. (*Of the
ready meal.*)

He feeds **Mark** *with a fork.*

Nice?

Mark Mmmmm.

Robbie Now give him some of yours.

Lulu Do you want some?

She feeds **Mark**.

Is that good?

Mark Delicious.

Robbie You've got a bit of blood.

Lulu Bit more?

Mark Why not?

Lulu *feeds him.*

Robbie My turn.

Robbie *feeds* **Mark**.

Mark, **Robbie** *and* **Lulu** *take it in turns to feed each other as the lights fade to black.*

The Beauty Queen of Leenane

Martin McDonagh

Martin McDonagh's first play, *The Beauty Queen of Leenane*, was the 1996 winner of the George Devine Award, won the Writers' Guild Award for Best Fringe Play and also the Evening Standard Award for Most Promising Newcomer. The play was nominated for six Tony awards, of which it won four, and a Laurence Olivier Award (the BBC Award for Best New Play). *The Beauty Queen of Leenane* is the first in Martin McDonagh's *Leenane Trilogy*; *A Skull in Connemara* and *The Lonesome West* (Royal Court and Druid Theatre Company co-productions, 1997) complete the cycle. *A Skull in Connemara* was nominated for an Olivier Award for Best New Comedy. *The Cripple of Inishmaan* (Royal National Theatre, 1996) and *The Lieutenant of Inishmore* (Royal Shakespeare Company, 2001) are the first and second in a trilogy of Aran Island plays.

The Beauty Queen of Leenane, a Druid Theatre Company/
Royal Court Theatre co-production, was first presented at
the Town Hall Theatre, Galway, on 1 February 1996,
marking the official opening of the theatre. It subsequently
opened at the Royal Court Theatre Upstairs on 5 March
1996. The cast was as follows:

Mag	Anna Manahan
Maureen	Marie Mullen
Ray	Tom Murphy
Pato	Brian F. O'Byrne

Directed by Garry Hynes
Designed by Francis O'Connor
Lighting by Ben Ormerod
Sound by David Murphy

Characters

Maureen Folan, *aged forty. Plain, slim.*
Mag Folan, *her mother, aged seventy. Stout, frail.*
Pato Dooley, *a good-looking local man, aged about forty.*
Ray Dooley, *his brother, aged twenty.*

Setting

Leenane, a small town in Connemara, County Galway.

Scene One

The living-room/kitchen of a rural cottage in the west of Ireland. Front door stage left, a long black range along the back wall with a box of turf beside it and a rocking-chair on its right. On the kitchen side of the set is a door in the back wall leading off to an unseen hallway, and a newer oven, a sink and some cupboards curving around the right wall. There is a window with an inner ledge above the sink in the right wall looking out into fields, a dinner table with two chairs just right of centre, a small TV down left, an electric kettle and a radio on one of the kitchen cupboards, a crucifix and a framed picture of John and Robert Kennedy on the wall above the range, a heavy black poker beside the range, and a touristy-looking embroidered tea towel hanging further along the back wall, bearing the inscription 'May you be half an hour in Heaven afore the Devil knows you're dead'. As the play begins it is raining quite heavily. **Mag Folan**, *a stoutish woman in her early seventies with short, tightly permed grey hair and a mouth that gapes slightly, is sitting in the rocking chair, staring off into space. Her left hand is somewhat more shrivelled and red than her right. The front door opens and her daughter,* **Maureen**, *a plain, slim woman of about forty, enters carrying shopping and goes through to the kitchen.*

Mag Wet, Maureen?

Maureen Of course wet.

Mag Oh-h.

Maureen *takes her coat off, sighing, and starts putting the shopping away.*

Mag I did take me Complan.

Maureen So you *can* get it yourself so.

Mag I can. (*Pause.*) Although lumpy it was, Maureen.

Maureen Well, can I help lumpy?

Mag No.

Maureen Write to the Complan people so, if it's lumpy.

Mag (*pause*) You do make me Complan nice and smooth. (*Pause.*) Not a lump at all, nor the comrade of a lump.

Maureen You don't give it a good enough stir is what you don't do.

Mag I gave it a good enough stir and there was still lumps.

Maureen You probably pour the water in too fast so. What it says on the box, you're supposed to ease it in.

Mag Mm.

Maureen That's where you do go wrong. Have another go tonight for yourself and you'll see.

Mag Mm. (*Pause.*) And the hot water too I do be scared of. Scared I may scould meself.

Maureen *gives her a slight look.*

Mag I *do* be scared, Maureen. I be scared what if me hand shook and I was to pour it over me hand. And with you at Mary Pender's, then where would I be?

Maureen You're just a hypochondriac is what you are.

Mag I'd be lying on the floor and I'm not a hypochondriac.

Maureen You are too and everybody knows that you are. Full well.

Mag Don't I have a urine infection if I'm such a hypochondriac?

Maureen I can't see how a urine infection prevents you pouring a mug of Complan or tidying up the house a bit when I'm away. It wouldn't kill you.

Mag (*pause*) Me bad back.

Maureen Your bad back.

Mag And me bad hand. (**Mag** *holds up her shrivelled hand for a second.*)

Maureen (*quietly*) Feck . . . (*Irritated.*) I'll get your Complan so if it's such a big job! From now and 'til doomsday! The one thing I ask you to do. Do you see Annette or Margo coming pouring your Complan or buying your oul cod in butter sauce for the week?

Mag No.

Maureen No is right, you don't. And carrying it up that hill. And still I'm not appreciated.

Mag You *are* appreciated, Maureen.

Maureen I'm not appreciated.

Mag I'll give me Complan another go so, and give it a good stir for meself.

Maureen Ah, forget your Complan. I'm expected to do everything else, I suppose that one on top of it won't hurt. Just a . . . just a blessed fecking skivvy is all I'm thought of!

Mag You're not, Maureen.

Maureen *slams a couple of cupboard doors after finishing with the shopping and sits at the table, after dragging its chair back loudly. Pause.*

Mag Me porridge, Maureen, I haven't had, will you be getting? No, in a minute, Maureen, have a rest for yourself . . .

But **Maureen** *has already jumped up, stomped angrily back to the kitchen and started preparing the porridge as noisily as she can. Pause.*

Mag Will we have the radio on for ourselves?

Maureen *bangs an angry finger at the radio's 'on' switch. It takes a couple of swipes before it comes on loudly, through static – a nasally male voice singing in Gaelic. Pause.*

Mag The dedication Annette and Margo sent we still haven't heard. I wonder what's keeping it?

Maureen If they sent a dedication at all. They only said they did. (**Maureen** *sniffs the sink a little, then turns to* **Mag**.)

Is there a smell off this sink now, I'm wondering.

Mag (*defensively*) No.

Maureen I hope there's not, now.

Mag No smell at all is there, Maureen. I do promise, now.

Maureen *returns to the porridge. Pause.*

Mag Is the radio a biteen loud there, Maureen?

Maureen A biteen loud, is it?

Maureen *swipes angrily at the radio again, turning it off. Pause.*

Mag Nothing on it, anyways. An oul fella singing nonsense.

Maureen Isn't it you wanted it set for that oul station?

Mag Only for Ceilidh Time and for whatyoucall.

Maureen It's too late to go complaining now.

Mag Not for nonsense did I want it set.

Maureen (*pause*) It isn't nonsense anyways. Isn't it Irish?

Mag It sounds like nonsense to me. Why can't they just speak English like everybody?

Maureen Why should they speak English?

Mag To know what they're saying.

Maureen What country are you living in?

Mag Eh?

Maureen What country are you living in?

Mag Galway.

Maureen Not what county!

Mag Oh-h . . .

Maureen Ireland you're living in!

Mag   *Ireland.*

Maureen   So why should you be speaking English in Ireland?

Mag   I don't know.

Maureen   It's Irish you should be speaking in Ireland.

Mag   It is.

Maureen   Eh?

Mag   Eh?

Maureen   'Speaking English in Ireland.'

Mag (*pause*)   Except where would Irish get you going for a job in England? Nowhere.

Maureen   Well, isn't that the crux of the matter?

Mag   Is it, Maureen?

Maureen   If it wasn't for the English stealing our language, and our land, and our God-knows-what, wouldn't it be we wouldn't need to go over there begging for jobs and for handouts?

Mag   I suppose that's the crux of the matter.

Maureen   It *is* the crux of the matter.

Mag (*pause*)   Except America, too.

Maureen   What except America too?

Mag   If it was to America you had to go begging for handouts, it isn't Irish would be any good to you. It would be English!

Maureen   Isn't that the same crux of the same matter?

Mag   I don't know if it is or it isn't.

Maureen   Bringing up kids to think all they'll ever be good for is begging handouts from the English and the Yanks. That's the selfsame crux.

Mag   I suppose.

Maureen   Of course you suppose, because it's true.

Mag (*pause*)   If I had to go begging for handouts anywhere, I'd rather beg for them in America than in England, because in America it does be more sunny anyways. (*Pause.*) Or is that just something they say, that the weather is more sunny, Maureen? Or is that a lie, now?

Maureen *slops the porridge out and hands it to* **Mag**, *speaking as she does so.*

Maureen   You're oul and you're stupid and you don't know what you're talking about. Now shut up and eat your oul porridge.

Maureen *goes back to wash the pan in the sink.* **Mag** *glances at the porridge, then turns back to her.*

Mag   Me mug of tea you forgot!

Maureen *clutches the edges of the sink and lowers her head, exasperated, then quietly, with visible self-control, fills the kettle to make her mother's tea. Pause.* **Mag** *speaks while slowly eating.*

Mag   Did you meet anybody on your travels, Maureen? (*No response.*) Ah no, not on a day like today. (*Pause.*) Although you don't say hello to people is your trouble, Maureen. (*Pause.*) Although some people it would be better not to say hello to. The fella up and murdered the poor oul woman in Dublin and he didn't even know her. The news that story was on, did you hear of it? (*Pause.*) Strangled, and didn't even know her. That's a fella it would be better not to talk to. That's a fella it would be better to avoid outright.

Maureen *brings* **Mag** *her tea, then sits at the table.*

Maureen   Sure, that sounds exactly the type of fella I would *like* to meet, and then bring him home to meet you, if he likes murdering oul women.

Mag   That's not a nice thing to say, Maureen.

Maureen Is it not, now?

Mag (*pause*) Sure why would he be coming all this way out from Dublin? He'd just be going out of his way.

Maureen For the pleasure of me company he'd come. Killing you, it'd just be a bonus for him.

Mag Killing *you* I bet he first would be.

Maureen I could live with that so long as I was sure he'd be clobbering you soon after. If he clobbered you with a big axe or something and took your oul head off and spat in your neck, I wouldn't mind at all, going first. Oh no, I'd enjoy it, I would. No more oul Complan to get, and no more oul porridge to get, and no more . . .

Mag (*interrupting, holding her tea out*) No sugar in this, Maureen, you forgot, go and get me some.

Maureen *stares at her a moment, then takes the tea, brings it to the sink and pours it away, goes back to* **Mag***, grabs her half-eaten porridge, returns to the kitchen, scrapes it out into the bin, leaves the bowl in the sink and exits into the hallway, giving* **Mag** *a dirty look on the way and closing the door behind her.* **Mag** *stares grumpily out into space. Blackout.*

Scene Two

Mag *is sitting at the table, staring at her reflection in a hand-mirror. She pats her hair a couple of times. The TV is on, showing an old episode of* The Sullivans. *There is a knock at the front door, which startles her slightly.*

Mag Who . . . ? Maureen. Oh-h. The door, Maureen.

She gets up and shuffles towards the kitchen window. There is another knock. She shuffles back to the door.

Who's at the door?

Ray (*off*) It's Ray Dooley, Mrs. From over the way.

Mag Dooley?

Ray   Ray Dooley, aye. You know me.

Mag   Are you one of the Dooleys so?

Ray   I am. I'm Ray.

Mag   Oh-h.

Ray (*pause. Irritated*)   Well, will you let me in or am I going to talk to the door?

Mag   She's feeding the chickens. (*Pause.*) Have you gone?

Ray (*angrily*)   Open the oul door, Mrs! Haven't I walked a mile out of me way just to get here?

Mag   Have you?

Ray   I have. 'Have you?' she says.

Mag *unlatches the door with some difficulty and* **Ray Dooley**, *a lad of about nineteen, enters.*

Ray   Thank you! An hour I thought you'd be keeping me waiting.

Mag   Oh, it's you, so it is.

Ray   Of course it's me. Who else?

Mag   You're the Dooley with the uncle.

Ray   It's only a million times you've seen me the past twenty year. Aye, I'm the Dooley with the uncle, and it's me uncle the message is.

Ray *stops and watches the TV a moment.*

Mag   Maureen's at the chickens.

Ray   You've said Maureen's at the chickens. What's on the telly?

Mag   I was waiting for the news.

Ray   You'll have a long wait.

Mag   I was combing me hair.

Ray   I think it's *The Sullivans*.

Mag   I don't know what it is.

Ray   You do get a good reception.

Mag   A middling reception.

Ray   Everything's Australian nowadays.

Mag   I don't know if it is or it isn't.

She sits in the rocking chair.

At the chickens, Maureen is.

Ray   That's three times now you've told me Maureen's at the chickens. Are you going for the world's record in saying 'Maureen's at the chickens'?

Mag (*pause. Confused*)   She's feeding them.

Ray *stares at her a moment, then sighs and looks out through the kitchen window.*

Ray   Well, I'm not wading through all that skitter just to tell her. I've done enough wading. Coming up that oul hill.

Mag   It's a big oul hill.

Ray   It *is* a big oul hill.

Mag   Steep.

Ray   Steep is right and if not steep then muddy.

Mag   Muddy and rocky.

Ray   Muddy and rocky is right. Uh-huh. How do ye two manage up it every day?

Mag   We do drive.

Ray   Of course. (*Pause.*) That's what I want to do is drive. I'll have to be getting driving lessons. And a car. (*Pause.*) Not a good one, like. A second-hand one, y'know?

Mag   A used one.

Ray   A used one, aye.

Mag   Off somebody.

Ray   Oul Father Welsh – Walsh – has a car he's selling, but I'd look a poof buying a car off a priest.

Mag   I don't like Father Walsh – Welsh – at all.

Ray   He punched Mairtin Hanlon in the head once, and for no reason.

Mag   God love us!

Ray   Aye. Although, now, that was out of character for Father Welsh. Father Welsh seldom uses violence, same as most young priests. It's usually only the older priests go punching you in the head. I don't know why. I suppose it's the way they were brought up.

Mag   There was a priest the news Wednesday had a babby with a Yank!

Ray   That's no news at all. That's everyday. It'd be hard to find a priest who hasn't had a babby with a Yank. If he'd punched that babby in the head, that'd be news. Aye. Anyways. Aye. What was I saying? Oh aye, so if I give you the message, Mrs, you'll be passing it on to Maureen, so you will, or will I be writing it down for you?

Mag   I'll be passing it on.

Ray   Good-oh. Mr brother Pato said to invite yous to our uncle's going-away do. The Riordan's hall out in Carraroe.

Mag   Is your brother back so?

Ray   He is.

Mag   Back from England?

Ray   Back from England, aye. England's where he was, so that's where he would be back from. Our Yankee uncle's going home to Boston after his holiday and taking those two ugly duckling daughters back with him and that Dolores whatyoucall, Healey or Hooley, so there'll be a little to-do in the Riordan's as a goodbye or a *big* to-do knowing hem show-off bastards and free food anyways, so me brother says ye're welcome to come or Maureen anyways, he knows you don't like getting out much. Isn't it you has the bad hip?

Mag   No.

Ray   Oh. Who is it has the bad hip so?

Mag   I don't know. I do have the urine infection.

Ray   Maybe that's what I was thinking of. And thanks for telling me.

Mag   Me urine.

Ray   I know, your urine.

Mag   And me bad back. And me burned hand.

Ray   Aye, aye, aye. Anyways, you'll be passing the message on to that one.

Mag   Eh?

Ray   You'll be remembering the message to pass it on to that one?

Mag   Aye.

Ray   Say it back to me so.

Mag   Say it back to you?

Ray   Aye.

Mag (*long pause*)   About me hip . . . ?

Ray (*angrily*)   I should've fecking written it down in the first fecking place, I fecking knew! And save all this fecking time!

He grabs a pen and a piece of paper, sits at the table and writes the message out.

Talking with a loon!

Mag (*pause*)   Do me a mug of tea while you're here, Pato. Em, Ray.

Ray   *Ray* my fecking name is! Pato's me fecking brother!

Mag I do forget.

Ray It's like talking to a . . . talking to a . . .

Mag Brick wall.

Ray Brick wall is right.

Mag (*pause*) Or some soup do me.

Ray *finishes writing and gets up.*

Ray There. Forget about soup. The message is there. Point that one in the direction of it when she returns from beyond. The Riordan's hall out in Carraroe. Seven o'clock tomorrow night. Free food. Okay?

Mag All right now, Ray. Are you still in the choir nowadays, Ray?

Ray I am *not* in the choir nowadays. Isn't it ten years since I was in the choir?

Mag Doesn't time be flying?

Ray Not since I took an interest in girls have I been in the choir because you do get no girls in choirs, only fat girls and what use are they? No. I go to discos, me.

Mag Good enough for yourself.

Ray What am I doing standing around here conversing with you? I have left me message and now I am off.

Mag Goodbye to you, Ray.

Ray Goodbye to you, Mrs.

Mag And pull the door.

Ray I was going to pull the door anyways . . .

He pulls the front door shut behind him as he exits.

(*Off.*) I don't need your advice!

*As **Ray**'s footsteps fade, **Mag** gets up, reads the message on the table, goes to the kitchen window and glances out, then finds a box of matches, comes back to the table, strikes a match, lights the message,* *goes to the range with it burning and drops it inside. Sound of footsteps approaching the front door.* **Mag** *shuffles back to her rocking chair and sits in it just as* **Maureen** *enters.*

Mag (*nervously*)   Cold, Maureen?

Maureen   Of course cold.

Mag   Oh-h.

Mag *stares at the TV as if engrossed.* **Maureen** *sniffs the air a little, then sits at the table, staring at* **Mag**.

Maureen   What are you watching?

Mag   I don't know *what* I'm watching. Just waiting for the news I am.

Maureen   Oh aye. (*Pause.*) Nobody rang while I was out, I suppose? Ah no.

Mag   Ah no, Maureen. Nobody did ring.

Maureen   Ah no.

Mag   No. Who would be ringing?

Maureen   No, nobody I suppose. No. (*Pause.*) And nobody visited us either? Ah no.

Mag   Ah no, Maureen. Who would be visiting us?

Maureen   Nobody, I suppose. Ah no.

Mag *glances at* **Maureen** *a second, then back at the TV. Pause.* **Maureen** *gets up, ambles over to the TV, lazily switches it off with the toe of her shoe, ambles back to the kitchen, staring at* **Mag** *as she passes, turns on the kettle, and leans against the cupboards, looking back in* **Mag**'s *direction.*

Mag (*nervously*)   Em, apart from wee Ray Dooley who passed.

Maureen (*knowing*)   Oh, did Ray Dooley pass, now?

Mag   He passed, aye, and said hello as he was passing.

Maureen   I thought just now you said there was no visitors.

Mag   There were no visitors, no, apart from Ray Dooley who passed.

Maureen   Oh, aye, aye, aye. Just to say hello he popped his head in.

Mag   Just to say hello and how is all. Aye. A nice wee lad he is.

Maureen   Aye. (*Pause.*) With no news?

Mag   With no news. Sure, what news would a gasur have?

Maureen   None at all, I suppose. Ah, no.

Mag   Ah, no. (*Pause.*) Thinking of getting a car I think he said he was.

Maureen   Oh aye?

Mag   A second-hand one.

Maureen   Uh-huh?

Mag   To drive, y'know?

Maureen   To drive, aye.

Mag   Off Father Welsh – Walsh – Welsh.

Maureen   Welsh.

Mag   Welsh.

Maureen *switches off the kettle, pours a sachet of Complan into a mug and fills it up with water.*

Maureen   I'll do you some of your Complan.

Mag   Have I not had me Complan already, Maureen? I have.

Maureen   Sure, another one won't hurt.

Mag (*wary*)   No, I suppose.

Maureen *tops the drink up with tap water to cool it, stirs it just* *twice to keep it lumpy, takes the spoon out, hands the drink to* **Mag**, *then leans back against the table to watch her drink it.* **Mag** *looks at it in distaste.*

Mag A bit lumpy, Maureen.

Maureen Never mind lumpy, Mam. The lumps will do you good. That's the best part of Complan is the lumps. Drink ahead.

Mag A little spoon, do you have?

Maureen No, I have no little spoon. There's no little spoons for liars in this house. No little spoons at all. Be drinking ahead.

Mag *takes the smallest of sickly sips.*

Maureen The whole of it, now!

Mag I do have a funny tummy, Maureen, and I do have no room.

Maureen Drink ahead, I said! You had room enough to be spouting your lies about Ray Dooley had no message! Did I not meet him on the road beyond as he was going? The lies of you. The whole of that Complan you'll drink now, and suck the lumps down too, and whatever's left you haven't drank, it is over your head I will be emptying it, and you know well enough I mean it!

Mag *slowly drinks the rest of the sickly brew.*

Maureen Arsing me around, eh? Interfering with my life again? Isn't it enough I've had to be on beck and call for you every day for the past twenty year? Is it one evening out you begrudge me?

Mag Young girls should not be out gallivanting with fellas . . . !

Maureen Young girls! I'm forty years old, for feck's sake! Finish it!

Mag *drinks again.*

Maureen 'Young girls'! That's the best yet. And how did Annette or Margo ever get married if it wasn't first out gallivanting that they were?

Mag I don't know.

Maureen Drink!

Mag I don't like it, Maureen.

Maureen Would you like it better over your head?

Mag *drinks again.*

Maureen I'll tell you, eh? 'Young girls out gallivanting.' I've heard it all now. What have I ever done but *kissed* two men the past forty year?

Mag Two men is plenty!

Maureen Finish!

Mag I've finished!

She holds out the mug. **Maureen** *washes it.*

Two men is two men too much!

Maureen To you, maybe. To you. Not to me.

Mag Two men too much!

Maureen Do you think I like being stuck up here with you? Eh? Like a dried-up oul . . .

Mag Whore!

Maureen *laughs.*

Maureen 'Whore'? (*Pause.*) Do I not *wish*, now? Do I not wish? (*Pause.*) Sometimes I *dream* . . .

Mag Of being a . . . ?

Maureen Of anything! (*Pause. Quietly.*) Of anything. Other than this.

Mag Well, an odd dream that is!

Maureen It's not at all. Not at all is it an odd dream.

(*Pause.*) And if it is it's not the only odd dream I do have. Do you want to be hearing another one?

Mag I don't.

Maureen I have a dream sometimes there of you, dressed all nice and white, in your coffin there, and me all in black looking in on you, and a fella beside me there, comforting me, the smell of aftershave off him, his arm round me waist. And the fella asks me then if I'll be going for a drink with him at his place after.

Mag And what do you say?

Maureen I say 'Aye, what's stopping me now?'

Mag You don't!

Maureen I do!

Mag At me funeral?

Maureen At your bloody wake, sure! Is even sooner!

Mag Well, that's not a nice thing to be dreaming!

Maureen I know it's not, sure, and it isn't a *dream*-dream at all. It's more of a day-dream. Y'know, something happy to be thinking of when I'm scraping the skitter out of them hens.

Mag Not at all is that a nice dream. That's a mean dream.

Maureen I don't know if it is or it isn't.

Pause. **Maureen** *sits at the table with a pack of Kimberley biscuits.*

I suppose now you'll never be dying. You'll be hanging on for ever, just to spite me.

Mag I *will* be hanging on for ever!

Maureen I know well you will!

Mag Seventy you'll be at my wake, and then how many men'll there be round your waist with their aftershave?

Maureen   None at all, I suppose.

Mag   None at all is right!

Maureen   Oh aye. (*Pause.*) Do you want a Kimberley?

Mag (*pause*)   Have we no shortbread fingers?

Maureen   No, you've ate all the shortbread fingers. Like a pig.

Mag   I'll have a Kimberley so, although I don't like Kimberleys. I don't know why you get Kimberleys at all. Kimberleys are horrible.

Maureen   Me world doesn't revolve around your taste in biscuits.

Maureen *gives* **Mag** *a biscuit.* **Mag** *eats.*

Mag (*pause*)   You'll be going to this do tomorrow so?

Maureen   I will. (*Pause.*) It'll be good to see Pato again anyways. I didn't even know he was home.

Mag   But it's all them oul Yanks'll be there tomorrow.

Maureen   So?

Mag   You said you couldn't stand the Yanks yesterday. The crux of the matter yesterday you said it was.

Maureen   Well, I suppose now, Mother, I will have to be changing me mind, but, sure, isn't that a woman's prerogative?

Mag (*quietly*)   It's only prerogatives when it suits you.

Maureen   Don't go using big words you don't understand, now, Mam.

Mag (*sneers. Pause*)   This invitation was open to me too, if you'd like to know.

Maureen (*half-laughing*)   Do you think you'll be coming?

Mag   I won't, I suppose.

Maureen   You suppose right enough. Lying the head off

you, like a babby of a tinker.

Mag I was only saying.

Maureen Well, don't be saying. (*Pause.*) I think we might take a drive into Westport later, if it doesn't rain.

Mag (*brighter*) Will we take a drive?

Maureen We could take a little drive for ourselves.

Mag We could now. It's a while since we did take a nice drive. We could get some shortbread fingers.

Maureen Later on, I'm saying.

Mag Later on. Not just now.

Maureen Not just now. Sure, you've only just had your Complan now.

Mag *gives her a dirty look. Pause.*

Maureen Aye, Westport. Aye. And I think I might pick up a nice little dress for meself while I'm there. For the do tomorrow, y'know?

Maureen *looks across at* **Mag***, who looks back at her, irritated. Blackout.*

Scene Three

Night. Set only just illuminated by the orange coals through the bars of the range. Radio has been left on low in the kitchen. Footsteps and voices of **Maureen** *and* **Pato** *are heard outside, both slightly drunk.*

Pato (*off, singing*) 'The Cadillac stood by the house . . .'

Maureen (*off*) Shh, Pato . . .

Pato (*off. Singing quietly*) 'And the Yanks they were within.' (*Speaking.*) What was it that oul fella used to say, now?

Maureen (*off*) What oul fella, now?

Maureen *opens the door and the two of them enter, turning the lights on.* **Maureen** *is in a new black dress, cut quite short.* **Pato** *is a good-looking man of about the same age as her.*

Pato   The oul fella who used to chase oul whatyoucall. Oul Bugs Bunny.

Maureen   Would you like a cup of tea, Pato?

Pato   I would.

Maureen *switches the kettle on.*

Maureen   Except keep your voice down, now.

Pato (*quietly*)   I will, I will. (*Pause.*) I can't remember *what* he used to say. The oul fella used to chase Bugs Bunny. It was something, now.

Maureen   Look at this. The radio left on too, the daft oul bitch.

Pato   Sure, what harm? No, leave it on, now. It'll cover up the sounds.

Maureen   What sounds?

Pato   The smooching sounds.

He gently pulls her to him and they kiss a long while, then stop and look at each other. The kettle has boiled. **Maureen** *gently breaks away, smiling, and starts making the tea.*

Maureen   Will you have a biscuit with your tea?

Pato   I will. What biscuits do you have, now?

Maureen   Em, only Kimberleys.

Pato   I'll leave it so, Maureen. I do hate Kimberleys. In fact I think Kimberleys are the most horrible biscuits in the world.

Maureen   The same as that, I hate Kimberleys. I only get them to torment me mother.

Pato   I can't see why the Kimberley people go making them at all. Coleman Connor ate a whole pack of

Kimberleys one time and he was sick for a week. (*Pause.*)
Or was it Mikados? It was some kind of horrible biscuits.

Maureen   Is it true Coleman cut the ears off Valene's
dog and keeps them in his room in a bag?

Pato   He showed me them ears one day.

Maureen   That's awful spiteful, cutting the ears off a dog.

Pato   It *is* awful spiteful.

Maureen   It would be spiteful enough to cut the ears off
anybody's dog, let alone your own brother's dog.

Pato   And it had seemed a nice dog.

Maureen   Aye. (*Pause.*) Aye.

Awkward pause. **Pato** *cuddles up behind her.*

Pato   You feel nice to be giving a squeeze to.

Maureen   Do I?

Pato   Very nice.

Maureen *continues making the tea as* **Pato** *holds her. A little
embarrassed and awkward, he breaks away from her after a second
and idles a few feet away.*

Maureen   Be sitting down for yourself, now, Pato.

Pato   I will. (*Sits at table.*) I do do what I'm told, I do.

Maureen   Oh-ho, do you now? That's the first time
tonight I did notice. Them stray oul hands of yours.

Pato   Sure, I have no control over me hands. They have
a mind of their own. (*Pause.*) Except I didn't notice you
complaining overmuch anyways, me stray oul hands. Not
too many complaints at all!

Maureen   I had complaints when they were straying over
that Yank girl earlier on in the evening.

Pato   Well, I hadn't noticed you there at that time,
Maureen. How was I to know the beauty queen of

Leenane was still yet to arrive?

Maureen   'The beauty queen of Leenane.' Get away with ya!

Pato   Is true!

Maureen   Why so have no more than two words passed between us the past twenty year?

Pato   Sure, it's took me all this time to get up the courage.

Maureen (*smiling*)   Ah, bollocks to ya!

Pato *smiles*. **Maureen** *brings the tea over and sits down.*

Pato   I don't know, Maureen. I don't know.

Maureen   Don't know what?

Pato   Why I never got around to really speaking to you or asking you out or the like. I don't know. Of course, hopping across to that bastarding oul place every couple of months couldn't've helped.

Maureen   England? Aye. Do you not like it there so?

Pato (*pause*)   It's money. (*Pause.*) And it's Tuesday I'll be back there again.

Maureen   Tuesday? This Tuesday?

Pato   Aye. (*Pause.*) It was only to see the Yanks off I was over. To say hello and say goodbye. No time back at all.

Maureen   That's Ireland, anyways. There's always someone leaving.

Pato   It's always the way.

Maureen   Bad, too.

Pato   What can you do?

Maureen   Stay?

Pato (*pause*)   I do ask meself, if there was good work in Leenane, would I stay in Leenane? I mean, there never will

be good work, but hypothetically, I'm saying. Or even bad
work. Any work. And when I'm over there in London and
working in rain and it's more or less cattle I am, and the
young fellas cursing over cards and drunk and sick, and the
oul digs over there, all pee-stained mattresses and nothing
to do but watch the clock . . . when it's there I am, it's
here I wish I was, of course. Who wouldn't? But when it's
here I am . . . it isn't *there* I want to be, of course not. But
I know it isn't here I want to be either.

Maureen And why, Pato?

Pato I can't put my finger on why. (*Pause.*) Of course it's
beautiful here, a fool can see. The mountains and the
green, and people speak. But when everybody knows
everybody else's business . . . I don't know. (*Pause.*) You
can't kick a cow in Leenane without some bastard holding
a grudge twenty year.

Maureen It's true enough.

Pato It is. In England they don't care if you live or die,
and it's funny but that isn't altogether a bad thing. Ah,
sometimes it is . . . ah, I don't know.

Maureen (*pause*) Do you think you'll ever settle down in
the one place so, Pato? When you get married, I suppose.

Pato (*half-laughing*) 'When I get married . . .'

Maureen You will someday, I'll bet you, get married.
Wouldn't you want to?

Pato I can't say it's something I do worry me head over.

Maureen Of course, the rake of women you have
stashed all over, you wouldn't need to.

Pato (*smiling*) I have no rake of women.

Maureen You have one or two, I bet.

Pato I may have one or two. That I know to say hello
to, now.

Maureen Hello me . . . A-hole.

Pato   Is true. (*Pause.*) Sure, I'm no . . .

Maureen (*pause*)   No what?

Pause. **Pato** *shrugs and shakes his head, somewhat sadly. Pause. The song 'The Spinning Wheel', sung by Delia Murphy, has just started on the radio.*

Maureen   Me mother does love this oul song. Oul Delia Murphy.

Pato   This is a creepy oul song.

Maureen   It *is* a creepy oul song.

Pato   She does have a creepy oul voice. Always scared me this song did when I was a lad. She's like a ghoul singing. (*Pause.*) Does the grandmother die at the end, now, or is she just sleeping?

Maureen   Just sleeping, I think she is.

Pato   Aye . . .

Maureen (*pause*)   While the two go hand in hand through the fields.

Pato   Aye.

Maureen   Be moonlight.

Pato (*nods*)   They don't write songs like that any more. Thank Christ. (**Maureen** *laughs. Brighter.*) Wasn't it a grand night though, Maureen, now?

Maureen   It was.

Pato   Didn't we send them on their way well?

Maureen   We did, we did.

Pato   Not a dry eye.

Maureen   Indeed.

Pato   Eh?

Maureen   Indeed.

Pato   Aye. That we did. That we did.

Maureen (*pause*)   So who *was* the Yankee girl you did have your hands all over?

Pato (*laughing*)   Oh, will you stop it with your 'hands all over'?! Barely touched her, I did.

Maureen   Oh-ho!

Pato   A second cousin of me uncle, I think she is. Dolores somebody. Healey or Hooley. Healey. Boston, too, she lives.

Maureen   That was illegal so if it's your second cousin she is.

Pato   Illegal me arse, and it's not *my* second cousin she is anyway, and what's so illegal? Your second cousin's boobs aren't out of bounds, are they?

Maureen   They are!

Pato   I don't know about that. I'll have to consult with me lawyer on that one. I may get arrested the next time. And I have a defence anyways. She had dropped some Taytos on her blouse, there, I was just brushing them off for her.

Maureen   Taytos me arsehold, Pato Dooley!

Pato   Is true! (*Lustful pause. Nervously.*) Like this is all it was . . .

Pato *slowly reaches out and gently brushes at, then gradually fondles,* **Maureen**'s *breasts. She caresses his hand as he's doing so, then slowly gets up and sits across his lap, fondling his head as he continues touching her.*

Maureen   She was prettier than me.

Pato   You're pretty.

Maureen   She was prettier.

Pato   I like you.

Maureen   You have blue eyes.

Pato   I do.

Maureen   Stay with me tonight.

Pato   I don't know, now, Maureen.

Maureen   Stay. Just tonight.

Pato (*pause*)   Is your mother asleep?

Maureen   I don't care if she is or she isn't. (*Pause.*) Go lower.

Pato *begins easing his hands down her front.*

Maureen   Go lower ... Lower ...

His hands reach her crotch. She tilts her head back slightly. The song on the radio ends. Blackout.

Scene Four

Morning. **Maureen**'s *black dress is lying across the table.* **Mag** *enters from the hall carrying a potty of urine, which she pours out down the sink. She exits into the hall to put the potty away and returns a moment later, wiping her empty hands on the sides of her nightie. She spots the black dress and picks it up disdainfully.*

Mag   Forty pounds just for that skimpy dress? That dress is just skimpy. And laying it around then?

She tosses the dress into a far corner, returns to the kitchen and switches the kettle on, speaking loudly to wake **Maureen**.

I suppose I'll have to be getting me own Complan too, the hour you dragged yourself in whatever time it was with your oul dress. (*Quietly.*) That dress just looks silly. (*Loudly.*) Go the whole hog and wear no dress would be nearer the mark! (*Quietly.*) Snoring the head off you all night. Making an oul woman get her Complan, not to mention her porridge. Well, I won't be getting me own porridge, I'll tell you that now. I'd be afeard. You won't catch me getting me own porridge. Oh no. You won't be catching me out so easily.

Pato *has just entered from the hall, dressed in trousers and pulling on a shirt.*

Pato   Good morning there, now, Mrs.

Mag *is startled, staring at* **Pato** *dumbfounded.*

Mag   Good morning there, now.

Pato   Is it porridge you're after?

Mag   It is.

Pato   I'll be getting your porridge for you, so, if you like.

Mag   Oh-h.

Pato   Go ahead and rest yourself.

Mag *sits in the rocking chair, keeping her eyes on* **Pato** *all the while as he prepares her porridge.*

Pato   It's many the time I did get me brother his porridge of a school morning, so I'm well accustomed. (*Pause.*) You couldn't make it to the oul Yanks' do yesterday so?

Mag   No.

Pato   Your bad hip it was, Maureen was saying.

Mag (*still shocked*)   Aye, me bad hip. (*Pause.*) Where's Maureen, now?

Pato   Em, having a lie-in a minute or two, she is. (*Pause.*) To tell you the truth, I was all for ... I was all for creeping out before ever you got yourself up, but Maureen said 'Aren't we all adults, now? What harm?' I suppose we are, but ... I don't know. It's still awkward, now, or something. D'you know what I mean? I don't know. (*Pause.*) The Yanks'll be touching down in Boston about now anyways. God willing anyways. Aye. (*Pause.*) A good oul send-off we gave them anyways, we did, to send them off. Aye. (*Pause.*) Not a dry eye. (*Pause.*) Aye. (*Pause.*) Was it a mug of Complan too you wanted?

Mag   It was.

Pato *fixes her Complan and brings it over.*

Pato   You like your Complan so.

Mag   I don't.

Pato   Do you not, now?

Mag   She makes me drink it when I don't like it and forces me.

Pato   But Complan's good for you anyways if you're old.

Mag   I suppose it's good for me.

Pato   It is. Isn't it chicken flavour?

Mag   I don't know what flavour.

Pato *(checking box)*   Aye, it's chicken flavour. That's the best flavour.

Pato *returns to the porridge.*

Mag *(quietly)*   With all oul lumps you do make it, never minding flavour. *And* no spoon.

Pato *gives* **Mag** *her porridge and sits at the table.*

Pato   There you go, now. *(Pause.)* Whatever happened to your hand there, Mrs? Red raw, it is.

Mag   Me hand, is it?

Pato   Was it a scould you did get?

Mag   It *was* a scould.

Pato   You have to be careful with scoulds at your age.

Mag   Careful, is it? Uh-huh . . .

Maureen *enters from the hall, wearing only a bra and slip, and goes over to* **Pato**.

Maureen   Careful what? We was careful, weren't we, Pato?

Maureen *sits across* **Pato**'s *lap.*

Pato (*embarrassed*)   Maureen, now . . .

Maureen   Careful enough, 'cos we don't need any babies coming, do we? We do have enough babies in this house to be going on with.

Maureen *kisses him at length.* **Mag** *watches in disgust.*

Pato   Maureen, now . . .

Maureen   Just thanking you for a wonderful night, I am, Pato. Well worth the wait it was. *Well* worth the wait.

Pato (*embarrassed*)   Good-oh.

Mag   Discussing me scoulded hand we was before you breezed in with no clothes!

Maureen   Ar, feck your scoulded hand. (*To* **Pato**.) You'll have to be putting that thing of yours in me again before too long is past, Pato. I do have a taste for it now, I do . . .

Pato   Maureen . . .

She kisses him, gets off, and stares at **Mag** *as she passes into the kitchen.*

Maureen   A mighty oul taste. Uh-huh.

Pato *gets up and idles around in embarrassment.*

Pato   Em, I'll have to be off now in a minute anyways. I do have packing to do I do, and whatyoucall . . .

Mag (*pointing at* **Maureen**. *Loudly*)   She's the one that scoulded me hand! I'll tell you that, now! Let alone sitting on stray men! Held it down on the range she did! Poured chip-pan fat o'er it! Aye, and told the doctor it was me!

Maureen (*pause. Nonplussed, to* **Pato**)   Be having a mug of tea before you go, Pato, now.

Pato (*pause*)   Maybe a quick one.

Maureen *pours out the tea.* **Mag** *looks back and forth between the two of them.*

Mag   Did you not hear what I said?

Maureen   Do you think Pato listens to the smutterings of a senile oul hen?

Mag   Senile, is it? (*She holds up her left hand.*) Don't I have the evidence?

Maureen   Come over here a second, Pato. I want you to smell this sink for me.

Mag   Sinks have nothing to do with it!

Maureen   Come over here now, Pato.

Pato   Eh?

Pato *goes into the kitchen.*

Maureen   Smell that sink.

Pato *leans into the sink, sniffs it, then pulls his head away in disgust.*

Mag   Nothing to do with it, sinks have!

Maureen   Nothing to do with it, is it? Everything to do with it, *I* think it has. Serves as evidence to the character of me accuser, it does.

Pato   What is that, now? The drains?

Maureen   Not the drains at all. Not the drains at all. Doesn't she pour a potty of wee away down there every morning, though I tell her seven hundred times the lavvy to use, but oh no.

Mag   Me scoulded hand this conversation was, and not wee at all!

Maureen   And doesn't even rinse it either. Now is that hygienic? And she does have a urine infection too, is even less hygienic. I wash me praities in thee. Here's your tea now, Pato.

Pato *takes his tea, sipping it squeamishly.*

Mag   Put some clothes on you, going around the house

half-naked! Would be more in your line!

Maureen   I do like going round the house half-naked. It does turn me on, it does.

Mag   I suppose it does, aye.

Maureen   It does.

Mag   And reminds you of Difford Hall in England, too, I'll bet it does...

Maureen (*angrily*)   Now you just shut your fecking...

Mag   None of your own clothes they let you wear in there either, did they?

Maureen   Shut your oul gob, I said ...!

Mag   Only long gowns and buckle-down jackets...

Maureen *approaches* **Mag**, *fists clenched.* **Pato** *catches her arm and steps between the two.*

Pato   What's the matter with ye two at all, now ...?

Mag   Difford Hall! Difford Hall! Difford Hall ...!

Maureen   Difford Hall, uh-huh. And I suppose...

Mag   Difford Hall! Difford Hall...!

Maureen   And I suppose that potty of wee was just a figment of me imagination?

Mag   Forget wee! Forget wee! D'you want to know what Difford Hall is, fella?

Maureen   Shut up, now!

Mag   It's a nut-house! An oul nut-house in England I did have to sign her out of and promise to keep her in me care. Would you want to be seeing the papers now?

She shuffles off to the hall.

As proof, like. Or to prove am I just a senile oul hen, like, or *who*'s the loopy one? Heh! Pegging wee in me face, oh aye ...

Quiet pause. **Maureen** *idles over to the table and sits.* **Pato** *pours his tea down the sink, rinses his mug and washes his hands.*

Maureen (*quietly*) It's true I was in a home there a while, now, after a bit of a breakdown I had. Years ago this is.

Pato What harm a breakdown, sure? Lots of people do have breakdowns.

Maureen A lot of dollally people, aye.

Pato Not dollally people at all. A lot of well-educated people have breakdowns too. In fact, if you're well-educated it's even more likely. Poor Spike Milligan, isn't he forever having breakdowns? He hardly stops. I do have trouble with me nerves every now and then, too, I don't mind admitting. There's no shame at all in that. Only means you do think about things, and take them to heart.

Maureen No shame in being put in a nut-house a month? Ah no.

Pato No shame in thinking about things and worrying about things, I'm saying, and 'nut-house' is a silly word to be using, and you know that well enough, now, Maureen.

Maureen I do.

Pato *goes over and sits across the table from her.*

Maureen In England I was, this happened. Cleaning work. When I was twenty-five. Me first time over. Me only time over. Me sister had just got married, me other sister just about to. Over in Leeds I was, cleaning offices. Bogs. A whole group of us, only them were all English. 'Ya oul backward Paddy fecking ... The fecking pig's-backside face on ya.' The first time out of Connemara this was I'd been. 'Get back to that backward fecking pigsty of yours or whatever hole it was you drug yourself out of.' Half of the swearing I didn't even understand. I had to have a black woman explain it to me. Trinidad she was from. They'd have a go at her too, but she'd just laugh. This big face she had, this big oul smile. And photos of Trinidad she'd show me, and 'What the hell have you left there for?' I'd

say. 'To come to this place, cleaning shite?' And a calendar
with a picture of Connemara on I showed her one day,
and 'What the hell have you left there for?' she said back
to me. 'To come to this place . . .' (*Pause.*) But she moved to
London then, her husband was dying. And after that it all
just got to me.

Pato (*pause*)   That's all past and behind you now anyways,
Maureen.

Pause. **Maureen** *looks at him a while.*

Maureen   Am I still a nut case you're saying, or you're
wondering?

Pato   Not at all, now . . .

Maureen   Oh no . . . ?

Maureen *gets up and wanders back to the kitchen.*

Pato   Not at all. That's a long time in the past is all I'm
saying. And nothing to be ashamed of. Put it behind you,
you should.

Maureen   Put it behind me, aye, with that one hovering
eyeing me every minute, like I'm some kind of . . . some
kind of . . . (*Pause.*) And, no, I didn't scould her oul hand,
no matter how doolally I ever was. Trying to cook chips on
her own, she was. We'd argued, and I'd left her on her
own an hour, and chips she up and decided she wanted.
She must've tipped the pan over. God knows how, the eej.
I just found her lying there. Only, because of Difford Hall,
she thinks any accusation she throws at me I won't be any
the wiser. I won't be able to tell the differ, what's true and
what's not. Well, I *am* able to tell the differ. Well able, the
smelly oul bitch.

Pato   You shouldn't let her get to you, Maureen.

Maureen   How can I help it, Pato? She's enough to drive
anyone loopy, if they weren't loopy to begin with.

Pato (*smiling*)   She is at that, I suppose.

Maureen (*smiling*)   She is. It's surprised I am how sane I've turned out!

They both smile. Pause.

Pato   I *will* have to be off in a minute now, Maureen.

Maureen   Okay, Pato. Did you finish your tea, now?

Pato   I didn't. The talk of your mother's wee, it did put me off it.

Maureen   It would. It would anybody. Don't I have to live with it? (*Sadly.*) Don't I have to live with it? (*Looking straight at him.*) I suppose I do, now.

Pato (*pause*)   Be putting on some clothes there, Maureen. You'll freeze with no fire down.

Pause. **Maureen**'s *mood has become sombre again. She looks down at herself.*

Maureen (*quietly*)   'Be putting on some clothes'? Is it ugly you think I am now, so, 'Be putting on some clothes . . .'

Pato   No, Maureen, the cold, I'm saying. You can't go walking about . . . You'll freeze, sure.

Maureen   It wasn't ugly you thought I was last night, or maybe it was, now.

Pato   No, Maureen, now. What . . . ?

Maureen   A beauty queen you thought I was last night, or you said I was. When it's 'Cover yourself', now, 'You do sicken me' . . .

Pato (*approaching her*)   Maureen, no, now, what are you saying that for . . . ?

Maureen   Maybe that was the reason so.

Pato (*stops*)   The reason what?

Maureen   Be off with you so, if I sicken you.

Pato   You don't sicken me.

Maureen (*almost crying*)   Be off with you, I said.

Pato (*approaching again*)   Maureen . . .

Mag *enters, waving papers, stopping* **Pato***'s approach.*

Mag   Eh? Here's the papers now, Difford Hall, if I'm such a senile oul hen. Eh? Who wants an oul read, now? Eh? Proof this is, let alone pegging sinks at me! (*Pause.*) Eh?

Pato   Maureen . . .

Maureen (*composed. Gently*)   Be going now, Pato.

Pato (*pause*)   I'll write to you from England. (*Pause. Sternly.*) Look at me! (*Pause. Softly.*) I'll write to you from England.

Pato *puts on his jacket, turns for a last look at* **Maureen***, then exits, closing the door behind him. Footsteps away. Pause.*

Mag   He won't write at all. (*Pause.*) And I did throw your oul dress in that dirty corner too!

Pause. **Maureen** *looks at her a moment, sad, despairing but not angry.*

Maureen   Why? Why? Why do you . . . ?

Pause. **Maureen** *goes over to where her dress is lying, crouches down beside it and picks it up, holding it to her chest. She lingers there a moment, then gets up and passes her mother.*

Just look at yourself.

Maureen *exits into hall.*

Mag   Just look at *yourself* too, would be . . . would be . . . (**Maureen** *shuts the hall door behind her.*) . . . more in your line.

She is still holding up the papers rather dumbly. Pause. She lays the papers down, scratches herself, notices her uneaten porridge and sticks a finger in it. Quietly.

Me porridge is gone cold now. (*Loudly.*) Me porridge is gone cold now!

She stares out front, blankly. Blackout.

Interval.

Scene Five

*Most of the stage is in darkness apart from a spotlight or some such
on* **Pato** *sitting at the table as if in a bedsit in England, reciting a
letter he has written to* **Maureen**.

Pato   Dear Maureen, it is Pato Dooley and I'm writing
from London, and I'm sorry it's taken so long to write to
you but to be honest I didn't know whether you wanted
me to one way or the other, so I have taken it upon myself
to try and see. There are a lot of things I want to say but
I am no letter-writer but I will try to say them if I can.
Well, Maureen, there is no major news here, except a
Wexford man on the site a day ago, a rake of bricks fell on
him from the scaffold and forty stitches he did have in his
head and was lucky to be alive at all, he was an old fella,
or fifty-odd anyways, but apart from that there is no major
news. I do go out for a pint of a Saturday or a Friday but
I don't know nobody and don't speak to anyone. There is
no one to speak to. The gangerman does pop his head in
sometimes. I don't know if I've spelt it right, 'Gangerman',
is it 'e-r' or is it 'a'? It is not a word we was taught in
school. Well, Maureen, I am 'beating around the bush' as
they say, because it is you and me I do want to be talking
about, if there is such a thing now as 'you and me', I don't
know the state of play. What I thought I thought we were
getting on royally, at the goodbye to the Yanks and the
part after when we did talk and went to yours. And I *did*
think you were a beauty queen and I *do* think, and it
wasn't anything to do with that at all or with you at all, I
think you thought it was. All it was, it has happened to me
a couple of times before when I've had a drink taken and
was nothing to do with did I want to. I would have been
honoured to be the first one you chose, and flattered, and
the thing that I'm saying, I was honoured then and I am
still honoured, and just because it was not to be that night,
does it mean it is not to be ever? I don't see why it should,
and I don't see why you was so angry when you was so

nice to me when it happened. I think you thought I looked
at you differently when your breakdown business came up,
when I didn't look at you differently at all, or the thing I
said 'Put on your clothes, it's cold', when you seemed to
think I did not want to be looking at you in your bra and
slip there, when nothing could be further from the truth,
because if truth be told I could have looked at you in your
bra and slip until the cows came home. I could never get
my fill of looking at you in your bra and slip, and some
day, God willing, I will be looking at you in your bra and
slip again. Which leads me on to my other thing, unless
you still haven't forgiven me, in which case we should just
forget about it and part as friends, but if you *have* forgiven
me it leads me on to my other thing which I was lying to
you before when I said I had no news because I do have
news. What the news is I have been in touch with me
uncle in Boston and the incident with the Wexford man
with the bricks was just the final straw. You'd be lucky to
get away with your life the building sites in England, let
alone the bad money and the 'You oul Irish this-and-that',
and I have been in touch with me uncle in Boston and a
job he has offered me there, and I am going to take him
up on it. Back in Leenane two weeks tomorrow I'll be, to
collect up my stuff and I suppose a bit of a do they'll
throw me, and the thing I want to say to you is do you
want to come with me? Not straight away of course, I
know, because you would have things to clear up, but after
a month or two I'm saying, but maybe you haven't
forgiven me at all and it's being a fool I'm being. Well, if
you haven't forgiven me I suppose it'd be best if we just
kept out of each other's way the few days I'm over and if I
don't hear from you I will understand, but if you *have*
forgiven me what's to keep you in Ireland? There's your
sisters could take care of your mother and why should you
have had the burden all these years, don't you deserve a
life? And if they say no, isn't there the home in Oughterard
isn't ideal but they do take good care of them, my mother
before she passed, and don't they have bingo and what
good to your mother does that big hill do? No good.

(*Pause.*) Anyways, Maureen, I will leave it up to you. My
address is up the top there and the number of the phone in
the hall, only let it ring a good while if you want to ring
and you'll need the codes, and it would be grand to hear
from you. If I don't hear from you, I will understand. Take
good care of yourself, Maureen. And that night we shared,
even if nothing happened, it still makes me happy just to
think about it, being close to you, and even if I never hear
from you again I'll always have a happy memory of that
night, and that's all I wanted to say to you. Do think about
it. Yours sincerely, Pato Dooley.

Spotlight cuts out, but while the stage is in darkness **Pato** *continues
with a letter to his brother.*

Dear Raymond, how are you? I'm enclosing a bunch of
letters I don't want different people snooping in on. Will
you hand them out for me and don't be reading them, I
know you won't be. The one to Mick Dowd you can wait
till he comes out of hospital. Let me know how he is or
have they arrested the lass who belted him. The one to
poor Girleen you can give to her any time you see her, it
is only to tell her to stop falling in love with priests. But
the one to Maureen Folan I want you to go over there the
day you get this and put it in her hand. This is important
now, in her hand put it. Not much other news here. I'll fill
you in on more of the America details nearer the time.
Yes, it's a great thing. Good luck to you, Raymond, and
P.S. Remember now, in Maureen's hand put it. Goodbye.

Scene Six

Afternoon. **Ray** *is standing near the lit range, watching TV,
somewhat engrossed, tapping a sealed envelope against his knee now
and then.* **Mag** *watches him and the letter from the rocking chair.
Long pause before* **Ray** *speaks.*

Ray   That Wayne's an oul bastard.

Mag   Is he?

Ray   He is. He never stops.

Mag   Oh-h.

Ray (*pause*)   D'you see Patricia with the hair? Patricia's bad enough, but Wayne's a pure terror. (*Pause.*) I do like *Sons and Daughters*, I do.

Mag   Do ya?

Ray   Everybody's always killing each other and a lot of girls do have swimsuits. That's the best kind of programme.

Mag   I'm just waiting for the news to come on.

Ray (*pause*)   You'll have a long wait.

The programme ends. **Ray** *stretches himself.*

That's that then.

Mag   Is the news not next? Ah no.

Ray   No. For God's sake, *A Country Fecking Practice*'s on next. Isn't it Thursday?

Mag   Turn it off, so, if the news isn't on. That's all I do be waiting for.

Ray *turns the TV off and idles around.*

Ray   Six o'clock the news isn't on 'til. (*He glances at his watch. Quietly, irritated.*) Feck, feck, feck, feck, feck, feck, feck, feck, feck. (*Pause.*) You said she'd be home be now, didn't you?

Mag   I did. (*Pause.*) Maybe she got talking to somebody, although she doesn't usually get talking to somebody. She does keep herself to herself.

Ray   I know well she does keep herself to herself. (*Pause.*) Loopy that woman is, if you ask me. Didn't she keep the tennis ball that came off me and Mairtin Hanlon's swingball set and landed in yere fields and wouldn't give it back no matter how much we begged and that was ten years ago and I still haven't forgotten it?

Mag   I do have no comment, as they say.

Ray   Still haven't forgotten it and I never will forget it!

Mag   But wasn't it that you and Mairtin were pegging yere tennis ball at our chickens and clobbered one of them dead is why your ball was in our fields . . . ?

Ray   It ws swingball we were playing, Mrs!

Mag   Oh-h.

Ray   Not clobbering at all. Swingball it was. And never again able to play swingball were we. For the rest of our youth, now. For what use is a swingball set without a ball?

Mag   No use.

Ray   No use is right! No use at all. (*Pause.*) *Bitch!*

Mag (*pause*)   Be off and give your letter to me so, Ray, now, and I'll make sure she gets it, and not have you waiting for a lass ruined your swingball set on you.

Ray *thinks about it, tempted, but grudgingly decides against it.*

Ray   I'm under strict instructions now, Mrs.

Mag (*tuts*)   Make me a mug of tea so.

Ray   I'm not making you a mug of tea. Under duress is all I'm here. I'm not skivvying about on top of it.

Mag (*pause*)   Or another bit of turf on the fire put. I'm cold.

Ray   Did I not just say?

Mag   Ah g'wan, Ray. You're a good boy, God bless you.

Sighing, **Ray** *puts the letter – which* **Mag** *stares at throughout – on the table and uses the heavy black poker beside the range to pick some turf up and place it inside, stoking it afterwards.*

Ray   Neverminding swingball, I saw her there on the road the other week and I said hello to her and what did she do? She outright ignored me. Didn't even look up.

Mag   Didn't she?

Ray   And what I thought of saying, I thought of saying,
'Up your oul hole, Mrs', but I didn't say it, I just thought
of saying it, but thinking back on it I should've gone ahead
and said it and skitter on the bitch!

Mag   It wouldn't been good enough for her to say it, up
and ignoring you on the road, because you're a good gasur,
Ray, fixing me fire for me. Ah, she's been in a foul oul
mood lately.

Ray   She does wear horrible clothes. And everyone agrees.
(*Finished at the range, poker still in hand,* **Ray** *looks over the tea
towel on the back wall.*) 'May you be half an hour in Heaven
afore the Devil knows you're dead.'

Mag   Aye.

Ray (*funny voice*)   'May you be half an hour in Heaven
afore the Devil knows you're dead.'

Mag (*embarrassed laugh*)   Aye.

Ray *idles around a little, wielding the poker.*

Ray   This is a great oul poker, this is.

Mag   Is it?

Ray   Good and heavy.

Mag   Heavy and long.

Ray   Good and heavy and long. A half a dozen coppers
you could take out with this poker and barely notice and
have not a scratch on it and then clobber them again just
for the fun of seeing the blood running out of them. (*Pause.*)
Will you sell it to me?

Mag   I will not. To go battering the polis?

Ray   A fiver.

Mag   We do need it for the fire, sure.

Ray *tuts and puts the poker back beside the range.*

Ray   Sure, that poker's just going to waste in this house.

He idles into the kitchen. Her eye on the letter, **Mag** *slowly gets out of her chair.*

Ah, I could get a dozen pokers in town just as good if I wanted, and at half the price.

Just as **Mag** *starts her approach to the letter,* **Ray** *returns, not noticing her, idles past and picks the letter back up on his way.* **Mag** *grimaces slightly and sits back down.* **Ray** *opens the front door, glances out to see if* **Maureen** *is coming, then closes it again, sighing.*

A whole afternoon I'm wasting here. (*Pause.*) When I could be at home watching telly.

Ray *sits at the table.*

Mag   You never know, it might be evening before she's ever home.

Ray (*angrily*)   You said three o'clock it was sure to be when I first came in!

Mag   Aye, three o'clock it usually is, oh aye. (*Pause.*) Just sometimes it does be evening. On occasion, like. (*Pause.*) Sometimes it does be *late* evening. (*Pause.*) Sometimes it does be *night*. (*Pause.*) *Morning* it was one time before she . . .

Ray (*interrupting angrily*)   All right, all right! It's thumping you in a minute I'll be!

Mag (*pause*)   I'm only saying now.

Ray   Well, stop saying! (*Sighs. Long pause.*) This house does smell of pee, this house does.

Mag (*pause. Embarrassed*)   Em, cats do get in.

Ray   Do cats get in?

Mag   They do. (*Pause.*) They do go to the sink.

Ray (*pause*)   What do they go to the sink for?

Mag   To wee.

Ray   To wee? They go to the sink to wee? (*Piss-taking.*) Sure, that's mighty good of them. You do get a very considerate breed of cat up this way so.

Mag (*pause*)   I don't know what breed they are.

Pause. **Ray** *lets his head slump down onto the table with a bump, and slowly and rhythmically starts banging his fist down beside it.*

Ray (*droning*)   I don't want to be here, I don't want to be here, I don't want to be here, I don't want to be here . . .

Ray *lifts his head back up, stares at the letter, then starts slowly turning it around, end over end, sorely tempted.*

Mag (*pause*)   Do me a mug of tea, Ray. (*Pause.*) Or a mug of Complan do me, even. (*Pause.*) And give it a good stir to get rid of the oul lumps.

Ray   If it was getting rid of oul lumps I was to be, it wouldn't be with Complan I'd be starting. It would be much closer to home, boy. Oh aye, much closer. A big lump sitting in an oul fecking rocking chair it would be. I'll tell you that!

Mag (*pause*)   Or a Cup-a-Soup do me.

Ray *grits his teeth and begins breathing in and out through them, almost crying.*

Ray (*giving in sadly*)   Pato, Pato, Pato. (*Pause.*) Ah what news could it be? (*Pause. Sternly.*) Were I to leave this letter here with you, Mrs, it would be straight to that one you would be giving it, isn't that right?

Mag   It is. Oh, straight to Maureen I'd be giving it.

Ray (*pause*)   And it isn't opening it you would be?

Mag   It is not. Sure, a letter is a private thing. If it isn't my name on it, what business would it be of mine?

Ray   And may God strike you dead if you do open it?

Mag   And may God strike me dead if I do open it, only

He'll have no need to strike me dead because I won't be opening it.

Ray (*pause*)   I'll leave it so.

He stands, places the letter up against a salt cellar, thinks about it again for a moment, looks **Mag** *over a second, looks back at the letter again, thinks once more, then waves a hand in a gesture of tired resignation, deciding to leave it.*

I'll be seeing you then, Mrs.

Mag   Be seeing you, Pato. *Ray*, I mean.

Ray *grimaces at her again and exits through the front door, but leaves it slightly ajar, as he is still waiting outside.* **Mag** *places her hands on the sides of the rocking chair, about to drag herself up, then warily remembers she hasn't heard* **Ray**'s *footsteps away. She lets her hands rest back in her lap and sits back serenely. Pause. The front door bursts open and* **Ray** *sticks his head around it to look at her. She smiles at him innocently.*

Ray   Good-oh.

Ray *exits again, closing the door behind him fully this time.* **Mag** *listens to his footsteps fading away, then gets up, picks up the envelope and opens it, goes back to the range and lifts off the lid so that the flames are visible, and stands there reading the letter. She drops the first short page into the flames as she finishes it, then starts reading the second. Slow fade-out.*

Scene Seven

Night. **Mag** *is in her rocking chair,* **Maureen** *at the table, reading. The radio is on low, tuned to a request show. The reception is quite poor, wavering and crackling with static. Pause before* **Mag** *speaks.*

Mag   A poor reception.

Maureen   Can I help it if it's a poor reception?

Mag (*pause*)   Crackly. (*Pause.*) We can hardly hear the tunes. (*Pause.*) We can hardly hear what are the dedications or from what part of the country.

Maureen   I can hear well enough.

Mag   Can ya?

Maureen (*pause*)   Maybe it's deaf it is you're going.

Mag   It's not deaf I'm going. Not nearly deaf.

Maureen   It's a home for deaf people I'll have to be putting you in soon. (*Pause.*) And it isn't cod in butter sauce you'll be getting in there. No. Not by a long chalk. Oul beans on toast or something is all you'll be getting in there. If you're lucky. And then if you don't eat it, they'll give you a good kick, or maybe a punch.

Mag (*pause*)   I'd die before I'd let meself be put in a home.

Maureen   Hopefully, aye.

Mag (*pause*)   That was a nice bit of cod in butter sauce, Maureen.

Maureen   I suppose it was.

Mag   Tasty.

Maureen   All I do is boil it in the bag and snip it with a scissor. I hardly need your compliments.

Mag (*pause*)   Mean to me is all you ever are nowadays.

Maureen   If I am or if I'm not. (*Pause.*) Didn't I buy you a packet of wine gums last week if I'm so mean?

Mag (*pause*)   All because of Pato Dooley you're mean, I suppose. (*Pause.*) Him not inviting you to his oul going-away do tonight.

Maureen   Pato Dooley has his own life to lead.

Mag   Only after one thing that man was.

Maureen   Maybe he was, now. Or maybe it was me who was only after one thing. We do have equality nowadays. Not like in your day.

Mag　There was nothing wrong in my day.

Maureen　Allowed to go on top of a man nowadays, we are. All we have to do is ask. And nice it is on top of a man, too.

Mag　Is it nice now, Maureen?

Maureen (*bemused that* **Mag** *isn't offended*)　It is.

Mag　It does sound nice. Ah, good enough for yourself, now.

Maureen, *still bemused, gets some shortbread fingers from the kitchen and eats a couple.*

Mag　And not worried about having been put in the family way, are you?

Maureen　I'm not. We was careful.

Mag　Was ye careful?

Maureen　Aye. We was nice and careful. We was *lovely* and careful, if you must know.

Mag　I'll bet ye was lovely and careful, aye. Oh aye. Lovely and careful, I'll bet ye were.

Maureen (*pause*)　You haven't been sniffing the paraffin lamps again?

Mag (*pause*)　It's always the paraffin lamp business you do throw at me.

Maureen　It's a funny oul mood you're in so.

Mag　Is it a funny oul mood? No. Just a normal mood, now.

Maureen　It's a funny one. (*Pause.*) Aye, a great oul time me and Pato did have. I can see now what all the fuss did be about, but ah, there has to be more to a man than just being good in bed. Things in common too you do have to have, y'know, like what books do you be reading, or what are your politics and the like, so I did have to tell him it was no-go, no matter how good in bed he was.

Mag   When was this you did tell him?

Maureen   A while ago it was I did tell him. Back . . .

Mag (*interrupting*)   And I suppose he was upset at that.

Maureen   He *was* upset at that but I assured him it was for the best and he did seem to accept it then.

Mag   I'll bet he accepted it.

Maureen (*pause*)   But that's why I thought it would be unfair of me to go over to his do and wish him goodbye. I thought it would be awkward for him.

Mag   It would be awkward for him, aye, I suppose. Oh aye. (*Pause.*) So all it was was ye didn't have enough things in common was all that parted ye?

Maureen   Is all it was. And parted on amicable terms, and with no grudges on either side. (*Pause.*) No. No grudges at all. I did get what I did want out of Pato Dooley that night, and that was good enough for him, and that was good enough for me.

Mag   Oh, aye, now. I'm sure. It was good enough for the both of ye. Oh aye.

Mag *smiles and nods.*

Maureen (*laughing*)   It's a crazy oul mood you're in for yourself tonight! Pleased that tonight it is Pato's leaving and won't be coming pawing me again is what it is, I bet.

Mag   Maybe that's what it is. I *am* glad Pato's leaving.

Maureen (*smiling*)   An interfering oul biddy is all you are. (*Pause.*) Do you want a shortbread finger?

Mag   I *do* want a shortbread finger.

Maureen   Please.

Mag   Please.

Maureen *gives* **Mag** *a shortbread finger, after waving it phallically in the air a moment.*

Maureen   Remind me of something, shortbread fingers do.

Mag   I suppose they do, now.

Maureen   I suppose it's so long since you've seen what they remind me of, you do forget what they look like.

Mag   I suppose I do. And I suppose you're the expert.

Maureen   I am the expert.

Mag   Oh aye.

Maureen   I'm the king of the experts.

Mag   I suppose you are, now. Oh, I'm sure. I suppose you're the king of the experts.

Maureen (*pause. Suspicious*)   Why wouldn't you be sure?

Mag   With your Pato Dooley and your throwing it all in me face like an oul peahen, eh? When . . . (**Mag** *catches herself before revealing any more.*)

Maureen (*pause. Smiling*)   When what?

Mag   Not another word on the subject am I saying. I do have no comment, as they say. This is a nice shortbread finger.

Maureen (*with an edge*)   When what, now?

Mag (*getting scared*)   When nothing, Maureen.

Maureen (*forcefully*)   No, when what, now? (*Pause.*) Have you been speaking to somebody?

Mag   Who would I be speaking to, Maureen?

Maureen (*trying to work it out*)   You've been speaking to somebody. You've . . .

Mag   Nobody have I been speaking to, Maureen. You

know well I don't be speaking to anybody. And, sure, who would Pato be telling about that . . . ?

Mag *suddenly realises what she's said.* **Maureen** *stares at her in dumb shock and hate, then walks to the kitchen, dazed, puts a chip-pan on the stove, turns it on high and pours a half-bottle of cooking oil into it, takes down the rubber gloves that are hanging on the back wall and puts them on.* **Mag** *puts her hands on the arms of the rocking chair to drag herself up, but* **Maureen** *shoves a foot against her stomach and groin, ushering her back.* **Mag** *leans back into the chair, frightened, staring at* **Maureen***, who sits at the table, waiting for the oil to boil. She speaks quietly, staring straight ahead.*

Maureen   How do you know?

Mag   Nothing do I know, Maureen.

Maureen   Uh-huh?

Mag (*pause*)   Or was it Ray did mention something? Aye, I think it was Ray . . .

Maureen   Nothing to Ray would Pato've said about that subject.

Mag (*tearfully*)   Just to stop you bragging like an oul peahen, was I saying, Maureen. Sure what does an oul woman like me know? Just guessing, I was.

Maureen   You know sure enough, and guessing me arse, and not on me face was it written. For the second time and for the last time I'll be asking, now. How do you know?

Mag   On your face it *was* written, Maureen. Sure that's the only way I knew. You still do have the look of a virgin about you you always have had. (*Without malice.*) You always will.

Pause. The oil has started boiling. **Maureen** *rises, turns the radio up, stares at* **Mag** *as she passes her, takes the pan off the boil and turns the gas off, and returns to* **Mag** *with it.*

(*Terrified.*) A letter he did send you I read!

Maureen *slowly and deliberately takes her mother's shrivelled hand, holds it down on the burning range, and starts slowly pouring some of the hot oil over it, as* **Mag** *screams in pain and terror.*

Maureen   Where is the letter?

Mag *(through screams)*   I did burn it! I'm sorry, Maureen!

Maureen   What did the letter say?

Mag *is screaming so much that she can't answer.* **Maureen** *stops pouring the oil and releases the hand, which* **Mag** *clutches to herself, doubled-up, still screaming, crying and whimpering.*

Maureen   What did the letter say?

Mag   Said he did have too much to drink, it did! Is why, and not your fault at all.

Maureen   And what else did it say?

Mag   He won't be putting me into no home!

Maureen   What are you talking about, no home? What else did it say?!

Mag   I can't remember, now, Maureen. I *can't* . . . !

Maureen *grabs* **Mag**'s *hand, holds it down again and repeats the torture.*

Mag   No . . . !

Maureen   What else did it say?! Eh?!

Mag *(through screams)*   Asked you to go to America with him, it did!

Stunned, **Maureen** *releases* **Mag**'s *hand and stops pouring the oil.* **Mag** *clutches her hand to herself again, whimpering.*

Maureen   What?

Mag   But how could you go with him? You do still have me to look after.

Maureen *(in a happy daze)*   He asked me to go to America with him? Pato asked me to go to America with him?

Mag (*looking up at her*)   But what about me, Maureen?

A slight pause before **Maureen**, *in a single and almost lazy motion, throws the considerable remainder of the oil into* **Mag**'s *midriff, some of it splashing up into her face.* **Mag** *doubles-up, screaming, falls to the floor, trying to pat the oil off her, and lies there convulsing, screaming and whimpering.* **Maureen** *steps out of her way to avoid her fall, still in a daze, barely noticing her.*

Maureen (*dreamily, to herself*)   He asked me to go to America with him . . . ? (*Recovering herself.*) What time is it? Oh feck, he'll be leaving! I've got to see him. Oh God . . . What will I wear? Uh . . . Me black dress! Me little black dress! It'll be a remembrance to him . . .

Maureen *darts off through the hall.*

Mag (*quietly, sobbing*)   Maureen . . . help me . . .

Maureen *returns a moment later, pulling her black dress on.*

Maureen (*to herself*)   How do I look? Ah, I'll have to do. What time is it? Oh God . . .

Mag   Help me, Maureen . . .

Maureen (*brushing her hair*)   Help you, is it? After what you've done? Help you, she says. No, I won't help you, and I'll tell you another thing. If you've made me miss Pato before he goes, then you'll *really* be for it, so you will, and no messing this time. Out of me fecking way, now . . .

She steps over **Mag**, *who is still shaking on the floor, and exits through the front door. Pause.* **Mag** *is still crawling around slightly. The front door bangs open and* **Mag** *looks up at* **Maureen** *as she breezes back in.*

Me car keys I forgot . . .

She grabs her keys from the table, goes to the door, turns back to the table and switches the radio off.

Electricity.

Maureen *exits again, slamming the door. Pause. Sound of her car starting and pulling off. Pause.*

Mag (*quietly*)   But who'll look after me, so?

Mag, *still shaking, looks down at her scalded hand. Blackout.*

Scene Eight

Same night. The only light in the room emanates from the orange coals through the grill of the range, just illuminating the dark shapes of **Mag**, *sitting in her rocking chair, which rocks back and forth of its own volition, her body unmoving, and* **Maureen**, *still in her black dress, who idles very slowly around the room, poker in hand.*

Maureen   To Boston. To Boston I'll be going. Isn't that where them two were from, the Kennedys, or was that somewhere else, now? Robert Kennedy I did prefer over Jack Kennedy. He seemed to be nicer to women. Although I haven't read up on it. (*Pause.*) Boston. It does have a nice ring to it. Better than England it'll be, I'm sure. Although where wouldn't be better than England? No shite I'll be cleaning there, anyways, and no names called, and Pato'll be there to have a say-so anyways if there was to be names called, but I'm sure there won't be. The Yanks do love the Irish. (*Pause.*) Almost begged me, Pato did. Almost on his hands and knees, he was, near enough crying. At the station I caught him, not five minutes to spare, thanks to you. Thanks to your oul interfering. But too late to be interfering you are now. Oh aye. Be far too late, although you did give it a good go, I'll say that for you. Another five minutes and you'd have had it. Poor you. Poor selfish oul bitch, oul you. (*Pause.*) Kissed the face off me, he did, when he saw me there. Them blue eyes of his. Them muscles. Them arms wrapping me. 'Why did you not answer me letter?' And all for coming over and giving you a good kick he was when I told him, but 'Ah no,' I said, 'isn't she just a feeble-minded oul feck, not worth dirtying your boots on?' I was defending you there. (*Pause.*) 'You will

come to Boston with me so, me love, when you get up the
money.' 'I will, Pato. Be it married or be it living in sin,
what do I care? What do I care if tongues'd be wagging?
Tongues have wagged about me before, let them wag
again. Let them never stop wagging, so long as I'm with
you, Pato, what do I care about tongues? So long as it's
you and me, and the warmth of us cuddled up, and the
skins of us asleep, is all I ever really wanted anyway.'
(*Pause.*) 'Except we do still have a problem, what to do with
your oul mam, there,' he said. 'Would an oul folks' home
be too harsh?' 'It wouldn't be too harsh but it would be
too expensive.' 'What about your sisters so?' 'Me sisters
wouldn't have the bitch. Not even a half-day at Christmas
to be with her can them two stand. They clear forgot her
birthday this year as well as that. "How do you stick her
without going off your rocker?" they do say to me. Behind
her back, like.' (*Pause.*) 'I'll leave it up to yourself so,' Pato
says. He was on the train be this time, we was kissing out
the window, like they do in films. 'I'll leave it up to
yourself so, whatever you decide. If it takes a month, let it
take a month. And if it's finally you decide you can't bear
to be parted from her and have to stay behind, well, I
can't say I would like it, but I'd understand. But if even a
year it has to take for you to decide, it is a year I will be
waiting, and won't be minding the wait.' 'It won't be a
year it is you'll be waiting, Pato', I called out then, the
train was pulling away. 'It won't be a year nor yet nearly a
year. It won't be a week!'

The rocking chair has stopped its motions. **Mag** *starts to slowly lean
forward at the waist until she finally topples over and falls heavily to
the floor, dead. A red chunk of skull hangs from a string of skin at
the side of her head.* **Maureen** *looks down at her, somewhat bored,
taps her on the side with the toe of her shoe, then steps onto her back
and stands there in thoughtful contemplation.*

'Twas over the stile she did trip. Aye. And down the hill
she did fall. Aye. (*Pause.*) Aye.

Pause. Blackout.

Scene Nine

A rainy afternoon. Front door opens and **Maureen** *enters in funeral attire, takes her jacket off and idles around quietly, her mind elsewhere. She lights a fire in the range, turns the radio on low and sits down in the rocking chair. After a moment she half-laughs, takes down the boxes of Complan and porridge from the kitchen shelf, goes back to the range and empties the contents of both on the fire. She exits into the hall and returns a moment later with an old suitcase which she lays on the table, brushing off a thick layer of dust. She opens it, considers for a second what she needs to pack, then returns to the hall. There is a knock at the door.* **Maureen** *returns, thinks a moment, takes the suitcase off the table and places it to one side, fixes her hair a little, then answers the door.*

Maureen   Oh hello there, Ray.

Ray (*off*)   Hello there, Mrs ...

Maureen   Come in ahead for yourself.

Ray   I did see you coming ahead up the road.

He enters, closing the door. **Maureen** *idles to the kitchen and makes herself some tea.*

I didn't think so early you would be back. Did you not want to go on to the reception or the whatyoucall they're having at Rory's so?

Maureen   No. I do have better things to do with me time.

Ray   Aye, aye. Have your sisters gone on to it?

Maureen   They have, aye.

Ray   Of course. Coming back here after, will they be?

Maureen   Going straight home, I think they said they'd be.

Ray   Oh aye. Sure, it's a long oul drive for them. Or fairly long. (*Pause.*) It did all go of okay, then?

Maureen   It did.

Ray   Despite the rain.

Maureen   Despite the rain.

Ray   A poor oul day for a funeral.

Maureen   It was. When it couldn't been last month we buried her, and she could've got the last of the sun, if it wasn't for the hundred bastarding inquests, proved nothing.

Ray   You'll be glad that's all over and done with now, anyways.

Maureen   Very glad.

Ray   I suppose they do only have their jobs to do. (*Pause.*) Although no fan am I of the bastarding polis. Me two wee toes they went and broke on me for no reason, me arsehole drunk and disorderly.

Maureen   The polis broke your toes, did they?

Ray   They did.

Maureen   Oh. Tom Hanlon said what it was you kicked a door in just your socks.

Ray   Did he now? And I suppose you believe a policeman's word over mine. Oh aye. Isn't that how the Birmingham Six went down?

Maureen   Sure, you can't equate your toes with the Birmingham Six, now, Ray.

Ray   It's the selfsame differ. (*Pause.*) What was I saying, now?

Maureen   Some bull.

Ray   Some bull, is it? No. Asking about your mam's funeral, I was.

Maureen   That's what I'm saying.

Ray (*pause*)   Was there a big turn-out at it?

Maureen   Me sisters and one of their husbands and nobody else but Maryjohnny Rafferty and oul Father Walsh – Welsh – saying the thing.

Ray   Father Welsh punched Mairtin Hanlon in the head once, and for no reason. (*Pause.*) Are you not watching telly for yourself, no?

Maureen   I'm not. It's only Australian oul shite they do ever show on that thing.

Ray (*slightly bemused*)   Sure, that's why I do like it. Who wants to see Ireland on telly?

Maureen   *I* do.

Ray   All you have to do is look out your window to see Ireland. And it's soon bored you'd be. 'There goes a calf.' (*Pause.*) I be bored anyway. I be continually bored. (*Pause.*) London I'm thinking of going to. Aye. Thinking of it, anyways. To work, y'know. One of these days. Or else Manchester. They have a lot more drugs in Manchester. Supposedly, anyways.

Maureen   Don't be getting messed up in drugs, now, Ray, for yourself. Drugs are terrible dangerous.

Ray   Terrible dangerous, are they? Drugs, now?

Maureen   You know full well they are.

Ray   Maybe they are, maybe they are. But there are plenty of other things just as dangerous, would kill you just as easy. Maybe even easier.

Maureen (*wary*)   Things like what, now?

Ray (*pause. Shrugging*)   This bastarding town for one.

Maureen (*pause. Sadly*)   Is true enough.

Ray   Just that it takes seventy years. Well, it won't take me seventy years. I'll tell you that. No way, boy. (*Pause.*) How old was your mother, now, when she passed?

Maureen   Seventy, aye. Bang on.

Ray   She had a good innings, anyway. (*Pause.*) Or an innings, anyway. (*Sniffs the air.*) What's this you've been burning?

Maureen   Porridge and Complan I've been burning.

Ray   For why?

Maureen   Because I don't eat porridge or Complan. The remainders of me mother's, they were. I was having a good clear-out.

Ray   Only a waste that was.

Maureen   Do I need your say-so so?

Ray   I'd've been glad to take them off your hands, I'm saying.

Maureen   (*quietly*)   I don't need you say-so.

Ray   The porridge, anyway. I do like a bit of porridge. I'd've left the Complan. I don't drink Complan. Never had no call to.

Maureen   There's some Kimberleys left in the packet I was about to burn too, you can have, if it's such a big thing.

Ray   I *will* have them Kimberleys. I do love Kimberleys.

Maureen   I bet you do.

Ray *eats a couple of Kimberleys.*

Ray   Are they a bit stale, now? (*Chews.*) It does be hard to tell with Kimberleys. (*Pause.*) I think Kimberleys are me favourite biscuit out of any biscuits. Them or Jaffa Cakes. (*Pause.*) Or Wagon Wheels. (*Pause.*) Or would you classify Wagon Wheels as biscuits at all now. Aren't they more of a kind of a bar ...?

Maureen   (*interrupting*)   I've things to do now, Ray. Was it some reason you had to come over or was it just to discuss Wagon Wheels?

Ray   Oh aye, now. No, I did have a letter from Pato the other day and he did ask me to come up.

Maureen *sits in the rocking chair and listens with keen interest.*

Maureen   He did? What did he have to say?

Ray   He said sorry to hear about your mother and all, and his condolences he sent.

Maureen   Aye, aye, aye, and anything else, now?

Ray   That was the main gist of it, the message he said to pass onto you.

Maureen   It had no times or details, now?

Ray   Times or details? No . . .

Maureen   I suppose . . .

Ray   Eh?

Maureen   Eh?

Ray   Eh? Oh, also he said he was sorry he didn't get to see you the night he left, there, he would've liked to've said goodbye. But if that was the way you wanted it, so be it. Although rude, too, I thought that was.

Maureen *(standing, confused)*   I did see him the night he left. At the station, there.

Ray   What station? Be taxicab Pato left. What are you thinking of ?

Maureen *(sitting)*   I don't know now.

Ray   By taxicab Pato left, and sad that he never got your goodbye, although why he wanted your goodbye I don't know. *(Pause.)* I'll tell you this, Maureen, not being harsh, but your house does smell an awful lot nicer now that your mother's dead. I'll say it does, now.

Maureen   Well, isn't that the best? With me thinking I did see him the night he left, there. The train that pulled away.

He looks at her as if she's mad.

Ray   Aye, aye. *(Mumbled, sarcastic.)* Have a rest for yourself.

(*Pause.*) Oh, do you know a lass called, em . . . Dolores
Hooley, or Healey, now? She was over with the Yanks
when they was over.

Maureen I know the name, aye.

Ray She was at me uncle's do they had there, dancing
with me brother early on. You remember?

Maureen Dancing with him, was it? Throwing herself as
him would be nearer the mark. Like a cheap oul whore.

Ray I don't know about that, now.

Maureen Like a cheap oul whore. And where did it get
her?

Ray She did seem nice enough to me, there, now. Big
brown eyes she had. And I do like brown eyes, me, I do.
Oh aye. Like the lass used to be on *Bosco*. Or I *think* the
lass used to be on *Bosco* had brown eyes. We had a black-
and-white telly at that time. (*Pause.*) What was I talking
about, now?

Maureen Something about this Dolores Hooley or
whoever she fecking is.

Ray Oh aye. Herself and Pato did get engaged a week
ago, now, he wrote and told me.

Maureen (*shocked*) Engaged to do what?

Ray Engaged to get married. What do you usually get
engaged for? 'Engaged to do what?' Engaged to eat a bun!

Maureen *is dumbstruck.*

Ray A bit young for him, I think, but good luck to him.
A whirlwind oul whatyoucall. July next year, they're
thinking of having it, but I'll have to write and tell him to
move it either forward or back, else it'll coincide with the
European Championships. I wonder if they'll have the
European Championships on telly over there at all?
Probably not, now, the Yankee bastards. They don't care
about football at all. Ah well. (*Pause.*) It won't be much of a

change for her anyways, From Hooley to Dooley. Only one letter. The 'h'. That'll be a good thing. (*Pause.*) Unless it's Healey that she is. I can't remember. (*Pause.*) If it's Healey, it'll be three letters. The 'h', the 'e' and the 'a'. (*Pause.*) Would you want me to be passing any message on now, when I'm writing, Mrs? I'm writing tomorrow.

Maureen   I get ... I do get confused. Dolores Hooley ...?

Ray (*pause. Irritated*)   Would you want me to be passing on any message, now, I'm saying?

Maureen (*pause*)   Dolores Hooley ...?

Ray (*sighing*)   Fecking ... The loons you do get in this house! Only repeating!

Maureen   Who's a loon?

Ray   Who's a loon, she says!

Ray *scoffs and turns away, looking out the window.* **Maureen** *quietly picks up the poker from beside the range and, holding it low at her side, slowly approaches him from behind.*

Maureen (*angrily*)   Who's a loon?!

Ray *suddenly sees something hidden behind a couple of boxes on the inner window ledge.*

Ray (*angrily*)   Well, isn't that fecking just the fecking best yet ...!

He picks up a faded tennis ball with a string sticking out of it from the ledge and spins around to confront **Maureen** *with it, so angry that he doesn't even notice the poker.* **Maureen** *stops in her tracks.*

Sitting on that fecking shelf all these fecking years you've had it, and what good did it do ya?! A tenner that swingball set did cost me poor ma and da and in 1979 that was, when a tenner was a lot of money. The best fecking present I did ever get and only two oul months' play out of it I got before you went and confiscated it on me. What

right did you have? What right at all? No right. And just
left it sitting there then to fade to fecking skitter. I
wouldn't've minded if you'd got some use out of it, if you'd
taken the string out and played pat-ball or something agin
a wall, but no. Just out of pure spite is the only reason you
kept it, and right under me fecking nose. And then you go
wondering who's a fecking loon? Who's a fecking loon, she
says. I'll tell you who's a fecking loon, lady. *You're* a fecking
loon!

Maureen *lets the poker fall to the floor with a clatter and sits in
the rocking chair, dazed.*

Maureen I don't remember why I did keep your
swingball on you, Raymond. I can't remember at all, now.
I think me head was in a funny oul way in them days.

Ray 'In them days,' she says, as she pegs a good poker
on the floor and talks about trains.

He picks the poker up and puts it in its place.

That's a good poker, that is. Don't be banging it against
anything hard like that, now.

Maureen I won't.

Ray That's an awful good poker. (*Pause.*) To show there's
no hard feelings over me swingball, will you sell me that
poker, Mrs? A fiver I'll give you.

Maureen Ah, I don't want to be selling me poker now,
Ray.

Ray G'wan. Six!

Maureen No. It does have sentimental value to me.

Ray I don't forgive you, so!

Maureen Ah, don't be like that, now, Ray . . .

Ray No, I don't forgive you at all . . .

Ray *goes to the front door and opens it.*

Maureen Ray! Are you writing to your brother, so?

Ray (*sighing*)   I am. Why?

Maureen   Will you be passing a message on from me?

Ray (*sighs*)   Messages, messages, messages, messages!
What's the message, so? And make it a short one.

Maureen   Just say . . .

Maureen *thinks about it a while.*

Ray   This week, if you can!

Maureen   Just say . . . Just say, 'The beauty queen of
Leenane says hello.' That's all.

Ray   'The beauty queen of Leenane says hello.'

Maureen   Aye. No!

Ray *sighs again.*

Maureen   *Goodbye.* Goodbye. 'The beauty queen of
Leenane says *goodbye.*'

Ray   'The beauty queen of Leenane says goodbye.'
Whatever the feck that means, I'll pass it on. 'The beauty
queen of Leenane says goodbye', although after this fecking
swingball business, I don't see why the feck I should.
Goodbye to you so, Mrs . . .

Maureen   Will you turn the radio up a biteen too, before
you go, there, Pato, now? *Ray*, I mean . . .

Ray (*exasperated*)   Feck . . .

He turns the radio up.

The exact fecking image of your mother you are, sitting
there pegging orders and forgetting me name! Goodbye!

Maureen   And pull the door after you . . .

Ray (*shouting angrily*)   I was going to pull the fecking door
after me!!

Ray *slams the door behind him as he exits. Pause.* **Maureen**
starts rocking slightly in the chair, listening to the song by the

Chieftains on the radio. The announcer's quiet, soothing voice is then heard.

Announcer   A lovely tune from the Chieftains there. This next one, now, goes out from Annette and Margo Folan to their mother Maggie, all the way out in the mountains of Leenane, a lovely part of the world there, on the occasion of her seventy-first birthday last month now. Well, we hope you had a happy one, Maggie, and we hope there'll be a good many more of them to come on top of it. I'm sure there will. This one's for you, now.

'The Spinning Wheel' by Delia Murphy is played. **Maureen** *gently rocks in the chair until about the middle of the fourth verse, when she quietly gets up, picks up the dusty suitcase, caresses it slightly, moves slowly to the hall door and looks back at the empty rocking chair a while. It is still rocking gently. Slight pause, then* **Maureen** *exits into the hall, closing its door behind her as she goes. We listen to the song on the radio to the end, as the chair gradually stops rocking and the lights, very slowly, fade to black.*

Methuen Drama Modern Plays

include work by

Edward Albee
Jean Anouilh
John Arden
Margaretta D'Arcy
Peter Barnes
Sebastian Barry
Brendan Behan
Dermot Bolger
Edward Bond
Bertolt Brecht
Howard Brenton
Anthony Burgess
Simon Burke
Jim Cartwright
Caryl Churchill
Noël Coward
Lucinda Coxon
Sarah Daniels
Nick Darke
Nick Dear
Shelagh Delaney
David Edgar
David Eldridge
Dario Fo
Michael Frayn
John Godber
Paul Godfrey
David Greig
John Guare
Peter Handke
David Harrower
Jonathan Harvey
Iain Heggie
Declan Hughes
Terry Johnson
Sarah Kane
Charlotte Keatley
Barrie Keeffe
Howard Korder

Robert Lepage
Doug Lucie
Martin McDonagh
John McGrath
Terrence McNally
David Mamet
Patrick Marber
Arthur Miller
Mtwa, Ngema & Simon
Tom Murphy
Phyllis Nagy
Peter Nichols
Sean O'Brien
Joseph O'Connor
Joe Orton
Louise Page
Joe Penhall
Luigi Pirandello
Stephen Poliakoff
Franca Rame
Mark Ravenhill
Philip Ridley
Reginald Rose
Willy Russell
Jean-Paul Sartre
Sam Shepard
Wole Soyinka
Shelagh Stephenson
Peter Straughan
C. P. Taylor
Theatre de Complicite
Theatre Workshop
Sue Townsend
Judy Upton
Timberlake Wertenbaker
Roy Williams
Snoo Wilson
Victoria Wood

Methuen Drama Contemporary Dramatists

include

John Arden (two volumes)
Arden & D'Arcy
Peter Barnes (three volumes)
Sebastian Barry
Dermot Bolger
Edward Bond (eight volumes)
Howard Brenton
  (two volumes)
Richard Cameron
Jim Cartwright
Caryl Churchill (two volumes)
Sarah Daniels (two volumes)
Nick Darke
David Edgar (three volumes)
David Eldridge
Ben Elton
Dario Fo (two volumes)
Michael Frayn (three volumes)
David Greig
John Godber (two volumes)
Paul Godfrey
John Guare
Lee Hall (two volumes)
Peter Handke
Jonathan Harvey
  (two volumes)
Declan Hughes
Terry Johnson (two volumes)
Sarah Kane
Barrie Keefe
Bernard-Marie Koltès
David Lan
Bryony Lavery
Deborah Levy
Doug Lucie
David Mamet (four volumes)

Martin McDonagh
Duncan McLean
Anthony Minghella
  (two volumes)
Tom Murphy (five volumes)
Phyllis Nagy
Anthony Nielsen
Philip Osment
Gary Owen
Louise Page
Stewart Parker (two volumes)
Joe Penhall
Stephen Poliakoff
  (three volumes)
David Rabe
Mark Ravenhill
Christina Reid
Philip Ridley
Willy Russell
Eric-Emmanuel Schmitt
Ntozake Shange
Sam Shepard (two volumes)
Simon Stephens
Shelagh Stephenson
Wole Soyinka (two volumes)
David Storey (three volumes)
Sue Townsend
Judy Upton
Michel Vinaver
  (two volumes)
Arnold Wesker (two volumes)
Michael Wilcox
Roy Williams
Snoo Wilson (two volumes)
David Wood (two volumes)
Victoria Wood

Methuen Drama World Classics

include

Jean Anouilh (two volumes)
Brendan Behan
Aphra Behn
Bertolt Brecht (eight volumes)
Büchner
Bulgakov
Calderón
Čapek
Anton Chekhov
Noël Coward (eight volumes)
Feydeau
Eduardo De Filippo
Max Frisch
John Galsworthy
Gogol
Gorky (two volumes)
Harley Granville Barker
   (two volumes)
Victor Hugo
Henrik Ibsen (six volumes)
Jarry

Lorca (three volumes)
Marivaux
Mustapha Matura
David Mercer (two volumes)
Arthur Miller (five volumes)
Molière
Musset
Peter Nichols (two volumes)
Joe Orton
A. W. Pinero
Luigi Pirandello
Terence Rattigan
   (two volumes)
W. Somerset Maugham
   (two volumes)
August Strindberg
   (three volumes)
J. M. Synge
Ramón del Valle-Inclán
Frank Wedekind
Oscar Wilde

Methuen Drama Student Editions

Jean Anouilh *Antigone* • John Arden *Serjeant Musgrave's Dance*
Alan Ayckbourn *Confusions* • Aphra Behn *The Rover* • Edward Bond
Lear • *Saved* • Bertolt Brecht *The Caucasian Chalk Circle* • *Fear and
Misery in the Third Reich* • *The Good Person of Szechwan* • *Life of Galileo* •
Mother Courage and her Children • *The Resistible Rise of Arturo Ui* • *The
Threepenny Opera* • Anton Chekhov *The Cherry Orchard* • *The Seagull* •
Three Sisters • *Uncle Vanya* • Caryl Churchill *Serious Money* • *Top Girls*
• Shelagh Delaney *A Taste of Honey* • Euripides *Elektra* • *Medea* •
Dario Fo *Accidental Death of an Anarchist* • Michael Frayn *Copenhagen*
• John Galsworthy *Strife* • Nikolai Gogol *The Government Inspector* •
Robert Holman *Across Oka* • Henrik Ibsen *A Doll's House* • *Ghosts* •
Hedda Gabler • Charlotte Keatley *My Mother Said I Never Should* •
Bernard Kops *Dreams of Anne Frank* • Federico García Lorca *Blood
Wedding* • *Doña Rosita the Spinster* (bilingual edition) • *The House of
Bernarda Alba* • (bilingual edition) • *Yerma* (bilingual edition) • David
Mamet *Glengarry Glen Ross* • *Oleanna* • Patrick Marber *Closer* • John
Marston *Malcontent* • Martin McDonagh *The Lieutenant of Inishmore* •
Joe Orton *Loot* • Luigi Pirandello *Six Characters in Search of an Author*
• Mark Ravenhill *Shopping and F***ing* • Willy Russell *Blood Brothers*
• *Educating Rita* • Sophocles *Antigone* • *Oedipus the King* • Wole
Soyinka *Death and the King's Horseman* • Shelagh Stephenson *The
Memory of Water* • August Strindberg *Miss Julie* • J. M. Synge *The
Playboy of the Western World* • Theatre Workshop *Oh What a Lovely
War* Timberlake Wertenbaker *Our Country's Good* • Arnold Wesker
The Merchant • Oscar Wilde *The Importance of Being Earnest* •
Tennessee Williams *A Streetcar Named Desire* • *The Glass Menagerie*

Methuen Drama Modern Classics

Jean Anouilh *Antigone* • Brendan Behan *The Hostage* • Robert Bolt *A Man for All Seasons* • Edward Bond *Saved* • Bertolt Brecht *The Caucasian Chalk Circle* • *Fear and Misery in the Third Reich* • *The Good Person of Szechwan* • *Life of Galileo* • *The Messingkauf Dialogues* • *Mother Courage and Her Children* • *Mr Puntila and His Man Matti* • *The Resistible Rise of Arturo Ui* • *Rise and Fall of the City of Mahagonny* • *The Threepenny Opera* • Jim Cartwright *Road* • *Two & Bed* • Caryl Churchill *Serious Money* • *Top Girls* • Noël Coward *Blithe Spirit* • *Hay Fever* • *Present Laughter* • *Private Lives* • *The Vortex* • Shelagh Delaney *A Taste of Honey* • Dario Fo *Accidental Death of an Anarchist* • Michael Frayn *Copenhagen* • Lorraine Hansberry *A Raisin in the Sun* • Jonathan Harvey *Beautiful Thing* • David Mamet *Glengarry Glen Ross* • *Oleanna* • *Speed-the-Plow* • Patrick Marber *Closer* • *Dealer's Choice* • Arthur Miller *Broken Glass* • Percy Mtwa, Mbongeni Ngema, Barney Simon *Woza Albert!* • Joe Orton *Entertaining Mr Sloane* • *Loot* • *What the Butler Saw* • Mark Ravenhill *Shopping and F***ing* • Willy Russell *Blood Brothers* • *Educating Rita* • *Stags and Hens* • *Our Day Out* • Jean-Paul Sartre *Crime Passionnel* • Wole Soyinka • *Death and the King's Horseman* • Theatre Workshop *Oh, What a Lovely War* • Frank Wedekind • *Spring Awakening* • Timberlake Wertenbaker *Our Country's Good*

For a complete catalogue of Methuen Drama titles
write to:

Methuen Drama
36 Soho Square
London
W1D 3QY

or you can visit our website at:

www.methuendrama.com